WESTMAR COLLEGE

W9-BWQ-940

SOCIAL PROBLEMS *on the* HOME FRONT

SOCIAL PROBLEMS
on the
HOME FRONT

A Study of
War-time Influences

FRANCIS E. MERRILL

PROFESSOR OF SOCIOLOGY
DARTMOUTH COLLEGE

HARPER & BROTHERS *Publishers* NEW YORK LONDON

HN
57
.M37

SOCIAL PROBLEMS ON
THE HOME FRONT

Copyright, 1948, by Harper & Brothers
PRINTED IN THE UNITED STATES OF AMERICA

All rights in this book are reserved.
No part of the book may be reproduced in any
manner whatsoever without written permission
except in the case of brief quotations embodied
in critical articles and reviews. For information
address Harper & Brothers

FIRST EDITION

A-X

14966

TO THE MEMORY OF
MY FATHER

CONTENTS

PREFACE

This is a study of social problems in the United States during World War II. A social problem is a situation that is believed to threaten an established social value and is considered capable of amelioration by social action. A social problem has three component elements: (a) a situation involving a number of persons; (b) a social value believed endangered thereby; (c) a realization that appropriate social action can (theoretically) be taken. The following situations defined as social problems are considered: desertion and divorce, emotional maladjustment of children, adolescent unsettlement, sexual promiscuity, prostitution, juvenile delinquency, crime, mental derangement, and suicide. This list merely represents some of the problems present in peacetime society and modified by the war. It does not claim to be inclusive.

War does not initiate social problems, but rather accentuates some, temporarily ameliorates others, and introduces still others hitherto unsuspected. The increased tempo of change during World War II intensified the difficulty of personal adjustment and thereby added to the extent and relative severity of many social problems. The war also changed certain conditions so completely that other problems were drastically, if temporarily, improved. This study is thus concerned with the "normal" problems of a dynamic society, intensified and modified by the American version of total war.

Certain necessary limitations have been placed upon the scope of the study. (1) A relatively few social problems are considered, out of a large number of possible problems. The selection is based upon the importance of the problems and the availability of the data. (2) The positive, integrative, or socially therapeutic effects of war do not fall within the purview of social problems and hence are not directly considered. (3) The discussion is limited to American society, with European experience treated only briefly for purposes of illustration

ix

and comparison. (4) The study is confined to social problems among the civilian population, except insofar as the behavior of the military directly affected the civilian population. (5) The study deals with the period from 1940-1945, although social problems obviously neither began with the war nor ended with it. Postwar problems merit extended discussion in their own right. (6) The complexity of the problems is such that the presentation is made in general and statistical terms, rather than in local and individual terms.

This study is one of a series sponsored by the Committee on War Studies of the Social Science Research Council. The author hereby expresses his appreciation to the Committee for its initial suggestion and subsequent assistance during the course of the project. My warmest thanks are extended to Dr. Shepard B. Clough of Columbia University, Executive Secretary of the Committee on War Studies, for his generous donations of time and resources and especially for his enthusiastic encouragement. In addition to Dr. Clough, the manuscript was read by Dr. Louis Wirth of the University of Chicago; by Dr. Mabel A. Elliott of Pennsylvania College for Women; and by Dr. Andrew G. Truxal of Dartmouth College. These busy people gave generously of their time and effort and their suggestions are hereby acknowledged with great appreciation. The errors of fact and interpretation should naturally be attributed solely to the author. Finally, to Emily Archibald Merrill, who assisted at every stage in the preparation of the manuscript, my deepest gratitude is accorded.

Francis E. Merrill

Hanover, New Hampshire
January 1, 1948

SOCIAL PROBLEMS on the HOME FRONT

CHAPTER ONE

WAR AND SOCIAL CHANGE

The Nature of Social Change

Total war brings many changes. World War II altered the lives of every man, woman, and child in the United States. Some of these alterations were almost imperceptible and the individuals relapsed quickly into the old patterns when the war was over. Other changes involved fundamental relationships between large numbers of persons which will never be the same again. The impact of the war was so severe that many individuals had their lives permanently modified. The old unregenerate days when wars were conducted by professionals with a minimum of disruption to the citizenry have gone forever and in their place has come total war, from whose impact no one can escape. The task of isolating and describing the social changes brought about by World War II is clearly beyond even the extensive scope of the series of studies of which this volume is a part.[1] The present study has a more modest goal; it deals with a representative group of situations commonly known as "social problems," which were initiated, aggravated, or modified by the social changes attendant upon World War II.

War has been juridically defined as "the *legal condition* which *equally* permits two or more *hostile groups* to carry on a *conflict* by *armed* force."[2] In the broader sociological sense, war is "a simultaneous conflict of armed forces, popular feelings, jural dogmas, and national cultures so nearly equal as to lead to an extreme intensification of each."[3] War is a condition recognized by all civilized states and carrying with it certain appropriate behavior patterns, the nature of which is determined by the character of the war itself. Modern war, as differentiated from the wars of less technologically advanced societies, is characterized by the "increased mechanization and size of armed forces, more general militarization and nationalization of the people, more comprehensive, intense, and extended operations"[4]—in short by all the

social phenomena known as total war. The present study is an attempt
to describe some of the effects of total war upon American society.

Social change in its simplest terms means that large numbers of
people do different things over a given period of time. Total war is
the most catastrophic instigator of social change the world has ever
seen, with the possible exception of violent revolution. War is set in
motion by social forces which initiate other forces, both internal and
external. Millions of persons find themselves doing things they have
never done before. Millions move from one part of the country to the
other, from the rural South to the urban North, from the East to
the Middle West, and from the Middle West to the Far West. Millions work at jobs they have never worked at before, in many cases
jobs which no one has ever done before. Millions of men are uncere-
moniously yanked from civil life and set to learning a new way of
life in the armed forces. Millions of families work out new adjustments, as the wife and mother plays many of the roles of the absent
husband and father. Millions of women go to work for the first time
in their lives, often at hard and exacting manual labor in shipyard
and aircraft factory. Millions of their children somehow learn to fend
for themselves and come home from school to an empty and motherless house. Millions of wives, sweethearts, mothers, and fathers are
under constant nervous tension with their loved ones in active theaters
of operations. Millions of wives learn to live without their husbands,
mothers without their sons, children without their fathers, girls without their beaux. America at war is people doing new things—grimly,
protestingly, gladly, semihysterically—but all changing the pattern of
their lives to some extent under the vast impersonality of total war.

The process of social change may be considered in other terms. In
the sociological frame of reference, wartime social change represents
population migration; social mobility; the evolution of new tech-
nologies and new industries; the rush of population to the congested
centers of war industry; the unprecedented increase in the labor force
from tapping new strata of the population; the imposition of new
social controls upon industry and the consumer; the increased number of broken families, some broken permanently by death or desertion, others temporarily by absence in the armed forces; housing
problems, as thousands of families move from farm to trailer or tene-
ment in a war boom town; family tensions, as the wage-earning wife
for the first time asserts her independence; ill-advised war marriages,

as boys and girl marry during a ten-day furlough; juvenile delinquency in the war centers; prostitution and sexual promiscuity as thousands of adolescent girls follow the glamour of the uniform to the camp towns and embarkation centers; racial tensions in population centers where the races come together under the frustrating circumstances of total war; religious and cultural conflict as accumulated tensions are directed toward the alien group at hand instead of the distant enemy—these are some of the aspects of social change as intensified by total war. These and similar problems represent the human stuff of war and social change. Many of the persons were in a sense casualties of World War II.

All of the social changes resulting from war do not bring about social disorganization, however. The social structure is strengthened by the patriotism enhanced by the wartime crisis. Certain internal controls are measurably strengthened by the presence of an external enemy, particularly when that enemy is Fascist Germany and Imperial Japan. Many formal controls are evidenced by the increased power of the central government, whose added powers are sanctioned by the necessities of war. Many new groups and institutions concern themselves with social problems—such as the control of commercialized vice for military protection—which under peaceful conditions are often not the business of any central authority. The mutually hostile attitudes experienced by various industrial, racial, religious, and nationality groups and expressed in the form of covert peacetime conflict are modified to a certain extent and directed toward the enemy outgroup in wartime. The sense of participation in a gigantic national effort enhances the national consensus and increases the temporary solidarity of the nation. Total war thus sets in motion certain forces tending to unify the nation under the stress of external threat to its existence, although their total net effect is probably less important than those forces making for the interruption of normal social relationships. Total war in general makes for social disorganization.

The Nature of Social Problems

The disorganization of certain social relationships produces a situation known as a social problem. Since we shall be concerned with the effect of World War II upon various selected social problems, it is well to understand clearly what we mean. In general, a social problem "is a condition which is an actual or imagined deviation from some social norm cherished by a considerable number of persons."⁵ The adjectives "actual or imagined" form an important part of the definition, for the reality of the social problem ultimately rests in the minds of the people defining it. A certain social situation—such as widespread discrimination against Negroes—may be observed on every hand throughout the South, but it is not considered a social problem by the majority of white southerners. No social values are threatened, for the values embody the principle of discrimination. In the North, Jim Crow segregation is considered a social problem and efforts are made to eliminate it. A social problem exists only when people are conscious of an infringement upon some cherished social value.

Social problems therefore are both subjective and objective in character. The objective aspect comprises human behavior on a sufficiently large scale to attract the attention of many people not directly concerned, or at least not conscious that they are concerned. The objective phase can be observed, measured, and verified by more or less objective means. Such measurement may take the form of vital statistics (using the term broadly), case histories, informal observation, or various secondary sources of information, in descending order of reliability. The Bureau of the Census acts as an extensive collector of information on different aspects of human behavior which may or may not be defined as social problems, depending on the values involved. Social problems are concerned with human behavior on a large scale, with activities performed by a considerable number of people, which can be measured more or less accurately, and which demand ameliorative action.

The mere existence of certain forms of behavior does not insure their consideration as social problems. To the objective and verifiable situation must be added a subjective evaluation, whereby the situation is judged to be inimical to group values. The situation, in short, must be so defined before it constitutes a social problem. Certain values must be called into question—such as the sanctity of private property, the belief in monogamous marriage, or the rights of free speech and assembly—before the behavior emerges as a full-fledged social problem. The violation may be either actual or imagined; many imaginary threats to established values are more serious than immediate and actual situations. The alleged infringement upon the rights of private initiative by the New Deal evoked more horrendous implications to many people than more serious threats to the same values from the Fascist International. Since values are subjective things, their safety rests in the minds of men, either on the conscious or the unconscious level.[6]

The role of social values is thus central to social problems. It is not necessary to enter the philosophical controversy as to whether values are social objects in themselves or merely the feeling we have toward those objects. For our purposes, social values are those standards and norms which have acquired emotional connotation and whose continued maintenance we believe vital to our social order. Every society has its own set of values, many of which are common to all societies; others are unique to the individual society, at least in emphasis. Many of the values of a capitalistic-democratic society differ from those of a socialist-authoritarian society. The complete abridgement of free speech or state ownership of the means of production are therefore considered social problems in one and not in the other. After the greatest war in history, it should not be necessary to point out that men and nations will die for the preservation of their values.

The present discussion is concerned with the extent to which World War II increased or decreased certain behavior customarily defined as social problems in a democratic society. This is admittedly a large order and one which we do not propose to fill completely. The selection of social problems will be based upon the availability of the information, the competence of the writer, and the assumed interests of the reader. Any study of social problems during World War II with any pretense at completeness (which this emphatically is not) might include impingements upon the following values, suggested as basic to a liberal-democratic society:

"Material well-being of the entire population, including physical health, adequate supply of goods and services; psychic security; opportunity to compete for the possession of necessarily scarce values on the basis of competence in the performance of tasks for which these scarce values are rewards; opportunity of the populace to participate in the determination of policies and measures affecting them; responsibility of elected and appointed officials to the populace or its elected or otherwise designated agents; the maintenance of civil rights, including freedom of speech, freedom of press and publication, freedom of association, freedom of worship; opportunities for personal self-development so as to enable the individual to realize those of his potentialities which are not socially deleterious, including freedom of occupational choice, freedom of consumption choice. . . ."[7]

In addition to these suggested values, concerned largely with economic well-being and the civil liberties, there are others relating to such problems as the employment of women; the care of children; the physical stability of the home; the education of adolescents; respect for the safety of property and the person; premarital chastity; postmarital fidelity against both promiscuity for hire and not for hire; the adequate mental adjustment of the individual to society; and finally the integrity of individual life against suicide. Many of the economic and political values enumerated in the previous paragraph will be considered by other studies in this series. The present writer will have quite enough to do to give even a partial picture of some of the social problems outlined immediately above. Many of the values most basic to our society were questioned during World War II.

Social values are more than passive agents in the germination of social problems. The problem cannot exist without the infringement of the value; when called into question, the value may further obstruct the solution of the problem and even cause more serious problems. The basic social institutions are founded upon certain social values, which serve as the dominant intellectual and emotional concepts keeping them (the institutions) going. To take an extreme example: private property is one of the central values in our social structure and any infringement upon it we view with the greatest alarm. At the same time, certain logical implications of private property lead to such social problems as bad housing, unemployment, and crimes against property. Most people do not suggest that we eliminate private property in order to get rid of these problems. When the relationship between the value and the problem is considered in this light, the latter is usually defined as the necessary price for maintaining the central value of private property. Likewise, divorce is considered as a social problem threatening the existence of the stable family. If the traditional family were not based upon the *value* of indissoluble marriage, however, divorce would not be considered a fundamental threat to its future.

Social values both cause social problems and obstruct their solution. It is no mere play on words to point out, for example, that the value of private property obstructs a complete solution of the housing problem. Slum properties continue to exist because they are highly profitable; having amortized their original investment, the operators are content to make a minimum of repairs, keep the building fully occupied at a high gross rent, and pay a high net return to the estate, corporation, bank, or religious institution owning the property. This is by no means the only consideration involved in the complex housing problem.[8] It should be clear from this example, however, that in our complex society contradictory values arise and remain long after their original validity has gone. These values conflict in any attempt to ameliorate the conditions leading to many social problems. A complete solution of a certain problem would thus satisfy one set of values but might run directly counter to another. This conflict of values is one reason why social problems, even when their origin and genesis are fully understood, are difficult to solve. Action in any direction may run foul of a social value.[9]

The conflict in values may also take the form of a denial that any problem exists. People who are convinced that sexual freedom is a desirable value may deny that the increase in such behavior during World War II constituted a social problem. Those who argue for freedom in marriage may contend with perfect sincerity that the increase in divorce prior to and during the war was a desirable indication of greater freedom and hence no social problem. The wartime increase in child labor, involving the employment of children and adolescents and their absence from school, may be considered an eminently satisfactory return to the old ways by those who believe in hard work and no education. Discrimination against the Negro in the South is not necessarily a social problem to the majority of people south of the Mason-Dixon line. For certain generals, war is not a social problem but the most desirable possible order of things, unfortunately broken by occasional outbursts of peace. And so it goes. Many situations do not constitute a threat to the social values of large numbers of people and for them are not social problems.[10]

The question of amelioration involves the final element in the analysis of social problems. Certain forms of behavior are almost universally defined as social problems, since they threaten values which are almost universal in their application. Juvenile delinquency, crime, mental deficiency, mental disease, poverty, ill health, and bad housing fall in this category. Virtually everyone agrees that, when large numbers of persons are delinquent, criminal, mentally deficient, mentally deranged, poor, ill, and badly housed, the conditions constitute a series of social problems. But when it comes to ameliorative action against these problems, the conflict of values becomes apparent and as often as not there is no consensus forthcoming. To control crime, some would increase the severity of punishment and others would eliminate it altogether; to alleviate poverty, the proposals range all the way from complete socialism to the abandonment of all central regulation; suggested cures for mental deficiency run from sterilization of the border-line feeble-minded to more education for the morons. Social programs for social problems are a babel of conflicting values, attitudes, and ideologies.[11]

War and a Dynamic Society

Modern society is dynamic. Social change takes place with bewildering rapidity even in peacetime. The rate at which new traits and social patterns are introduced under "normal" conditions insures a constant state of disequilibrium. Social techniques, economic institutions, social institutions, and ideological elements are all changing at a differential rate of speed, bringing social maladjustment in their wake.[12] This condition is chronic to American society and can be mitigated, but not eliminated, by welfare provisions, social planning, and the resources of those private and public agencies whose business it is to rehabilitate the demoralized individual. The human effects of these social maladjustments which have been defined as inimical to the welfare of the group are called social problems. Total war is highly productive of social problems.

The outbreak of World War II found the United States at the end of a decade which had seen depression, partial recovery, the ominous threat of armed conflict, and the beginning of rearmament. Many group patterns had been weakened by the crisis of unemployment and its attendant dislocations. The dramatic role of the Federal Government in attacking these problems for the first time on a large scale added a new and unprecedented factor to the national equation. The great debate between the isolationists and interventionists had brought certain basic differences of opinion into sharp emotional focus. Race prejudice, religious bigotry, and hostility to various ethnic groups were coming to the national attention, highlighted by similar trends abroad. Organized labor was moving swiftly to consolidate its newly-won gains with the resultant pressure of class tensions. Social mobility, always one of the most characteristic features of American society, had not appreciably subsided from its mid-depression height. Large-scale migration to new industries had already begun, as hundreds of thousands of persons moved to the defense centers, shortly to be followed by millions of others. Social change and social maladjustment were familiar aspects of the American scene on the eve of Pearl Harbor.[13]

The outbreak of the war burst like another bombshell upon an American society already beset with serious social problems. The war set in motion a series of forces which tremendously increased the already rapid rate of social change. The gap between the rate of technological change and related social institutions was increased as public attention became centered upon winning the war at all costs, no matter what the human toll might be. This disparity between technological and social considerations was symbolized by Willow Run. This mammoth bomber plant embodied the latest in technical skill for the manufacture of the most dramatic instruments of modern warfare; the thousands of employees lived in squalid trailer camps, in pestilential shanty towns with privies in the back yard, or commuted forty miles per day to and from their homes in Detroit. Total war was defined in the quantitative terms of the invention, production, and distribution of unlimited quantities of munitions of war. The human implications of these necessary material factors were, with certain outstanding exceptions, largely ignored. As a result, America suffered casualties on the home front which compared in severity with those on the battlefield. Public opinion defined the situation in material terms. Many of its human implications were overlooked.[14]

This concentration on techniques undoubtedly enabled the United States to perform a miracle of production. The traditional American ingenuity which was responsible for the high material standard of living in a prewar world was applied to the business of war production.[15] Our own huge military establishment was largely, and that of our allies partially, equipped by these inventive skills combined with the industrial potentialities of this country. The result was a source of pride to ourselves, thanks from our allies, and apprehension to our enemies. The productive facilities of the country were co-ordinated with superlative skill to the business of war.[16] The effects of this co-ordination were apparent on every battlefield of the world. A considerable segment of the nation's industrial plant was converted almost overnight from a peacetime to a wartime basis.

The dynamics of society on the industrial and technological level thus received an unparalleled impetus, as billions of dollars of government money were poured into the erection of new plant facilities, more billions into the subsidization of other plants, and still more billions into war orders from established industrial concerns. These changes on the industrial level set in motion others on the institutional level, as millions of persons shifted their jobs and their homes simultaneously. The industrial changes were measured in the figures for the production of four-engine bombers, landing craft, destroyer escort vessels, and finally in the miracle of the atomic bomb. The accompanying social changes could not be measured in such satisfactory terms. Neither the national administration nor the people most directly concerned had the time or the energy to interest themselves in many wartime social problems.

World War II thus made a dynamic society more dynamic, increased the rate of change in an already rapidly changing society, and intensified many of the social problems deriving from the disparity in the rate of change between the various segments of this society. The normal processes of social change characteristic of our society were stimulated by the impact of the war. Many of the social problems arising from wartime maladjustments were thus much the same as those apparent in peacetime, with their severity enhanced by accelerated wartime change.

Reactions to Wartime Change

In the process of social change, social attitudes, values, and ideologies change less rapidly than do the corresponding technological, economic, and institutional structures.[17] This lag is particularly evident in wartime, when the universal experience of social change in perhaps its most drastic form is combined with a strong desire to maintain the *status quo*. The motivation for this idealization of the past and the absent is clear enough in the case of members of the armed forces who are forced to live away from their homes, families, and familiar surroundings for periods ranging up to several years.[18] Under such circumstances millions of men wish to keep America just as it was so that they may return to a country similar to the one they remembered during their enforced exile. These images do not adequately represent reality, a fact which contributes to the inevitable disillusionment of returning soldiers.[19] The importance of these mental constructs, however, rests not in their scientific validity but in their emotional value. Under the stress of battle and the cumulation of boredom, men do not live in a colorless and abstract world. They live in a colorful world of their own thinking and their own desiring, a world peopled with images of things as they would like to have them.[20]

More germane to our own interest, however, was the civilian reaction to the changes brought about by the war. Members of the civilian population saw changes in society going on before their very eyes. These alterations ranged in severity from the mild deprivations arising from rationing to those accompanying the voluntary cross-country migration of families and the employment of mothers in an aircraft factory. Social change means modifications in the behavior of millions of persons, modifications which are accelerated by war as by no other social phenomenon. In spite of the personal character of these innovations, the average individual is often unable to adjust his emotional life to them. He continues to live in a world of symbols derived from his formative years, symbols which were not accurately descriptive of his youthful world, let alone of his mature world. This failure of the individual to adjust his definitions to the dynamic reality accentuates the maladjustments of wartime society.

The combination of emotional conservatism and vested interests in connection with social change in peacetime applies most directly to technological innovations.[21] Many of these same factors are present in wartime to an accentuated degree because of the increased rate of change. The difference in the degree of acceptance is even more evident between those elements that are strictly technological and those connected with social institutions and related ideologies. Innovations at the technological level are defined as vital to the successful prosecution of the war, as indeed they are in the race between the belligerents to perfect the most efficient and lethal weapons and counterweapons. Improvements in the construction of atomic weapons, superbombers, rockets, jet-propelled aircraft, antitank weapons, and all the other devices useful in the conduct of the war are welcomed in the same spirit as technological developments in peacetime.

Attitudes toward institutional and ideological changes are not so favorable. These attitudes consist of (a) denying that any significant changes have taken place, and (b) tacitly accepting their reality but denying both their permanence and relative importance. These reactions take the form of an emotional denial that any significant modification has taken place in the family, the democratic state, the church, and the institutions of a *laissez-faire* economy. These institutions live in symbolic form in the minds of the average citizen, a form which he finds satisfactory for his emotional needs and for a rule-of-thumb adjustment to the world as it is. His life is organized about these symbols. They represent reality to him and he refuses to modify them even under the impact of total war. From his point of view, indeed, the war was fought for the preservation of these symbols in their traditional form. Any substantial modification thereof would be tantamount to treason and defeatism. Therefore, the average person refuses to believe that any permanent alterations have taken place in his institutional pattern and its ideological counterpart, both of which exist as stereotypes in his mind.

The importance of this "pseudo-environment" of stereotypes, symbols, and myths lies in the fact that the individual bases his actions upon it. If he were content merely to mull over the changes brought about by war and do nothing about them, the resultant effect upon the real world would be negligible. His symbolic environment, however, motivates his actions in the real environment of political issues, economic relationships, religious pressures, and family attitudes. A knowledge of the pictures in his head is thus important to an understanding of his social behavior.[22] Many illustrations of this psychological maladjustment will be apparent in the various aspects of wartime behavior. It seems clear that the social maladjustments of wartime society are further intensified by these negativistic definitions of change itself. By denying the existence of the institutional changes, the individual places a psychological roadblock in the way of subsequent adjustment. People unaware of the necessity for social readjustment do not take kindly to efforts to bring about the necessary changes.

Many phases of economic, social, and cultural life have traditionally been intrusted to private initiative in our society. The field of private housing, for example, has been left largely to the individual who is expected to provide for his family to the best of his ability without outside assistance. This procedure operated with reasonable efficiency while America was still primarily a rural society. It operated with less efficiency during the rise of the large city, particularly in the crowded slum areas of those urban agglomerations. It operated with still less efficiency during World War II, when small urban communities doubled and tripled in population in a few months following the establishment of an army camp, explosives factory, or port of embarkation.

Under such conditions, private enterprise is inadequate, as the housing situation is still defined in terms of traditional individualism. Clinging to the symbolic vestiges of a pioneer day, the local people may shrug their shoulders at the plight of the migrant families brought in to work in the new factory. They may categorically deny the necessity of government housing on the ground that this is in violation of the American way. They may even actively oppose any such efforts on the assumption that the migrant families will be left at the termination of hostilities and thereby swell the local relief rolls.[23] On whatever symbolic terms the rationalization is made, the result tends to be the same—namely, an intensification of social maladjustment through failure to realize the reality and importance of social change.[24]

This aggravation of wartime social maladjustment was not confined to the field of defense housing. Changes took place in almost every important field of human relationship,[25] intensifying the gap between present behavior and its traditional definition. Some of these changes were readily discernible in the statistical data collected and tabulated by public and private agencies. Others were apparent only in the subjective analyses of the changing roles, attitudes, and definitions of the situation of the millions of persons whose behavior was modified by the war. In our subsequent consideration of these modifications in behavior, we shall examine both the changes themselves and their social definitions. Only by understanding both the objective and the subjective manifestations of wartime social problems can their full implications be grasped. A knowledge of the definition of the situation, as well as the situation itself, is necessary to complete understanding.[26]

War and Employment

War on the home front meant that many people performed a variety of new activities. Millions of persons either worked at new jobs or at any job outside the home for the first time. The Bureau of Labor Statistics estimated that from the summer of 1940 to April, 1944 the number of persons in the armed forces or in civilian jobs increased by approximately 16 million over the total number employed in 1940. This total was achieved by absorbing approximately seven million who were unemployed in 1940 and adding nine million additional persons to the labor force. Under normal conditions, the labor force would have been increased over this period by less than three million; the additional six million represented a variety of persons who would not otherwise have entered the labor force—"students, housewives, retired workers, or others not working or seeking work in paid employment."[27]

This large group was composed of people whose way of life was drastically modified by the war, since it represented those who were not previously working as well as many millions who would not under normal circumstances ever have worked at gainful employment. Other millions should also be included in the war readjustment, inasmuch as they were performing functions which they were not performing four years before. A complete picture of social change on the employment level alone would further augment this 16 million persons by the number who were employed in 1940 at a peacetime job and subsequently changed to one connected with the war. This group did not represent a net increase in the labor force, but it did figure in any consideration of the impact of war upon the employment of the American people.

The "long arm of the job" reached into every other level of behavior in wartime America. This influence was particularly apparent in the members of the new working group who would not have been working under peacetime conditions. Approximately 3.3 million of the "abnormal" wartime expansion of the labor force came from boys and girls who would ordinarily have been attending school on a full-time basis, instead of going part-time and working after school. The behavior of these young people underwent profound alterations during the war. The 1,380,000 employed wives of service men also perforce adjusted to a changed situation, as they simultaneously learned new jobs and tried to adapt themselves to the absence of their husbands. The adjustments faced by these young women were perhaps more severe than those of any other group in the civilian population. Finally, the labor force in April, 1944 included about 800,000 *extra* male workers over 55. These were men who would normally have retired but instead continued working, plus many who came back from retirement to lend their skills and training to the war effort. These representative segments of the employed population in the Spring of invasion year represented different aspects of the problem of changed behavior under wartime conditions. Equally drastic changes took place among many of the remainder of the 59.5 million members of the armed and labor forces of the nation.[28]

War and Social Mobility

The United States is the most mobile society the world has ever seen. Millions of restless men and women are constantly on the move. The resultant social fluidity is unprecedented both in range and extent. More than 15 million persons, or approximately 12 per cent of the population, changed their residence at least once in the five years from 1935 to 1940.[29] The tremendous physical distances in the country have largely been conquered by modern transportation and communication, so that the individual is substantially at home in any of the regional subcultures of the nation, even though some of the local mores may be unfamiliar to him. Search for better economic opportunities—and often for any opportunity at all—is still the basic motivating factor in our social mobility. From the pioneer movements into the East and Middle West, the settlement of the Great Plains, the opening of the Far West, and the closing of the last frontier, Americans have been a nation of wanderers. The defense program and the war accelerated tendencies which have been evident for many years.

Social mobility in the United States reached its highest point during World War II. Estimates by the Bureau of the Census indicate that approximately 15,300,000 members of the civilian population (12 per cent of the nonmilitary total) were residing in a different county in March, 1945 than they were on December 7, 1941. This total does not include the 12,000,000 men and women in the armed forces, whose wartime mobility was proverbial, nor does it include the persons who moved away from their county of residence after Pearl Harbor but returned by March, 1945. Such persons were not counted as migrants. Even without this last undetermined number, the combined total of civilian and military migrants between our entrance into the war and the final few months of the conflict was 27,300,000 persons. "Never before in the history of our country," comments the Bureau of the Census, "has there been so great a shuffling and redistribution of population in so short a time."[30]

The impetus of World War II surpassed the hitherto unequaled movement of the late depression years, even when the movements of the armed forces were not included. The volume of civilian migration during the war was approximately two-thirds greater, on an average annual basis, than that of the last half of the turbulent 1930's. With certain corrections, the yearly number of migrants in the 1935-40

period was approximately 2,800,000, while during the war years the
number rose to approximately 4,700,000 annually. The compulsive forces
operative during World War II were even more powerful than those
of the depression years. High wages in the war industries, the desire
to participate actively in the war effort, the wish to be near husbands
and sweethearts, and finally the sad migration back to the parental
home when the soldier was shipped overseas—these were among the
wartime factors contributing to the five-million annual civilian mobility. Many of the 7,100,000 women comprising the majority of the
11,800,000 civilian migrants over 14 years of age came in one of these
latter categories. Their movements were determined by those of their
men.[31]

Striking regional differences were apparent in the pattern of wartime mobility. The trend of long-distance migration during the war
followed that evident before the war, namely, from north and south
toward the West. The West quickly became the most expansive of the
war-booming areas, with aircraft and ship-building industries thriving
and attracting large numbers of migrants (many of them young men
and women) from all parts of the country. These young and well-
paid persons continued to swell marriage and birth records in the
West long after the rest of the country had lapsed into normalcy or
even subnormalcy in this respect.[32] In the period from Pearl Harbor
to the Spring of 1945, the West showed a net gain of approximately
1,200,000 in civilian population, with the South contributing some
900,000 of this total and the North about 300,000. This net gain of the
West becomes even more significant when the figures for gross migration are considered. Approximately 1,600,000 wartime migrants invaded
the West during this period, of whom 900,000 came from the North
and 700,000 from the South. Only 400,000 left the West in these years,
leaving a net wartime gain of almost a million and a quarter citizens.[33]

In spite of the increased industrialization of the South during the
war and the large number of military installations established there,
this region was the chief loser by wartime migration, contributing
hundreds of thousands of its men, women, and children to the North
as well as the West. Some 1,000,000 persons moved from the South
to the North, many of them to the urban centers of the North Central
States, where they were attracted by the high wages in the war industries. The counter-migration from North to South was only 600,000,
leaving the latter with a net deficit of some 400,000 persons. When the

total gross migration from the South to the North and West is considered, the South saw some 1,600,000 of its sons and daughters leave the land of cotton and move to some other part of the country.[34] The ultimate effects of this migration upon social attitudes in the field of race, religion, and industrial problems will no doubt be considerable, as the migrants interact with persons of different cultural backgrounds.

Another significant impact of wartime mobility was that taking place upon the social structure of the South itself. The war accelerated the prewar migration from the rural areas to the rapidly growing industrial areas, with a consequent modification of the extreme cultural isolation which formerly characterized farm life in this region. Southern migration within a state amounted to the considerable total of 3,200,000 and interstate migration within the South to 1,600,000. The war thus stimulated nearly five million persons to move within the South alone, not counting the other hundreds of thousands who left the region altogether. At no time since the Civil War has the South undergone such a tremendous social ferment, characterized in this instance by the numbers of persons abruptly brought into contact with new social patterns, either in the industrial areas of their own region or in similar areas of new and unfamiliar regions.[35]

One of the important effects of mobility is the necessity to adjust to another group of friends, social institutions, and social attitudes. This necessity was experienced by all of the 27,300,000 civilian and military migrants during World War II, every one of whom entered into new social relationships in their wartime peregrinations. The 15,300,000 civilian migrants were all obliged to adapt themselves to new social institutions—schools, churches, businesses, and governmental agencies —manned by strange employees and functionaries with different personal characteristics and new ways. The 12,000,000 men and women in the armed forces made the most drastic adjustment when they stepped from civilian into military life. Once adjusted, however, it made no basic difference whether they were stationed in South Carolina, Texas, or California. The change to military life had been made and military life was everywhere distressingly similar.

To the civilian migrants who moved long distances from one region to another, the social adjustments presented additional complications. A family moving from the backwoods of Georgia to the suburbs of Detroit was faced with all the adjustments of any family moving from one community to another. In addition, it had to adapt its behavior from rural to urban life. Finally, this migrant southern family had to make the change from one regional pattern to another, involving accommodative adjustments to such highly emotional situations as new racial, religious, and industrial relations. During the war, regional migration was undertaken by approximately 3,600,000 persons, with 7,800,000 crossing state lines. In the peacetime five-year period from 1935 to 1940, interregional migrants were 2,600,000 in number, while interstate migrants were 6,500,000. The war exhibited the same high degree of long-range mobility as the immediate prewar period, with an acceleration of previous trends from 1941 to 1945.[36]

Social Problems and Wartime Mobility

The loosening of group patterns characteristic of peacetime mobility was also apparent in wartime, whether the individual moved during the defense or actual war period. A considerable proportion of the 15,300,000 persons who moved from one county to another between 1941 and 1945 severed many of the ties of neighborhood and community life in the process. In the new community, these migrants were considered as transients by many of the permanent residents and often not admitted to full equality in local affairs. The temporary character of the war emergency caused many of the migrants to consider themselves as semitransient residents of the new community and hence not subject to the same obligations and restraints as those with more permanent ties. These attitudes produced a certain degree of maladjustment in the community, as well as in the persons defined as transients therein. Many of the social problems related to wartime mobility grew out of this decline in the informal controls of the social group. These problems may be considered briefly here in terms of the larger society, the family, and the person—categories which are actually but three different aspects of the same social whole.

1. *Mobility and society.* When millions of persons move from one community to another, many social relationships are modified or broken.[37] When this move takes place over a period of four or five years and the bulk of the migrant population is crowded into a relatively few heavily congested areas, the resulting maladjustments are compounded. When 12 per cent of the civilian population live in a different county in 1945 than they did less than four years before, the resultant process involves millions of individual adjustments and thousands of group adjustments. Some adjustments are completely suc-

cessful, others less so, and still others frankly unsuccessful, both to the migrants and the recipient population. The "cake of custom" was broken in many places by persons leaving local groups and institutions, as well as by those attempting to make contact with similar organizations in the new community. The war was like the ladle of a gigantic soup cauldron, stirring up the normal ingredients, tossing them from side to side and place to place, bringing about new mixtures of the component parts, and finally removing some elements completely and depositing them in various remote corners of the world.

The appearance of persons with new behavior patterns may bring about social tensions in the recipient communities. This was an important effect of wartime mobility upon the structure of American society as a whole. Racial patterns of accommodation, attitudes of religious tolerance, accommodative relationships with various ethnic groups tend to mitigate social conflict when these diverse groups live in close contact for prolonged periods.[38] A period of intensified mobility scatters the bearers of these patterns and brings them into contact with other situations in which accommodation is not similarly established. Many of the conflict patterns which in peacetime remain covert were fanned into open flame in World War II by persons whose prejudices were offended by unfamiliar relationships. Many of these new contacts were made on a highly emotional level; tempers were short on crowded streetcars in Washington, Baltimore, Detroit, and St. Louis, as white migrants from the South were jostled by Negroes who had long breathed the heady northern air of comparative freedom. Serious race rioting arose in more than one city from a series of such episodes.[39]

2. *Mobility and the family.* The family as a social institution is peculiarly dependent upon a fixed physical locus. Parents need the stabilizing force of local institutions as well as the informal controls of neighborhood opinion. Children need the continuity of regular school attendance and the emotional security of a familiar group of playmates in which their status is firmly established. These elements are lacking, at least in part, when the family moves from one community to the other, no matter what its economic circumstances. The family will ordinarily participate more completely in a new community if the father has a responsible job, although even then many of the elements of social stability are lacking. The nomadic life of the migrant was formerly confined almost exclusively to men and boys.

During the depression, the effects of social uprooting were applied to thousands of families, a trend continued under the defense and wartime mobilization of the industrial and human resources of the nation.

The economic condition of the wartime migrant family was relatively good and few requests for financial aid came to the social agencies during the defense and wartime boom. Many of the economic problems ordinarily associated with transiency were not evident until cutbacks in the military production programs began to cause local unemployment. Welfare authorities were fearful that many wartime migrants would be stranded in unsympathetic communities when the war was over. These communities did everything they could to encourage the influx of migratory labor, only to regard the newcomer as a social pariah when the rush began to slacken. The general attitude toward these millions of mobile individuals and families, upon whose willingness to move much of the success of the war program depended, was indicated by the failure of the majority of local communities and states to make the new workers eligible for public assistance. In any prolonged period of postwar unemployment, the plight of thousands of migrant families will become desperate. The honored warworker may easily again become the despised Okie.[40]

The unity of the family was often broken by the wartime mobility of the breadwinner. Divorce figures do not indicate the results of this situation and accurate desertion figures are nonexistent. We can only judge by indirection that the effect of wartime migration upon family stability was anything but salutary. Although the majority of the families temporarily broken by migration were ultimately reunited, there were many families whose head vanished without a trace into the vast mass of the mobile population.[41] Many men who left home to find defense and war jobs may never have had any intention of sending for their families. Others gradually grew apart through no design on either side. Still others eventually granted their wives divorces on the grounds of desertion. Whatever the process of deterioration, whether premeditated or accidental, the end result upon the family was unfortunate. Many families suffered eventual disintegration under the impact of wartime mobility.[42]

3. *Mobility and the person.* The effects of wartime mobility upon the person were but different aspects of its effects upon the larger social group and the family. Whatever the social unit, it is the person who in the last analysis is cut off from the normal contacts of settled

community life. The hostile or indifferent attitude of many members of the local community toward the warworker was often equaled only by the lack of interest of the migrants themselves in the intimate life of their new home. No matter how honest, industrious, and patriotic the newcomer might have been, the old resident often tended to define him as a stranger, a migrant, and a shiftless wanderer, unable to sink his roots deeply in any one place. The stereotype of the wretched Okie was a difficult one for the wartime migrant to overcome.[43]

The children of migration are the chief victims when this way of life is carried to extremes. During the wartime peregrinations of their families from one industrial center to another, many children were taken out of school and were unable to establish the permanent social contacts so important in building a stable life organization. These children were often forced to live under inadequate housing conditions, in trailer camps or crowded slum areas in the outskirts of mushrooming industrial cities.[44] In many cases, these new homes were no worse than those in which they existed before the war emergency. These former dwellings, such as they were, nevertheless represented home to the migrant children, something the new ones would never become.

The demand for war workers brought another group into the field, themselves but scarcely older than the children who played in the mud of the trailer camps. These were the adolescents from 14–18 years of age who were lured from home by the prospect of lucrative work in war plants or related industries and whose help was sought by war and service industries as long as the emergency lasted. Although these new migrants experienced few of the employment difficulties of their older brothers and sisters in the depression decade, they were still faced by many of the problems growing out of a mobile way of life.[45] These young people, at an impressionable age, were often obliged to live in cheap hotels, rooming houses, and trailer camps in the least desirable areas of the city. These were the centers which, after a fashion, had housed transients for decades. Institutions and social patterns had sprung up in these sections to cater to the homeless man of the predepression period. These institutions were notably unsuitable for young people. The postwar repercussions of such experiences in the lives of thousands of young people will not be salutary.[46]

Many of these changes brought about by wartime mobility will be continued after the war. A considerable minority (estimated by some authorities as one half) of the wartime migrants stated that they were not planning to return "home" after the war. Some were planning to settle in the community where they found temporary employment, others to move on to other fields. The readiness of the wartime migrants to remigrate varied with the apparent security of their future employment, the length of time they had been in the new community, the place they had made in it, the degree to which they had become identified with its institutions, their relative social status in their former home town, and their general satisfaction with the new social milieu. "It seems safe to conclude, therefore," suggests one student of population movements, "that whatever conditions exist after the war— full employment or mass unemployment—this war will have effected some permanent changes in our distribution of population."[47] The egg cannot be unscrambled.

War and Consensus

Many recurrent conflict situations between white and black, native-born and foreign-born, workers and management, Catholic and Protestant, and Jew and Gentile are latent in peacetime society and indicate that the United States has not yet achieved the cultural, racial, and class homogeneity that makes for harmonious social adjustments. Perfect or even approximate agreement is not found in our peacetime population; the frustrations, deprivations, and anxieties of wartime living combined to make consensus all the more difficult. "These conflicts," comments one observer, "can be visualized as the acceleration of trends previously present in our culture to a degree where they seriously impair the efficiency of any collective effort. Time as a dimension of adjustment in this case will only serve to intensify the conflicts and perpetuate them at the expense of sound post-war reconstruction."[48] The national effort was directed toward winning the war with all possible dispatch. On that level, consensus was virtually unanimous. On the level of institutional, class, and ideological alignments, such unanimity did not exist. With negligible exceptions, the nation was united about the central aim of victory over the Axis powers. On many of the practical applications of democracy at home, however, the situation was not so clear.

More than a century ago, De Tocqueville described the concept of censensus in terms as clearly applicable to American society in World War II as to the then struggling young republic. "A society can exist," he suggested, "only when a great number of men consider a great number of things in the same point of view; when they hold the same opinions upon many subjects, and when the same occurrences suggest the same thoughts and impressions to their minds."[49] Long before the war was over, there was no longer any question of the *physical* safety of an America which had become the most powerful military force in the world. The conflicting pressures of interest groups during the war left some doubt, however, of the type of social structure which would emerge from the crisis. Postwar efforts must be made on the domestic front commensurate in scope and daring with those made on the battle front if the nation is not to lose many of the democratic fruits of victory. The difficulty is more than making democracy work; it is also a question of making large numbers of people *want* it to work, of making sure that "a great number of men consider a great number of things in the same point of view" when they think of democracy.

The concept of wartime consensus is essentially the same as morale, a popular expression whose implications are often little understood. Blumer has defined group morale as "a disposition to act together toward a goal,"[50] a definition which combines aphoristic brevity with sociological soundness. The war strengthened national morale on the exalted level of victory, but it did not exert a corresponding influence upon morale on the level of conflicting groups, classes, and ideologies. Certain powerful pressure groups may indeed have attempted to use the war emergency to promote their own ends.[51] A lack of consensus on many fundamental democratic issues was evident throughout World War II.

The normal processes of social change characteristic of our dynamic society were clearly intensified by total war. The maladjustments arising from the differential rate of change between the several aspects of wartime society were intensified by the negative definitions placed upon many of these changes. Social problems growing out of wartime maladjustments were thus aggravated by conflicting social values. Certain difficulties arose from the conviction that no change had taken place and hence that there was no problem of adjustment. Other difficulties grew out of the conflicting definitions of what should be done, admitting that a problem actually existed. This confusion increased the complexity of adjustment to both material and institutional changes and thereby further confounded the situation.

A central hypothesis emerges from this preliminary discussion. The hypothesis is that World War II intensified, but did not substantially modify, the social problems of a peacetime society. We shall examine this hypothesis in the light of various aspects of wartime behavior. The facts may confirm the hypothesis that total war is a great accelerator, but not a great modifier, of social problems. On the other hand, the facts may indicate that total war not only intensifies old problems but at the same time temporarily alleviates others. A third possibility is that total war also creates still other problems not ordinarily found in peacetime. If either or both of these alternatives proves to be the case, we shall have to revise our hypothesis.

CHAPTER TWO

WAR AND FAMILY DISORGANIZATION

Social Change and Family Disorganization

The family is an outgrowth of the society as a whole. By changing the social structure, World War II brought about such modifications in the family as a rising marriage rate, an accelerated birth rate, and an increased participation of married women in gainful activity outside the home. The war also brought about important changes in the functions which the family has traditionally performed in our society. The war introduced new conditions under which marriage took place and modified the internal relationships and external contacts of the members of the family. The war so changed the way of life of millions of people that many new stresses and strains were generated within the pattern of family relationships. Some of these changes will be reflected for generations. This chapter will consider some of the principal wartime tensions communicated to the family, as well as the extent to which the secular trend toward an increasing rate of family disorganization was affected by the war. Finally, we shall consider briefly the impact of World War II upon the future stability of the family, particularly in terms of its immediate prospects.

The dynamic society of prewar America set in motion many individual tensions which were ultimately communicated to the family. Just as a static society tends to imply a stable family, so a dynamic society is reflected in an unstable family, maintained at high psychic stress and predisposed to tensions, disorganization, and disintegration. Approximately a quarter of a million divorces took place in the prewar year of 1937, which was the highest absolute number up to that time. The divorce rate in that year was 1.93 per 1,000 of estimated population, the highest rate in the history of the country.[1] These two figures provided an index to the state of matrimony in a nation emerging from its greatest depression and to the pent-up tensions which had been temporarily repressed during this period.

The rate of prewar divorce was also an indication of another basic trend in the American family—a trend marked by new functions and new expectations. Deprived of many of the utilitarian functions which formerly kept it together, the family has increasingly become a relationship providing personal affection, sexual excitement, and emotional security for its adult members. These functions are difficult to perform to the complete satisfaction of the participants, nourished as they are upon the ideals of romantic love. The disorganization of the modern family is thus often the aftermath of a frustrated idealism.[2]

Family tensions come both from within and without. Internal tensions reflect the hopes and expectations, the personal whimsies, and the temperamental differences of husband and wife. External tensions grow more directly out of the society in which the family operates and reflect the technological, economic, and institutional maladjustments therein.[3] Both forms of tensions are apparent in the family in peace and war. The divorce rate declined during the early years of the depression and slowly increased during the years immediately thereafter. The rate continued to rise steadily throughout World War II, so that by the end of hostilities in 1945 it had reached its highest point.

The war brought about the prolonged separation of between three and four million families.[4] Such a prolonged mass separation had never been previously experienced by the American family. The effects of this phenomenon cannot be completely ascertained until long after the war, since many of the resultant frustrations and deprivations were not apparent until the millions of families had been reassembled for some time. Many families were broken by the military death of the' husband. The majority of these men would normally have expected to finish their middle and declining years in the comforting security of their homes and families. In the temporary separation of millions of families and the permanent disruption of thousands of others, the war exerted a new and unforeseen influence upon this central institution.

All of the effects of the war upon the family were neither so new nor so radical as this mass separation. In other respects, the war largely tended to accelerate the changes of a peacetime society which had long been threatening the stability of the family. The mobility of wartime families, the personal frustrations of their members, the modifications in family functions, the growing importance of the romantic aspects, and the changing economic roles of husband and wife—all these were present in prewar society and were intensified by the war. Under the dynamism of twentieth-century America, families had long been more mobile; the traditional functions had been rapidly assumed by other agencies; marriage was becoming more a personal and temporary relationship and less an impersonal and permanent institution; more married women were entering business and industry; and patriarchal roles were deteriorating as women increasingly assumed masculine prerogatives. None of these changes was initiated by the war; all of them were immensely accelerated by it. The family underwent a corresponding modification; with this modification went an increased difficulty in maintaining its old-fashioned solidarity.

War and Family Tensions (Personal)

Since personality is the subjective aspect of culture, changes in the culture will be ultimately reflected in the personality of its participants. The members of a family reflect in their personalities many of the tensions immanent in a wartime society. The frustrations, anxieties, bewilderments, hates, aggressions, and uncertainties generated in a society undergoing the fears and regimentation inevitable in wartime are reflected in the family circle. "Many of the minor tensions in family life," remarks Mowrer, "grow out of the fact that the members of the family become the convenient scapegoats for the hatreds and animosities generated in the communal life of the individual, which, in the interest of maintaining his prestige, his job, and the accomplishments of his goal, he has to hold in check. The family circle," he concludes, "becomes the convenient locale within which these emotions can with some safety find expression, even at the expense of producing tensions in family relations."[5] By serving as a safety valve for the emotional release of the frustrated individual, the family suffers a certain weakening of its own solidarity. The tie binding husband and wife can resist many corrosive tensions and expressions of ill-temper. When these manifestations are multiplied by the conflicts of a wartime society, however, the cumulative effect may ultimately bring disaster to the individual family. The conjugal boiling point is eventually reached, even if "there *is* a war on."

Personal tensions also grow out of different behavior patterns of husband and wife. Rare indeed is the family whose members do not experience some small irritations from certain habits and mannerisms of the others. Under the peacetime conditions in a functioning family, these petty annoyances are generally overlooked or condoned. Even those marriages which come to the parting of the ways on apparently minor differences are generally riven by fundamental maladjustments of whose real nature the participants may or may not be fully aware. Married people suffering from wartime tensions and frustrations may find it more difficult to forgive and forget. Annoyances ordinarily ignored become magnified in homes overshadowed by the tensions of war. Such deeper fears as the loss of a loved one may serve temporarily to bring the family together, as the members turn to each other to assuage their sorrow. On another level, however, the tensions arising from clashing personalities may be more pronounced in wartime.

The response pattern in marriage includes not only sex relations but also the intimate exchanges on the personal level which play such an important role in the modern family.[6] In peacetime, the response tension may arise from sexual incompatibility or the different definitions which husband and wife place upon the sexual problem. In wartime, the problem becomes one of total or partial deprivation of the sexual response and the resultant lack of emotional security in husband and wife. The lonely wife and the soldier husband present far too complex a subject for complete treatment here. A revealing monograph might be based upon the emotional difficulties arising from this situation in a representative sample of the three to four million families temporarily broken during World War II. This crisis in the response tension is one of the unique and unprecedented effects of the war upon the intimate relationships of the family. The majority of peacetime situations involving such tensions are concerned with the unwillingness of the wife to submit to the physical attentions of the husband, the progressive lack of excitement with which the husband views such attentions, or the divergent points of view concerning the relative importance of personal intimacy in marriage. In wartime, the emphasis shifted. Husbands and wives no longer complained of boredom or incompatibility. They complained of loneliness.

The role of jealousy in wartime family tensions is another problem on which information is lacking, save fragmentary and inconclusive case material. From isolated cases, it appears that a wide disparity in familial definition existed between married couples during the war. In some instances, the husband tacitly understood that the wife would not live a completely monastic life during his absence but would go out with other men and even accept an occasional good-night kiss. In other cases, the husband exacted and the wife obeyed a rigid code of behavior which permitted her no more than a civil word to any potential male companion and restricted her completely to the society of other war widows. Whatever the arrangements between husband and wife, the relationship was not productive of serious tensions as long as it was maintained in mutual good faith. Tension and jealousy arose when the situation was defined in a different manner by husband and wife or when one or the other was unfaithful to the code established between them. The extent to which good faith, however defined, was maintained between the majority of war-separated families will never be known with any degree of accuracy or completeness. The opportunity was there for serious marital tensions, whose number and severity will come to light, and that only partially, from the statistics of postwar divorces.

Just as the search for affection in an uncertain world is a primary motive for wartime marriage, so its maintenance becomes a basic problem once the marriage is established. To the young husband and wife who have compressed their marriage and honeymoon into a five-day leave, the memory of those five days and the symbolic relationship resulting therefrom becomes an important factor in maintaining their morale both as individuals and as members of a family. The importance attributed to the personal intimacy of the two young people means that its deprivation produces tensions which are difficult to remedy. The complete inability of either party to do anything about the separation may further increase the psychological difficulties in maintaining the marital relationship *in absentia*. These difficulties are enhanced by the cultural definitions placed upon the romantic impulse in the American scene and the important role it plays in the family pattern. This does not mean that the British, French, Russian, or German soldier did not miss his wife and family during the long separation. It does mean, however, that on the level of romantic response—which is the only possible tie between two young persons recently married —the family tensions in the American Army and on the American home front were perhaps more intense than those of any nation. As a people, we have placed the highest premium on the delights of romantic love. Deprived of it, we naturally would be more inclined to miss it than would those peoples who, because of differences in cultural emphasis, had never experienced it.

The traditional conception of sex behavior was in the process of redefinition during the decades before the war.[7] The double standard of morals was undergoing a drastic change. "Moralists still striving to maintain the value of chastity," Burgess suggests, "are losing the full force of their stock arguments, namely: the fear of pregnancy, now diminished by the use of contraceptives, and the danger of venereal infection, now lessened by preventives and prophylaxis and by the discovery of chemical and fever treatments for syphilis and of sulfathiosol cure for gonorrhea."[8] It is probable that prewar codes of behavior were generally maintained during the war, allowing for the greater sexual laxity traditionally allowed the soldier as a partial recompense for the risk of his life. It remains to be seen how young married persons in wartime, who were the increasingly emancipated youth of the thirties, maintained the abstinence demanded of the husband and wife by tradition and how much this generation actually redefined the situation in the face of a changing world. World War II in all probability accelerated the sexual emancipation of unmarried boys and girls that was already well under way. The effects of this emancipation upon the millions of families established during the war years may be equally significant.

War and Family Tensions (Social)

Social tensions refer to those elements of family friction whose sources are largely outside the personality of husband and wife. The distinction between personal and social tensions becomes more unreal in wartime, since the over-all conflict pervades the atmosphere so completely that it finds inevitable reflection in the personalities of the marriage partners. Nevertheless, it is possible to make certain valid distinctions between the tensions which are primarily outgrowths of personality differences accentuated by wartime frustrations and those which grow out of factors external to the individual and over which he or she has no control. Tensions growing out of the employment of women (and the extensive modification in family roles resulting therefrom), the physical mobility of the family in a war-industrial economy, and the crowding of families in congested production areas were some of the aspects of family relationships which were essentially social in origin.

Changes in family roles may be inferred from representative figures on the employment of married women during the war. In the Detroit-Willow Run Congested Production Area, for example, the labor force increased from 1,063,434 workers in March, 1940 to 1,202,685 workers in June, 1944. Almost the entire increase was concentrated in the category of employed women, whose numbers rose from 246,467 to 396,605 in the four-year period. These additions to the labor force were largely married women with no children. Figures for the Detroit Metropolitan District in 1940 and 1944 indicate an increase from 24.1 to 37.0 per cent in the proportion of female workers 18 to 64 years of age who were married, widowed, or divorced and had no children under ten years of age. The labor force was increased by some 76,055 women in this category. Women in the labor force with one or more children under ten also increased from 7.7 per cent of the total workers in 1940 to 15.6 per cent in 1944. This group represented an addition to the total labor force of some 22,890 workers.[9]

The traditional role of the husband has been defined as provider and chief money-maker, while the wife has been restricted by custom to the home. The employment of many thousands of married women in vital war production generated family tensions, whose exact causes were often unknown to the husband himself. As one social worker puts it, ". . . in our complicated society, with its traditional concept of employment as a masculine prerogative, a woman's working may have symbolic meaning for her husband and may be a threat to him if he is not altogether secure in his masculinity."[10] Case evidence suggests that the participation of many women in industry generated such family tensions, particularly where the earnings of the wife were equal to or greater than those of the husband. The emotional bases of the tensions may have been already present in the personal relationships of the couple and were only aggravated by the overt demonstration of equality evidenced in the successful employment of the wife. In such instances the war again acted as a catalytic agent, speeding up a process that was already in motion under peacetime conditions.

Many of the economic tensions which customarily plague the family in peacetime were considerably curtailed by the material prosperity of the civilian population in World War II. With employment at the highest rate in history, and with the national income at astronomical levels, many difficulties arising from poverty and unemployment were either minimized or eliminated entirely from millions of economically marginal homes. Employment was possible for the great majority of persons, married and single, who were willing and able to work. The total number of unemployed reached the minimal figure of 840,000 in January 1945, as compared with 50,960,000 persons gainfully employed in the civilian labor force at the same time.[12] To the element of virtually full employment was added the feeling of participation in the national purpose which is an important therapeutic concomitant of nationalism in crisis. The 51 million persons in the civilian labor force, the 12 million men and women in the armed forces, and the remaining 42 million over 14 years of age in the civilian population not gainfully employed were all animated by the sense of common effort directed toward an end in which the vast majority heartily approved. The effect of this high morale upon the personal relationships of the wartime family was very great.

Other effects of the war did not have such a uniformly felicitous effect upon the family as did the virtually total employment. In the Congested Production Areas, for example, housing conditions were often such that families had to double up with parents or strangers. In the Detroit-Willow Run Area alone, 39,050 couples in 1944 were living in private households where the husband was not listed as the household head—i.e., where some person other than the husband was the dominant figure. Of this group, 25,575 couples were living with their parents or relatives, while 13,475 were lodging in the households of persons to whom they were not related. An additional 6,765 couples were living in "hotels, dormitories, lodging-houses, etc.," where they could not have had any privacy.[13] Other Congested Production Areas were similarly affected, with 23,450 couples in the San Francisco Bay Area living in private households where the husband was not the household head. Of this group, 14,630 were living with parents or relatives, while 8,820 lodged in households where they were not related.[14] Similar experience was indicated in the other Congested Production Areas throughout the country, as well as in many other communities where the congestion of wartime mobility, plus the rapid increase in the marriage rate, placed housing facilities for married couples at a premium.[15]

Doubling-up was also evident during the prolonged crisis of the depression, when thousands of young couples, often with children, were forced to return to the parental roof. The motivating force differed during World War II, when housing shortages rather than unemployment were the principal reasons for the doubling-up. Many of the strictly economic anxieties, born of the uncertainties of the depression, were absent during the war. Some of the basic reasons for family tensions still existed, however, as concomitants of any situation where two married generations live together in a non-patriarchal culture. The head of a new family is traditionally invested with social dominance over his wife. Under conditions of dual authority, no matter how well-intentioned, tensions tend to arise. The loyalties of husband and wife are inevitably divided, as the wife may unconsciously look to her father and the husband to his mother as the symbols of authority or compassion. Many of the 25,575 crowded couples in the Detroit-Willow Run Area, the 14,630 in the San Francisco Bay Area, and the thousands of others similarly affected all over the country doubtless experienced considerable friction from this type of situation.

The mobility of wartime, both industrial and military, was an important source of tensions which combined with other irritations eventually to disorganize the family relationship. The mobile individual in any industrial center, living as a single man cut off from the stable ties of a settled domestic existence, may gradually become estranged from his family. He may come in contact with other persons, male and female, who may wean him away from the settled but prosaic joys of monogamy. The homeless man, no matter what his economic status, is by his very absence often an inadequate husband and father, since the proper exercise of these roles implies his physical presence in the home. Fortunately, the bulk of wartime migration was not of this solitary type of men without their women and children. Indeed, one observer has remarked that "The age and sex composition of the 1944 migrant population suggests that wartime migration has been much more a 'family' type of migration than might have been expected. The fairly even balance of males and females and the large number of children, who do not migrate without their families, provoke this observation."[16] In spite of this limitation, however, mobility as a source of wartime family tensions was by no means a negligible factor.

War and Desertion

In the highly mobile society of a peacetime industrial America, many families are annually broken through desertion. This action is often unpremeditated on the part of the husband, who merely leaves his family in the hope of finding work in a distant city, a search which may continue indefinitely with gradually decreasing contacts with wife and children. Others deliberately leave their wives and/or children with no intention of returning; such persons use the vast anonymity of the United States to swallow them up and relieve them permanently of family responsibilities without the formality of a divorce. Desertion is thus a tacit indication of the disorganization of the family, a situation which may or may not eventually be recognized through formal divorce proceedings. Desertion also constitutes legal grounds for divorce in all but three states, although many divorces granted on this ground are merely rationalizations for other underlying marital tensions. In the present context, desertion will be considered as the permanent and deliberate departure from the home by husband or wife, leaving the remaining members of the family to shift for themselves. Desertion is the product of a mobile and secular society, in which the physical facilities for movement are great, the economic opportunities in distant fields putatively promising, and traditional family ties correspondingly loosened. This combination of circumstances is characteristic of peacetime society.[17] It was even more characteristic of American society at war.

The dynamic aspects of society were accentuated in World War II. Mobility was immensely speeded in all respects, with men and women continually moving from farm to city, from region to region, from camp to camp, from city to industrial city, and from east to west. Separation of husband and wife was the inevitable concomitant of service in the armed forces and often of service on the industrial front. The exigencies of the war not only brought about the forced separation of many families but made such separation socially respectable. For an indeterminate number of persons, both in and out of the army, this enforced separation became the conscious or unconscious basis for the subsequent desertion of their families. The informal dissolution of many individual families brought about by the war became habitual after the war. Whether intentional at the outset or not, many "temporary" wartime desertions became permanent.

In peace or war, there is little precise information on the extent of desertion. Figures for divorces granted on the ground of desertion are of little value in indicating the extent of the practice, since desertion is frequently only the "legal" reason for family disorganization which has but a negligible relationship to the "real" reasons. Information on the total number of deserted husbands or wives at any one time is incomplete, both because of the difficulty of defining desertion and the reluctance of many persons to admit themselves deserted. The logic of *a priori* reasoning would suggest that desertion substantially increased during World War II, since the elements which in peacetime contribute thereto increased in intensity. The actual figures, such as they are, neither confirm nor deny this hypothesis.

The nearest approach to a nationwide enumeration of the trends in "potential" desertion during the war years is offered by the Special Surveys Division of the Bureau of the Census. In April, 1940, there were 30,090,488 married females over 14 years of age in the United States. This total increased to 32,850,000 in February, 1944 and by February, 1946 had declined slightly to 32,070,000. In 1940, 28,516,937 of these women had their husbands present in the home; in 1944 the number of women in this fortunate condition had increased only slightly to 28,630,000, while by February 1946 the number had grown to 31,420,000. In 1940, there were 1,573,551 married women whose husbands were absent for any reason, as compared to 4,220,000 at the height of World War II. Of this wartime total, an estimated 2,760,000 husbands were absent in the armed forces, leaving a total of 1,460,000 in 1944 and 1,150,000 in 1946 absent for "other" reasons, presumably including potential or actual desertion. Since the number of husbands absent in the armed forces in 1940 was negligible for statistical purposes, the figures of 1,573,551 in 1940, 1,460,000 in 1944, and 1,150,000 in 1946 represent the best approximation of the number of families broken for various nonmilitary reasons, including desertion. Commenting upon the situation between 1940 and 1944, the Bureau of the Census remarks that "in spite of the migration of war workers from one part of the country to another there has been practically no change in the proportion of married couples living apart, other than that represented by the women with husbands absent in the armed forces."[18]

These figures seem to indicate that, in spite of the increase in wartime mobility, the proportion of husbands and wives living apart (and hence potential candidates for desertion) did not increase but appreciably decreased during World War II. The percentage of married women over 14 with husbands absent for reasons other than service in the armed forces decreased from 3.1 in 1940 to 2.8 in 1944 and 2.1 in 1946. The only qualification of these figures is that an indeterminate number of the 2,760,000 husbands in the armed forces in 1944 and the 1,240,000 still there in 1946 had thus temporarily solved their family difficulties. Some of the men listed as happily married and hence safe from family disorganization for the duration conceivably would have swelled the roster of absent husbands if they had remained in civilian life.

The other important source of wartime data on potential, if not actual, desertions comes from the ten Congested Production Areas throughout the country. In each case, the inmigrant population from 1940 to 1944 contained a considerable number of married persons temporarily separated from their husbands or wives. The majority of persons so enumerated probably duplicated the 1,460,000 estimated nationally as temporarily separated. The ten areas contained some two and one half million persons who had not lived there in 1940 and hence offer a considerable sample of the marital condition of the migrant population as a whole.[19] A substantial proportion of desertions undoubtedly existed within this group of people who, by their very act of mobility, had experienced the repercussions of war to a greater extent than those who stayed at home. Just as the community facilities of the Congested Production Areas bore witness to the stresses and strains of wartime congestion, so the migrants crowding into these areas bore in their personal and family relationships many of the maladjustments of a wartime society.

An enumeration of the ten areas, with the numbers and percentages of inmigrants living apart from their husbands and wives, therefore throws additional light on the numbers and distribution of temporarily deserted families, whatever the reason for desertion. The number of

Table I

Men and Women in Congested Production Areas Living Apart from their Husbands or Wives in First Six Months of 1944*

Area	Men Without Wives	Percentage	Women Without Husbands	Percentage
1. Charleston, S.C. Area	1,885	12.6	1,480	10.2
2. Detroit-Willow Run Area	8,745	12.7	10,340	14.4
3. Hampton Roads Area	7,112	13.4	7,266	13.2
4. Los Angeles Area	20,174	9.3	44,891	18.2
5. Mobile Area	5,096	20.0	3,073	13.0
6. Muskegon Area	875	15.8	713	13.1
7. Portland-Vancouver Area	8,556	13.4	9,292	14.4
8. Puget Sound Area	4,932	6.7	14,832	17.5
9. San Diego Area	3,360	6.8	12,285	20.8
10. San Francisco Bay Area	19,425	13.0	28,945	18.0

* Adapted from Bureau of the Census, Population, *Characteristics of the Population, Labor Force, Families, and Housing, for Ten Congested Production Areas,* Series CA-1, CA-2, and CA-3.

men living apart from their wives was more indicative of the possible extent of desertion than the number of women, inasmuch as the majority of the latter were the wives of service men who had moved to the war centers in order to be near their husbands in training or about to go overseas. This was particularly evident in the Congested Areas of the Pacific Coast, where the percentage of men without wives was appreciably smaller than that of wives without husbands. In the other areas, the percentages were more nearly equal, with the Mobile Area even showing a higher proportion of migrant solitary husbands than wives.

The full extent of the problem of potentially deserted husbands and wives in the Congested Production Areas is apparent when the absolute numbers of solitary married persons among the nonmigrant population (i.e., those living in the Area on April 1, 1940) are also considered. The total numbers of such lonely married persons were appreciably swelled in view of the larger population groups involved, even though the percentages of husbands without wives and wives without husbands were not so great among the nonmigrant population as among the migrant. Out of a total of 990,010 married persons in the San Francisco Bay Area (including both nonmigrants and inmigrants), some 110,880 were living apart from their husbands or wives. Of this number, 73,535 were women, one third of them under 25 years of age, a group composed largely of the wives of service men.[20] In the Detroit-Willow Run Area, 107,140 out of a total of 1,375,990 married persons were living apart from their husbands or wives; 77,220 of this separated group were women. More than 50 per cent of these 77,220 lonely women were under 30 years of age and many were the wives of men in the services.[21] In the Los Angeles Area, 193,578 men and women out of a total of 1,796,256 married persons were living apart from their husbands or wives; 149,303 of this group were women, the majority under 30 and in all probability the wives of service men. These representative areas illustrate the amount of temporary family disorganization during World War II. The figures are by no means conclusive even of the amount of potential desertion in the areas themselves, let alone that of the country as a whole. Failing more pertinent data, however, these are better than none.[22]

The majority of this large group of husbands and wives temporarily deserted by their spouses, whether voluntarily or involuntarily, eventually found their way back to the familial roof, if any, after the war.

The bulk of the families broken by the war were reconstituted after it was over, many with renewed ties of affection after the crisis which the family had weathered. Many men and women, on the other hand, who lived in the Congested Production Areas and other centers without their husbands and wives probably were never reunited on any basis, permanent or temporary, with their prewar marital partner. Thousands of cases of family desertion were set in motion by the war. Whether this number was larger or smaller than that of a "normal" society is impossible to determine. As a form of family disintegration, desertion plays a much larger role in an industrial and mobile society than in a stable and agrarian society such as prewar France. In the present state of information, however, we can only guess at the exact role of World War II in bringing about or accelerating this form of family breakdown.

War and Divorce

The secular trend toward an increasing rate of family disorganization through divorce has been evident since the year 1887, when the Bureau of the Census first collected statistics on the subject. The early years of the depression decade of the 1930's saw a temporary decline in this long-term trend, which decline was arrested with the gradual betterment of economic conditions in the latter half of the decade.[23] The early years of World War II, when America was not yet involved but when the defense program had "improved" economic conditions, saw a continued increase in both the absolute number of divorces and the divorce rate per 100 marriages.[24] During the years following Pearl Harbor, when America was actively participating in the war, the rate continued to rise. In the period immediately after the war, there is every indication that both the number of divorces and the rate per 100 marriages will rise to the highest point in our history.[25]

This study is primarily concerned with the effect of World War II upon social problems. Hence we will not undertake an elaborate discussion of conditions prior to 1940. The trends in wartime family disorganization are, however, not completely understandable without a minimum knowledge of the peacetime trends. Table II, on Page 39, provides this information.

The upward trend in divorce continued during the war. The situation is apparent in Table III, on Page 40, which shows the steady yearly increase in the period from 1940 to 1945.

Table II

Number of Divorces, Rate Per 1,000 of Estimated Population, and
Rate Per 100 Marriages: 1922-1940*

Year	Number of Divorces	Number per 1,000 of Estimated Population	Rate per 100 Marriages
1922	148,815	1.35	13.7
1923	165,096	1.48	15.0
1924	170,952	1.51	15.2
1925	175,449	1.53	15.1
1926	180,853	1.55	15.6
1927	192,037	1.62	16.4
1928	195,939	1.63	16.7
1929	201,468	1.66	16.9
1930	191,591	1.56	16.0
1931	183,664	1.48	15.5
1932	160,338	1.28	13.6
1933	165,000	1.31	14.2
1934	204,000	1.61	17.8
1935	218,000	1.71	18.9
1936	236,000	1.84	20.1
1937	250,000	1.93	21.0
1938	244,000	1.9	20.1
1939	251,000	1.9	20.5
1940	264,000	2.0	21.3

* Divorce figures through 1932 taken from Bureau of the Census, *Statistical Abstract of the United States: 1943*, Washington, 1944, p. 92; Figures from 1933 through 1937 taken from Samuel A. Stouffer and Lyle M. Spencer, "Recent Increases in Marriage and Divorce," *American Journal of Sociology*, 45:551-554 (January, 1939); Figures for 1938-1940 estimated by the Bureau of the Census. Rates per 100 marriages determined by Hornell Hart and Henrietta Bowne, "Divorce, Depression, and War," *Social Forces*, 22:191-194 (December, 1943). These rates are based on the average number of marriages during the ten years prior to the year under consideration.

World War II saw a steady increase in the absolute number of divorces, the number per 1,000 of the estimated population (excluding armed forces not in the continental United States), and the rate per 100 marriages. This trend presumably represented the cumulative effect of various wartime tensions, which increased the rate of family disorganization even in the face of various cohesive factors also operating upon the wartime family.

This experience was not typical of World War I, although the brevity of American participation in the first conflict makes valid comparison difficult. The divorce rate per 1,000 of estimated population increased from .95 in 1913 to 1.20 in 1917 when this country entered the war. In 1918 the rate dropped to 1.12 per 1,000 of estimated population, only to resume its upward progression in 1919 with 1.35. By 1920, when the full effects of demobilization and war marriages began to be apparent, the rate soared to 1.60, a figure which it did not equal again for several years. The immediate postwar years saw rates of 1.47 for 1921,

Table III

Estimated Divorces in the United States:
1940-1945*

Year	Number of Divorces	Number per 1,000 of Estimated Population	Rate Per 100 Marriages
1940	264,000	2.0	16.5
1941	293,000	2.2	17.3
1942	321,000	2.4	18.1
1943	359,000	2.6	22.8
1944	400,000	2.9	27.5
1945	502,000	3.6	31.0

* Adapted from Federal Security Agency, National Office of Vital Statistics, *Marriage and Divorce in the United States, 1937 to 1945,* Vital Statistics-Special Reports, Vol. 23, No. 9 (September 10, 1946), Tables 1 and 7.

1.35 for 1922, 1.48 for 1923, and 1.51 for 1924. World War II did not follow the pattern of World War I in the decreased number of divorces granted during its progress. It remains to be seen whether or not the sharp rise in divorces after the first war will be duplicated after the second.

Basing their predictions upon the decline in the divorce rate in World War I, many persons writing in the early years of World War II suggested that a similar pattern would prevail. Certain factors in the wartime situation contributed to the postponment of many divorces during the war, but these preventive factors were not sufficient to overcome the trend toward a rising divorce rate. Added to these disruptive factors was the boom in marriage accompanying the prosperity of the defense period and the early years of American participation. The marriage rate was already high in 1940, rose further in 1941, and reached an even higher point in 1942.[26] Many of these boom and wartime marriages appeared in the divorce statistics in subsequent years. Many other divorces were postponed until after the war.[27]

"Many men," suggested Burgess early in the war, "temporarily solve their marital difficulties by enlisting. Marriages on the brink of disaster will be saved 'for the duration' by the husband entering the armed forces through Selective Service."[28] No matter what the degree of prewar tensions, many such families remained technically together and did not seek the divorce courts until after the war. The shock of Pearl Harbor and the emotional participation of the American people in the task of defeating Germany and Japan characterized this general marital attitude. This artificial cohesion of the wartime family was compounded of several factors.

1. *Prudential factors.* "Wives who might otherwise sue for separate maintenance or divorce," said Burgess, "postpone such action until after the war, a prudential course in view of compulsory allowances to dependents of men in the service."[29] At the end of June, 1944, the Office of Dependency Benefits of the Army Service Forces was mailing monthly Class A benefit checks to 2,485,908 wives of men in the Army alone.[30] The category of Divorced Wife was also considered a Class A dependent and some 3,867 divorced wives were receiving checks as of June 30, 1944. The eligibility for such allowances was carefully defined as a "Former wife divorced who has not remarried and to whom alimony has been decreed and is still payable."[31] Under wartime conditions, the number of young, able-bodied, and childless wives granted divorces *with alimony* from an absent soldier fighting for his country was small. As long as the formal bonds of matrimony were not openly violated by the wife, no questions were asked by the Office of Dependency Benefits and the monthly allotments continued to arrive with pleasant regularity. The majority of wives obviously remained married to their absent husbands for other reasons than a few paltry dollars. Nevertheless, these pecuniary considerations undoubtedly operated in an appreciable number of cases to keep husband and wife together during the war. The relative importance of these prudential factors might be partially answered by knowing the number of the 2,485,908 wives who started divorce proceedings within five years after the end of the war.

2. *Mechanical factors.* Closely allied to the prudential factor in this connection was the mechanical difficulty of obtaining a divorce from a soldier husband, particularly if he did not wish to be divorced.

Soldiers did not have to answer a divorce summons unless they wanted to,[32] a privilege which had the practical effect of making it impossible to divorce a service husband without his consent. Many wives who, for fanciful or whimsical reasons, might have wished to divorce their soldier husbands in order to marry some new (and possibly temporary) love were thus rendered incapable of legal action. The amount of marital unfaithfulness engendered by such a situation was problematical, but the divorce rate was presumably kept down. Many judges were reluctant to grant divorces under these circumstances even when the husband had indicated his lack of opposition to the proceedings. The sanctity of the family became magnified as other institutional ties were destroyed; extra efforts were made by conscientious judges to maintain at least the formal integrity of the family.

3. *Morale factors.* War produced a feeling of solidarity throughout the nation and particularly between the civilian members of the family and those in the armed forces.[33] Mutual idealization took place among the absent members, whereby each was seen as unusually attractive. Individuals thus deprived of one another—the soldier in the field and the wife in the empty apartment—tended to remember the other in the most favorable light. Divorce under such conditions often became unthinkable. The return of the soldier and the resumption of normal family relationships partially dispelled this roseate aura. The actuality was seldom as glamorous as the dream. For the duration, however, the idealization of the absent one tended to keep many marriages together, even though some were later dissolved under the corrosive force of postwar disillusionment. All the social forces of the community were directed toward instilling a feeling of family co-operation. The morale of the soldier was partially dependent upon the solidarity of his family. Wives who complained to their absent husbands or threatened them with infidelity or divorce thus undermined the morale of the armed forces. The retention of family ties was defined as a patriotic duty in wartime and the force of public opinion was mobilized in this direction. Many divorces were thereby temporarily postponed.

4. *Emotional factors.* The individual need for emotional assurance in the midst of war combines with the centralization of attention on the overpowering fact of war itself to render family ties more solid. In explaining this complex psychological phenomenon, one sociologist said that "social necessity, that is, the need for intimate companionship and affectional security, becomes greater; the emotions, instead of being

focused mainly on the personal, are centered on the societal objective of war. . . . Under these conditions, equilibrium within the marital state is made more possible, personal likes and dislikes are subordinated, and divorce and other forms of marital disorganization tend toward the minimum."[34] The same deep desire for human assurance that increases the marriage rate in wartime helps also to maintain the solidarity of the family once it is established. In the immensity of war, men and women often hesitate to break the one human relationship which promises to give them sanctuary in a chaotic world. They may cling desperately to the form of the relationship, although the substance may long since have departed.

Many families, in short, demonstrate an increased protectiveness and cohesiveness in the face of the group crisis of war. A pervasive sense of danger seems to be the chief motivating factor. A variety of family behavior characterizes this drawing together of the primary group: "Maternal feelings are enhanced. Fathers and sons show increased interest and responsibility in their homes. In certain cases husbands and wives, previously separated, become reconciled. Wives . . . feel more kindly toward husbands, now in military service. Sons, previously irresponsible and disinterested, contribute money and work out careful plans for the security of their families."[35] These reactions of solidarity may be complicated by feelings of guilt of men who have heretofore been remiss in their duty toward their families. Unconscious hostility toward a member of the family may plague the holder when the object of the hostility is in danger. Guilt reactions may also figure in the complex group of sentiments affecting the wartime family.

Divorce in the Postwar World

The evidence points to a continuation of the high wartime divorce rate for several years after the war. The basis for this prediction is both quantitative and qualitative. The quantitative evidence lies in the increase in the number and rate of marriages during the early years of the war. The probability is good that a large number of divorces will result from this increased number of marriages. The qualitative evidence lies in the nature of the wartime marriages, compounded as they were of many elements making for instability. The effect of some of these early wartime marriages was apparent in the high divorce rates of 1944 and 1945. Many more will come to the parting of the ways in the years from 1945 to 1950.

The experience during and after World War I offers suggestive although by no means conclusive evidence of an increased divorce rate in the postwar period. Marriages contracted during and immediately after the earlier conflict produced a greater number of divorces than would normally have been expected from a comparison with the divorce rates of other years.[36] In France, Belguim, and Germany, the rates increased at an unprecedented pace after World War I. In France, the rate increased from a low point of 13 per 100,000 in 1915 to 92 in 1919. The German rate rose from 15 per 100,000 in 1916 to 63 per 100,000 in 1921.[37] The neutral Scandinavian countries reported only comparatively small increases in the postwar period.[38] It is probable that this country will see a continued rise over the already high wartime figure in the *immediate* postwar years, to be followed by a subsequent decrease from the highest figure during the decade of the 1950's. This decreased rate, however, will be higher than the prewar rate, indicating that the secular trend toward an increasing rate of divorce was not interrupted by the war.

The basic hypothesis underlying this study is that the war accentuated but did not permanently modify the forces making for social problems in America. This brief glimpse at the effect of World War II upon the family has, in general, confirmed this hypothesis. The war saw a steady increase in the number and rate of divorces. Certain factors may have kept the wartime rate from rising even faster than it did. This rise will probably continue for several years after the war. Some of the reasons for this belief are as follows:

1. *Statistical factors.* The increase in the number of wartime marriages would, even with other things equal, increase the probability of subsequent divorce. With a larger proportion of the population married, the mathematical chances of divorce will therefore be correspondingly greater. The decennial census in 1940 showed that 30,-100,000, or 60 per cent, of the female population 14 years and older was married. A sample census conducted in February, 1944 showed that this number had increased to 32,900,000, or 63 per cent of the same population group. During the decades between 1920 and 1940, however, the percentage of married women increased by only a fraction of 1 per cent. The most spectacular increase during World War II in the proportion of the female population who were married took place among women in their early twenties. In 1940, approximately five-tenths of the young women in the age group 20 to 24 years were mar-

ried, whereas in 1944 nearly six-tenths of this group were married. In the age group 25 to 34, the proportion increased by approximately five per cent during the four-year period. The proportion of married persons in the total population was higher in 1944 than in any previous time for which reliable statistics are available.[39]

2. *Prolonged absence.* During the long period of enforced separation, a process of maturation took place in millions of husbands and, to a somewhat lesser extent, in their wives. This process undoubtedly meant that many husbands and wives came together again as partial strangers, even where the patterns of a happy marriage were already well established before the war. Some of these virtual strangers found that their definitions of marriage had changed materially during the years apart. Divorce will often be the solution, whereby both parties may start again with other husbands and wives more in keeping with their mature ideals.

3. *Romantic marriage.* One of the most important factors bringing about the high divorce rate in the United States is the cluster of attitudes comprising romantic love.[40] These attitudes define both the circumstances under which marriage is begun and those under which it is continued. Wartime conditions produce romantic marriages, wherein young people are bemused by a pretty face, a manly figure, the glamour of the uniform, the desire to participate in the brief and romantic joys of marriage, and the often inchoate wish for some personal symbol in the hurly-burly of war. Marriages on short notice between boys and girls virtually unknown to each other, with different cultural backgrounds, attitudes, and values, tend to occur in wartime even more than peacetime. Many of these romantic war marriages will end in romantic postwar divorces.

4. *Prudential marriage.* An indeterminate number of wartime marriages, on the other hand, occurred in which the predominant reason was anything but romantic. These were marriages undertaken to avoid Selective Service, to become eligible for the allotments of a living soldier husband, or to qualify as the recipient of the insurance benefits of a dead husband. "Such rational motives as these," according to one sociologist, . . . "lead to highly unstable unions, for they mean that the marriage is in many cases treated as a means for reaching an end which will either not exist in peacetime or will not be served by the continuance of this particular match."[41] The cultural milieu of America is so permeated by the expectations of romantic love that

persons who marry without these attitudes often find themselves as unhappily wedded as those whose marriage was motivated by nothing else. Men who married to avoid the draft probably did not look happily upon their marriages when they returned from the wars. Girls who married for the sake of a Class A allotment may not have been pleased with their husbands when the war was over.

5. *Changing economic roles.* The war brought millions of married women into business and industry for the first time. The growing economic independence of women has long been one of the factors responsible for the upward trend in the divorce rate. Women who can support themselves will not remain permanently tied to an unpleasant marriage. Economic independence was experienced by many women earning equal wages with men in the war industries of World War II. Married women with absent husbands developed attitudes in keeping with the economic roles they were playing in the family and society. Furthermore, many of these working women moved their families from rural areas and small towns to larger centers. The change to life in the metropolitan community is in itself part of the social forces that have contributed to the increase in divorce.[42]

6. *Postwar marriage.* We have considered chiefly the postwar implications of marriages contracted before and during the war. Many marriages begun *after* the war will likewise be so inherently unstable as to eventuate in divorce within a comparatively short time. The dissolution of these marriages will further swell the postwar divorce figures. The factors causing people to contract such marriages have been summarized as follows: "first, the emotional and sexual intensity of contact after long separation; second, the feeling of moral and nervous release from war tension; and third, the fulfillment of engagements made during the conflict."[43]

Some men returning from long years of separation may marry the first American girl who is nice to them, thus symbolizing their emancipation from the army and the belated assumption of civilian joys. Others will marry the home town girl who wore their diamond, high school ring, or fraternity pin during the years of military service. Many of the men have changed greatly from the boys who joined the Marines on the day of their graduation from high school. These reluctant and bewildered husbands may ultimately seek release in divorce.

These and other factors should mean that the divorce rate in the immediate postwar years will be even higher than in the war years. Economic conditions will partially determine the trends, with a prolonged postwar boom accelerating the divorce rate and a short period of prosperity followed by a long depression exerting a moderating effect. Whatever the economic conditions, the postwar rate should be high, how high nobody knows. Predictions made before the end of the war by Hart and Bowne [44] and Kingsley Davis [45] suggested that the peak annual number of divorces in the postwar period would be 575,-000 and 461,000, respectively. In terms of the known figure of 502,000 for 1945, these estimates do not appear as high as they did when originally made. On the basis of the secular trend in divorce, which continued throughout World War II, the Bureau of the Census predicts that "divorces will continue to rise sharply in 1946, reach a peak in 1947, then decline rather sharply in 1948 and 1949, reach the normal trend by 1950, and follow this trend until 1960."[46] This means that 1947 will have perhaps 600,000 divorces, with a gradual decline over the following few years to a "normal" annual figure of perhaps 300,000 by 1950.[47]

Other social factors operative upon the postwar family may in some measure counteract these influences. Such possible tendencies may be summarized as follows:

1. *Increased birth rate.* The wartime increase in marriages was accompanied by an increase in births. Since approximately two-thirds of all divorces are granted to childless couples,[48] this factor may maintain the legal solidarity of many families that might otherwise seek divorce. The exact relationship between childlessness and divorce has never been established; it is reasonable to assume that the relationship is more than mere concomitant variation, even though desertions and informal separations should also be considered for an accurate correlation between family disorganization and the lack of children.[49]

2. *Premarital blood tests.* These tests are now mandatory in a number of states and serve very effectively to delay the time between the spontaneous desire to be married and the legal possibility thereof. This waiting period so delayed some over-hasty marriages in wartime that they never took place, thus decreasing somewhat the postwar candidates for divorce. The same procedure might conceivably operate similarly in the postwar period, thus indirectly limiting the number of completely inadequate marriages.

3. *Desire for marital sanctuary.* A certain number of married men

who served long years in the armed forces will so value their family
ties that they will go to great lengths to retain them in the postwar
period. Some such idealizations will merely augment the disillusionment of the postwar transitional period, while others will so cement the
integrity of the family that it can surmount many tensions which
would otherwise wreck it. The family will thus become to some people
a symbol of emotional security which must not be broken at any cost.[50]

It is doubtful if these and other counteractive influences will be sufficient to overcome the factors causing increased family disorganization
in the postwar period. The 1945 rate of approximately one divorce to
every three marriages will not continue to increase indefinitely.
Many of the contributory factors to this 1945 figure represent wartime
accumulations and postponements of divorces, which will ultimately
work themselves out in the immediate postwar years. It is doubtful,
however, if divorce will decrease to the prewar figure, when the ratio
of divorces to marriages was one to five (21.3 per 100 marriages in
1940). The trend toward an increasing rate of divorce has, with
relatively short-lived interruptions, been consistent since 1887. World
War II accelerated this trend.

CHAPTER THREE

WAR AND CHILDHOOD

Total War and the Child

In January, 1940, the White House Conference on Children in a Democracy issued a statement defining the standards, goals, and aspirations considered desirable for the child in a democratic America, either in war or in peace. The concluding paragraph of this pronouncement was as follows:

Whatever the degree of excellence of the democratic setting of life—political, economic, educational, religious, cultural—some children are handicapped in the enjoyment of its blessings. These handicaps may be physical or mental; they may arise out of unhappy home life, the loss of parents, or discriminations against minority groups; they may be the result of economic destitution or insecurity, or of a pathological condition in the child's own make-up. In a democracy every effort will be made to counterbalance these handicaps by providing for all children as nearly as possible the equal opportunity in life and in the pursuit of happiness that was assumed to be the foundation of this nation in its Declaration of Independence.[1]

This credo was delivered only four months after the outbreak of the war in Europe and almost two years before America's involvement therein. In March, 1942, the problems related to the child and arising from our active participation in World War II were considered in their new light by the Children's Bureau Commission on Children in Wartime. This Commission formulated "The Children's Charter in Wartime," which began with this stirring exhortation:

We are in total war against the aggressor nations. We are fighting again for human freedom and especially for the future of our children in a free world. Children must be safeguarded—and they can be safeguarded in the midst of this total war so that they can live and share in that future. They must be nourished, sheltered, and protected even in the stress of war production so that they will be strong to carry forward a just and lasting peace.[2]

At a meeting of the Commission in March, 1944, two years after its foundation, the problems facing children in World War II were further defined by Miss Katherine F. Lenroot:

We have a three fold task. We must hold the line now in the face of mounting strains and dislocations by strengthening homes and maintaining services for children throughout the Nation; we must anticipate the problems of the transition from war to peace and we must lay the foundations for a post-war world in which the needs of children and youth shall be given first consideration.[3]

Many of these problems had been met in the interval between the two meetings of the Commission by close working relationships between state and local committees and the national agencies of the Federal Government. As of March 1, 1944, 21 states were reported with operating defense-council committees, one of whose functions was planning for the needs of children in wartime. Local committees were in turn organized under local defense-councils for the purpose of implementing these programs. The maladjustments brought upon the children of the country by rapid wartime change were thus defined as social problems on a national, state, and local scale as an initial step in their eventual amelioration.[4]

The Commission on Children in Wartime carried forward an aggressive program on many fronts toward the betterment of conditions for children during the greatest war in history. Through the national facilities of the Children's Bureau of the Department of Labor, the Commission issued a series of pamphlets on the problems of children in war, as well as suggestions toward the amelioration of these problems.[5] In the following discussion, we shall draw heavily upon these documents, insofar as they throw light upon the nature and extent of children's problems brought about or aggravated by the social change attending World War II. The discussion will emphasize the problems themselves, rather than the measures adopted by the various private, community, state, or federal agencies to alleviate them. The limitations of this study make such a course necessary. The problems arising out of wartime social change will be considered as extensively as space permits. The measures that were taken to alleviate these problems must be left to others.

During the years of World War II, approximately one-third of the population of the United States was composed of children under 16.

The Sixteenth Census indicated that in 1940 there were 10,597,891 children under five years, 10,725,873 from five to nine years, and 11,790,934 from ten to fourteen years. Extending the age of childhood in this context to 16 years, we find that there were approximately 36 million children under 16 in 1940, more than 40 million under 18, and more than 46 million young people under 20.[6] The proportion of children under five increased during the war because of the high birth rates. Approximately 3,000,000 births took place in both 1942 and 1943, as compared to an average of some 2,000,000 in "normal" years.[7] A substantial proportion of the population was thus at an age where it could not conceivably be faced with the immediate prospect of taking an active part in the war. In spite of this freedom from physical participation, however, World War II clearly affected directly or indirectly every one of the 36 million children, with particular repercussions evident upon those born during the war years or who spent them without their fathers. In this chapter we shall point out some of the effects of war upon the life organizations of these future citizens, who were faced with many drastic changes at a time when their personalities were still in the formative stage.[8]

Social Problems and the Child

The child is born into a society already functioning, with its folkways, mores, and configurations of accepted behavior. The child adjusts to these social patterns in the process of growing up. In primitive societies, with their relatively simple culture patterns, this adjustment is comparatively easy, particularly when the culture is virtually static. Although these primitive societies do not offer the material comforts available in our own society, they nevertheless provide an emotional security that is often lacking in the dynamic and heterogeneous society of western Europe and America. This feeling of emotional security is one of the most important elements in the early life of the child; without it, he may suffer irreparable damage in the most plastic state of his personality. The years of the depression, with a deprivation of economic security facing millions of families, did not provide the most favorable social environment for the children directly affected. The war years raised the question of security on an even more fundamental level, not in the persons of the children themselves, but in those of their fathers and elder brothers. The effects of this psychological insecurity were not immediately apparent in the life organizations of the younger part of the nation. Only in later years may the possible implications be fully realized.

In the early months of American participation in World War II, fear was expressed by those in authority for the *physical* security of the children. The Children's Bureau published a guarded pamphlet entitled *To Parents in Wartime*, in which mothers and fathers of American children were admonished to "Prepare yourselves to face whatever may come," and "help your children to continue living their everyday lives with as little change as possible." When these admonitions were made in the early spring of 1942, possible attack by sea or air seemed very real, particularly on the Atlantic and Pacific coasts. Parents were advised to face the facts with their children and not invent euphemisms for such grim phrases (and possible experiences) as "black-outs," "alarms," and "explosions." Furthermore, "It is always best for him [the child] to hear of possible dangers from those he loves most. . . . This frank appraisal of dangers where they actually exist is an important step toward the sort of behavior that parents want to achieve even though they cannot escape their anxiety for their children."[9]

Fortunately these fears of physical violence to the children of America never materialized, as they did for the children of virtually every other belligerent nation. It would be fatuous to compare the personal and family adjustments faced by American children with the starvation, bombings, and utter personal disorganization experienced by the children of the other United Nations. Nevertheless, the rapidity of social change in wartime America, coupled with the long periods of deprivation of the father, left psychological scars on the personalities of many children. The family was subjected to diverse stresses and strains, some merely the accentuation of peacetime strains and others unprecedented in nature and scope. The greater the change, the more difficult is the social adjustment.

The war caused millions of men and women to perform new functions, often in new physical locations and under new social conditions. These changes in function naturally impinged upon the children, whose world was largely that of their mothers and fathers. Particularly to the infants and children of preschool age, the war was a reality in terms of the changes in circumstance of their parents. This relationship was made clear early in the war by the Children's Bureau: "The adults in the family are under new pressures in regard to work, to financial problems, to shifts in living conditions. Husbands will have longer hours of work; the rise in prices will affect the food budget; some items and some materials may be short and others may have to be substituted; the place of work or the home itself may be moved—any or all of these changes will bring along with them perplexing problems for the grown people in the family to solve."[10] These changes in the social situation of the family had important psychological impacts upon the children. Their physical world was modified. Even more changed was their mental world, which was subject to the dislocations and interruptions of war. The world furthermore was full of hostile people—Germans and Japanese—who if not actually present were at least psychologically as near as the radio, the movies, the black-out, and the air-raid drill.[11]

In a study of the effect of the war upon the children of London, Dr. Robert D. Gillespie, psychiatrist of the Royal Air Force, found that the most devastating factor in the experience of bombed-out children was *the interruption of their regular routine.* Whether the child were evacuated from the city or not, if his regular schedule of eating, sleeping, going to school, and recreation were interrupted, his emotional stability might be seriously threatened.[12] This situation was naturally worsened for those children who lost one or more parents in the blitz. Anna Freud, indeed, suggests that the most important consideration is not necessarily the change in social routine but rather the continued presence of the parents, with the love they alone can provide. "One year of work with England's refugee children," she states, "has revealed that a child can be bombed out, yet smile two minutes afterwards, or sleep peacefully while a bomb makes a big crater in a garden less than fifty yards away. Love for the parents is so great that it is a far greater shock for a child to be suddenly separated from its mother than to have a house collapse on top of him."[13] These conclusions of Miss Freud should be considered in the light of her father's emphasis upon the importance of the family in the emotional life of the child. Nevertheless, it is obvious that the emotional security of the child is seriously jeopardized by the absence of the parents. Such separation is often defined as rejection by the parents, who would in the childish mind certainly arrange some way of remaining with him if they wished to strongly enough.

The problems of the child in wartime America were not defined in terms of bombing and evacuation. Rather were they somewhat similar to those of normal times, accentuated in areas of social mobility and social congestion, where the impact of the war upon the civilian front was particularly crucial. Some of these problems were seen in a new light because of their close relationship to manpower needs, as well as the general problem of civilian morale in wartime. Such problems were not isolated phenomena but were intimately related to others in the complex framework of American society. Some of the more pressing of these social problems were summarized as follows, with particular reference to their relationship to the child:

Inadequate and insanitary housing is a serious hazard to the health of families in communities where war industries have brought a sudden influx of workers. Living conditions which make normal home life difficult, absence of fathers for military service, employment of mothers of young children, and night work and unusual strain of parents employed in war industries undermine family life and endanger the well-being of children.[14]

Other elements had such specific influences upon wartime children as the following:

Absence of parental guidance, freedom from restraints, and lack of protection of youth from dangerous influences in the community create problems of juvenile delinquency. Relaxation of school-attendance and child-labor laws, coupled with adolescent unrest, permits boys and girls to leave school before they are physically and mentally equipped for work. Unprecedented increases in child labor and youth employment due to wartime demands have increased manyfold the child-labor problems of normal years.[15]

The problems of the child are those of society as a whole. The social change of the war years made the child more than ever "a stranger and afraid" in a world he never made. Social mobility and congestion intensified many of the problems of wartime adjustment in a new environment for families and their children. The changes in social control, with the intensification of formal controls and the relaxation of many informal ones, had their effect upon the life of the wartime child. Social conflict, latent or overt, with its attendant discrimination, prejudice, and hatred was reflected in the emotional lives of millions of children of minority groups.

The problems of the wartime family were likewise in large part those of the child. Changes in the structure, functions, and relationships within the family had their repercussions in the personalities of the younger members, from infancy to adolescence. The disorganiza-

tion and interruption of the family, either through separation, desertion, or death, had injurious effects upon the emotional security of
the child whose father deserted his family, divorced them, or died in
battle. Finally, many of the problems of the individual as such—
adolescence, juvenile delinquency, sexual maladjustment, adult crime,
personal maladjustment, and personal disorganization—are intimately
related to problems impinging upon the child. In a complex and inter-
related modern society, the individual, no matter which of the seven
ages of man he represents, need never send to know for whom the
bell tolls. It tolls for him.

Emotional Impact of Social Change

The child is exceedingly vulnerable to war and social change. In the
normal course of events, his personality has not yet become fully
integrated. He is, furthermore, "continually in the process of change,
which is ever creating new doubts, new deprivations, new dependen-
cies, new hostilities, and new anxieties, which may make him vulnerable to conditions and attitudes peculiar to war . . . his devices for
handling his emotional disturbances are not well intrenched, so that
one may anticipate a more ready crash of previous modes of adjustment than in the case of the adult who has attained a relatively good
adjustment."[16] The child may also "internalize" his war experiences by
incorporating them in his unconscious mind, whence they may return
in later years to disorganize his personality. Because of this plasticity
and inarticulateness, the child may have experiences which he is unable
to verbalize or otherwise discharge in the same way as the more
articulate adult. These insecurities may come to light long after the
war is over, when the child has become an adolescent or an adult.
The emotional stresses and strains of wartime upon the nascent personality may conceivably, like the sins of the fathers, be visited upon
the third and fourth generations.[17]

The emotional impact of war presumably had a different effect
upon different age groups in the child population. While there is much
overlapping in the following sequence, nevertheless there would appear
to be certain broad differentiations based upon previous knowledge
of emotional behavior at the various stages of childhood.

1. *Infant level.* Many persons assume that the sole requisite for
adequate personality development in infancy is good physical care.
This point of view avers that, provided the child is adequately fed,

warmed, and otherwise physically cared for, the war cannot harm
him but will pass him by as he lies in his snug air-raid shelter. This
assumption does not accord with the facts of emotional security, which
is related to but not synonymous with physical security. The employment of mothers of very young children in war industries or related
service occupations made more difficult the intimate rapport between
members of the family. In addition, the infant in wartime sensed many
of the anxieties of the mother as communicated to him on an intimate
emotional level. The bases of these wartime anxieties have been enumerated as follows: (1) "the mother's anxiety that her husband or close
relative will go to war or her constant anxiety if he or they are already
in service; (2) crowded living conditions in the defense areas, where
inadequate housing is unavoidable, or in other areas due to the
doubling-up of families, bring conflicts between relatives which
tax the mother's relationship to the child; and (3) changes in living
arrangements may be timed with points of stress in the infant's life, as
the weaning and toilet-training period."[18]

The world of the infant is a small one, bounded physically by the
four walls of his home and socially by his parents and immediate
family. He can develop fully "only through a relationship of affection
with his mother (or one person who regularly stands in place of the
mother). It is only through the cumulative daily detail of small acts
making up the mother's care, through which the mother expresses her
affection for the child, that an infant can develop the capacity to give
and receive affection so important throughout his life."[19] So stated a
group of authorities in the fields of psychiatry, child welfare, child
health, and child development, following a Children's Bureau Conference on the wartime care of children under two years. When the
infant is deprived of these relationships, the effect is apparent in
"slower mental development, social ineptness, weakened initiative,
and damage to the child's capacity in future life to form satisfactory
relationships."[20] If the customary social relationships between himself
and the other members of the family as expressed in his own routines
and the expressions of affection directed toward himself remain
constant, his own personality will remain comparatively unaffected by
the war. If these relationships are interrupted or disorganized, his
personality may suffer. With a world at war, it was often difficult for
parents to provide a full measure of emotional security in the home.[21]

2. *Preschool level.* When the child passes from infancy and makes

contact with persons outside the home, he is experiencing his first direct social role. These contacts take place with his contemporaries, who are similarly trying their wings in a new environment. Here the child must learn for the first time to curtail or inhibit many of the aggressive impulses which have hitherto received direct satisfaction from his parents. This process is considerably more difficult in wartime, where the patterns of aggression are encouraged on every side. When the child learns from his parents and fellows of the day-to-day progress of the most concentrated forms of violence perpetrated upon the enemy, it is difficult not to personify the enemy in one of his small playmates who has momentarily appropriated one of his possessions. The neighbor who uses his wagon may be violently expropriated, with the obvious justification in the mind of the small owner that the other is a "nasty Jap" or a "dirty Nazi." The child may become confused during wartime as to whether he should inhibit his aggressive impulses. This confusion may appear in later years in the form of adolescent personality disorders, juvenile delinquency, adult crime, or personal maladjustment.

3. *School level.* At this age, the child normally begins to strive for self-dependence from his parents, particularly his mother. This process may take an exaggerated form under the stress of wartime, with children indulging in many forms of behavior defined as antisocial in our society. Early in the war, the executives of eighteen public and private social agencies in Illinois reported among young children an increase in "acts of vandalism and pilfering; noisy, combative, roughhouse play in which there is destruction of property and injury to the participants. Truancy, running away, staying out nights, less interest in organized games, and a general tendency to restless, random activity . . ." [22]

The reasons for this behavior were almost as various as the social stresses and strains themselves. War encourages the aggression of the child at the very time when that aggression is normally channeled into other forms of behavior considered more socially desirable. Dr. Karl A. Menninger points out that "War stimulates the wish to exert power over other people, to be aggressive, dominant, commanding, possessive. Civilization restricts such impulses in all of us only with great difficulty. . . . Much as we talk of peace, all of us have secret yearnings, of which we are a little ashamed, to act in ways that would be permissible only if war existed." [23] When this aggressive behavior among children takes the form of organized games and sports, it is defined as normal and desirable. When, as a direct outgrowth of war-time stimulation, it assumed other forms, the resulting behavior was defined as a social problem. As the child advances into adolescence and his physiological equipment matures, the failure to curb his aggressive impulses becomes even more serious in the eyes of society.[24]

In speaking of the wartime problems of children of school age, one psychiatrist pointed out that social planning has lagged behind in connection with this age group on the assumption that as long as they are in school their difficulties are automatically solved. Infants and adolescents have, she continued, been the recipients of more solicitude on the basis of their own special problems, while those of elementary school age have been left largely to their own devices in the afterschool periods.[25] Much of the basic pattern of personality is established during these years; in the years of the war the social basis of personality underwent drastic modification for hundreds of thousands of children. Many of the elements in a changing social order combined to influence this development of personality in directions not previously anticipated. We shall consider three of these types of wartime social change below, as they impinged upon the social environment of the family and hence of the children.

The most severe cases of emotional disorder among children in World War II were found in the belligerent countries, with Britain providing much of the available information on this score. A child-guidance clinic in London reported that the largest group of symptoms exhibited by children who had been subjected to such war strains as bombing or the loss of one or both of their parents were psychosomatic in character—that is, physiological symptoms with an emotional basis. These evidences of emotional insecurity included "bed-wetting, soiling, hysterical vomiting, sleep-walking, fits and tics (like habitual grimacing, blinking, and shrugging, and so on)." In other large groups, such reactions as "anxiety states, depressions, hysteria, and the like" were observed. Other behavior took the form of "truancy, stealing, destructiveness, noisy and aggressive behavior, and running away," while still other children developed such personality traits as "seclusiveness, irritability, over-submissiveness, and defiance. . . ."[26]

American psychiatrists and social workers point out that similar symptoms could be unearthed in the files of any child-guidance clinic in the United States.[27] Many children and adults in this country apparently reacted to the *possibility* of bombing and attack as they

would have to the real thing. In such cases, the fear was a very real
emotion, even though the basis for it rested in fantasy rather than
fact.[28] Many children who were emotionally unstable from some temperamental or previous environmental factor were unable to cope with
these new difficulties. Their emotional insecurity was heightened by
changes in their routine, interruptions in their accustomed pattern of
life, or the deprivation of one or both parents. This feeling of insecurity had many symptoms in the American child, even though the
psychosomatic responses were not as serious as those observed among
the children of London who had been forced to undergo real and
tangible terrors.[29]

The emotional impact of the war upon the child seems, in short, to
have been a function of his other social relationships. If these relationships were satisfactory, many of the emotional repercussions of the
war appear to have passed him by. If, on the other hand, he had
other personality disorders, they tended to be enhanced by the environmental changes of the war. A study of children between the ages of
seven and thirteen undertaken at Bellevue Hospital indicated "the
rather striking tendency of the children with severe personality disorders to weave their conflicts and anxieties into the war situation . . .
[which] was used in such cases as a medium of expressing basic conflicts not necessarily created by the war."[30] The anxieties of the children in Bellevue were most clearly aroused by situations related to the
family and their relation to it. Behavior difficulties could therefore be
expected "with a child who has had a home in which there has been
a constant marked threat to his relationship with the parents. The
frustrations and deprivations which such a child has been experiencing
as a result of this unsatisfactory relationship will most probably become reinforced by any further threat to this relationship as a result
of the war."[31] Neurotic children, whose latent fears were already
aroused by the denial of affection or by insecurity in the parental
relationship, were most vulnerable to the strains of a wartime society.

Wartime Mobility and the Child

The emotional impact of wartime social changes on the child can
only be inferred from his behavior. Many of the results upon the personality cannot be adequately determined at the time but must be
taken into consideration in the behavior of later years. These basic
aspects of personality do not readily lend themselves to quantitative

measurement and hence cannot be presented as direct evidence of the effects of war. There are, however, certain aspects of child behavior during wartime which do lend themselves to measurement. These data are related to the changes in social circumstances which have brought about some of the personality changes adumbrated above. These environmental changes resulted from the mobility of families, the employment outside the home of hundreds of thousands of married women, and the separation of families in which the link between father and children was broken for years at a time.

As indicated above, social mobility reached its highest point during World War II.[32] The traditional form of social mobility in the United States has been the unattached boy or man, wandering from place to place in search of work. This stereotype was modified during the depression by the appearance of hundreds of thousands of families with children in a desperate search for a meager livelihood.[33] The mobility of the war years was even more domestic. The most accurate data for the composition of this migration were gathered in ten Congested Production Areas in 1944 by the Bureau of the Census at the request of the President's Committee for Congested Production Areas. Total inmigration into the ten Areas from 1940 to 1944 was 2,452,212 persons, of whom 419,703 were under 15 years of age.[34] This number represented 17 per cent of the migratory population, a percentage which would be considerably increased if children under four years of age had been included. In the sample census, children under four were included in the nonmigrant rather than the migrant population, since they had been born since April 1, 1940 and hence had no place of residence when the decennial census was taken. It is impossible to determine exactly the number of children under five in the migratory group, which should be added to the 419,703 enumerated above. The magnitude of the problem of mobility and children in wartime is apparent, however, from the number involved in the ten Congested Production Areas alone, without counting the migration in and out of all the other centers in the United States.

The majority of these nearly half a million children probably moved but once or twice during the emergency period. Their lives thus were not in any sense as peripatetic as those of the members of the Joad family, whose only home was a dilapidated automobile in which they constantly moved from place to place in search of work. Nevertheless, the interruption of the lives of the wartime children during their formative years was considerable. Their new social circumstances ranged all the way from new playmates, a new teacher, and new recreational activities to a new home, new hours of work for parents, and an entirely new social milieu. Some children who had always lived in the country had to adjust themselves to the city, often under crowded housing conditions and with inadequate recreational facilities. Children of minority groups faced difficult adjustments when they moved from areas of ethnic and racial toleration to areas where these

Table IV

Total Inmigrants and Those under 15 Years of Age in Ten Congested Production Areas 1940-1944*

Congested Production Area	Total Inmigrants	Total Under 15
1. Charleston	46,825	9,120
2. Detroit-Willow Run	254,485	46,530
3. Hampton Roads	165,760	27,678
4. Los Angeles	782,705	126,742
5. Mobile	12,068	2,086
6. Muskegon	19,083	4,192
7. Portland-Vancouver	222,134	45,770
8. Puget Sound	269,352	50,760
9. San Diego	164,985	23,490
10. San Francisco Bay	514,815	83,335
	2,452,212	419,703

* Adapted from Bureau of the Census, Series CA-3, *op. cit.*

patterns were not fully developed. In a society such as our own, accustomed to considerable mobility, these readjustments were not so difficult as those of the bombed-out children of London's East End, suddenly faced by the new world of the open country. The roots of the average American family are not so firmly planted in a traditional social environment as those of the European family; nevertheless the difficulty of personal adjustment of the children was great.

Another aspect of wartime migration among children occurred with the hundreds of thousands of families engaged in migrant agricultural labor.[35] The role of World War II in accelerating or retarding this type of migration is not exactly known, although such movement was probably not accelerated to the same extent as migration to the congested production areas. The number of children involved in this agricultural migration was very large, with one authority estimating the number between six and sixteen years of age at one million. These children move at least once during the school year with their families; large numbers of them attend school only one or two months in the year and many do not attend at all.[36] Their problems of personal adjustment were even greater than those of the young people involved in industrial migration, inasmuch as the transitory nature of such agricultural labor generally meant a whole series of moves for the children. If such children were to be educated at all, some Federal efforts should be mobilized, since the problem was clearly one transcending state boundaries.

The child is dependent upon the primary group for the well-rounded development of personality. The most important primary group is his own family, which accompanies him (or vice versa) on his wartime wanderings. The other groups in his life—the play group, the school group, and the rest—are left behind as he follows his parents from one community to another. One of the important elements in his personality is the series of roles in these primary groups which he must abandon when he leaves the community. Even the plasticity of childhood cannot always bridge the gap between moves and the child is often left for a considerable time in the new environment without the friends he needs. The more retiring the child, the more difficult it is for him to make new contacts; at the same time, such a child is acutely in need of the emotional security that status in several groups can give him. Temporary rejection by the new group is difficult; permanent rejection may be demoralizing.

The child in the wartime environment of a congested production area often could not count upon the emotional support of his parents during the period of gaining status in the new groups. The parents were often handicapped in this vital role by three factors: (1) They were forced to devote an undue amount of attention to their own adjustment; (2) The father often had to work on the swing or graveyard shift and saw his children only infrequently; (3) Many of the mothers themselves took jobs in war production and were unable to support their children emotionally in time of need. Figures are not available for the exact number of working women with children among the migrant group in the congested production areas. We do know, however, that 45 per cent of all female migrants 14 years of age and over were in the labor force, a group which included many thousands

of mothers with young children.[37] The contribution of these mothers
to the war effort was great, but in the process of becoming workers
they were unable to perform many of their functions as mothers.

Working Mothers and Children

A second important change in the social circumstances of children
in World War II was the employment of their mothers in full or
part-time industry or service activities. In March 1940, there were
833,000 married women aged 18–64 in the labor force with one or more
children under ten years of age. By February 1944, this number had
grown to 1,470,000, an increase from 7.8 per cent to 12.1 per cent of the
population. This number was divided as to age brackets with 270,000
in the group from 18–24 years, 710,000 from 25–34 years, 400,000 from
35–44, and a small number from 45–64 years. The wartime trends in
the employment of women with small children may be seen in the
following table:

Table V

Married Women Aged 18–64 in the Civilian Labor Force with Children
Under Ten, March 1940 and February 1944*

Age Group	1940 Total	1944 Total
Total, 18–64 Years	833,000	1,470,000
18–24 Years	118,000	270,000
25–34 Years	449,000	710,000
35–44 Years	223,000	400,000
45–64 Years	43,000	a

* "Sources of Wartime Labor Supply in the United States," *Monthly Labor Review*,
59:264-278 (August, 1944), Table 4, p. 275.

a Number of persons in this category too small to permit estimate on the basis of 1944
sample statistics.

The implications of this increase in working mothers in terms of
the functions of the family are various. One of these functions is the
physical protection and education of the children in their formative
years. In hundreds of thousands of families this function was modified
during the war with consequent changes in the social environment of
millions of children. These modifications were injurious to the welfare
of the child, although not sufficiently so to forbid the employment of
mothers under these conditions. This dilemma is stated by Katharine
F. Lenroot as follows: "During the war we have not placed sufficient
emphasis upon what a child needs from his mother and what contribu-

tion the mother makes when she devotes the major part of her time and attention to the management of a home and the care of young children."[38]

If the situation were defined as important enough to warrant the employment of mothers with young children, it should also have been defined as sufficiently important to provide adequate care of the child during the hours of employment. Like many of the other war-time readjustments in the lives of infants and children, the results of this change must largely be inferred at this time, since the subjects are neither sufficiently articulate to express their reactions nor sufficiently mature to come in contact with those agencies which record their unusual behavior. The deprivation of emotional security coming from the absence of the mother will be apparent only in the future.

Early in the war, the War Manpower Commission issued a statement concerning "Policy on Employment in Industry of Women with Young Children," in which it suggested that the employment of women in this category be postponed as long as possible. When this step became vitally necessary, in certain areas where the labor shortage was acute, the Commission suggested that "(a) they should be employed at suitable hours and on such shifts and part-time schedules as will cause the least disruption in their family life, and that (b) if they are unable to arrange for the satisfactory care of their children at home during working hours, adequate facilities should be provided for the care of their children.[39] This supervision in some places took the form of foster-home care, day-care centers, nursery schools, kindergartens, and various forms of homemaker services, all of which attempted to act as substitute mothers for the child of school and pre-school age. These extensions of the protective and educational functions of the family were initiated before World War II, for the problems of working mothers with young children were by no means unique to the war period. The emergency merely accelerated the process of social change which made these readjustments more vitally necessary, not only to the family but to the war effort as well.

The problems involved in the day care of the different age groups varied considerably, and different social mechanisms were evolved to meet them. Homemaker services were made available for children of all ages who did not adjust happily to group companionship or presented some special problem of health or behavior. Foster-home day care was particularly desirable in the case of infants under two, whose problems must be met on an individualized basis. Day nurseries made it possible for children from the age of two to experience group contacts at an earlier age than was hitherto considered either possible or desirable. Some form of wartime day care for children in school was important because of the insecurity felt by many children when they returned from school to a motherless home.[40]

These various surrogates for maternal care operated in an indeterminate number of the million and a half homes with young children in which the mother was gainfully employed. These arrangements ranged in formality from a group of young children casually chaperoned by an older sister to well-equipped day nurseries manned by trained social workers and financed by the Works Progress Administration or the Office of Defense Health and Welfare Services. This range of group and institutional character makes difficult any generalizations concerning the relative success of these wartime adjustments, particularly since there are no adequate criteria for assessing them. Considered in terms of their success in mobilizing all available labor for war production, these arrangements were a highly successful means to an end. Considered in terms of their adequacy as substitutes for the mother-child relationship, the comparison becomes virtually meaningless, inasmuch as there are no definite standards of maternal care. Furthermore, the results of these changes upon the personalities of the children directly affected will not be known for years or even decades, at which time the wartime changes will be inextricably intermingled with other cultural factors in the personality of the individual.

These changes in social circumstance for the child were frank makeshifts for the normal care of the mother. Our society is based upon the small, compact, conjugal family, in which the care and early training of the child falls largely upon the mother. Other societies have evolved their own behavior patterns about some form of the consanguine family, where the family group is larger and the "maternal" functions are shared by several maternal or paternal aunts. Still other societies have started with the conjugal family and have, in a few decades, progressed toward a drastic modification of its traditional functions, particularly regarding child care. The results of these innovations upon the personality of the child are not clear. Our own society is still committed, in theory at least, to the constant and exclusive care of the young children by the mother during the preschool years. Children deprived of this care do not have the same social environment as the majority of their fellows. Furthermore, such atypical children are considered as a social problem, merely because of their atypicality. This definition in turn helps to accentuate the possible maladjustment of the children immediately affected. Large numbers of children came into this problem category for the first time during World War II.

Even under the best of material circumstances, many of the young children in the million and a half homes with working mothers were deprived of certain social relationships believed important to the normal child. Those who considered the problem solved when public provision for child care was provided were not viewing the situation in all its human implications. Such persons "forget what it may mean to take little children from their parents in the early morning and hurry them to a day-care center. They forget that many children develop a feeling of insecurity when they are away from their mothers from dawn to dark. . . . They forget what may happen to school-age children when they do not have the anchor of knowing that mother is at home."[41] The world is a strange and terrifying place to the little child, even when it is not complicated by the fears, fantasies, and frustrations of total war. The child in our society has acute psychic need of his parents to furnish the emotional security he can find in no other place.

Examples of the unfortunate effects of maternal neglect under these circumstances could be found in any agency dealing with children during World War II. In a report based upon compilations from a number of such agencies, as well as case histories from individual psychiatrists, Dr. David M. Levy summarized some of the typical forms of neglect by the working mother. "The neglect," he states, "varies from improper feeding to complete abandonment of the children. The tempting, lucrative job becomes a rough test of maternal responsibility, even allowing for economic necessity."[42] When a position beckoned in war work in another city, many mothers traveled to the place of work with no thought of any provision for the children. Others continued to work long after members of the local community complained that their children were demoralizing not only themselves but other children. Other mothers were reluctant to give up their jobs even when their children became public charges. Others remarked that, since the war was so important, why bother about the problems of their children? Others imposed undue responsibilities upon their older children to take care of the younger while they (the mothers) continued to work.[43]

The responses of the children to these evidences of neglect were varied, depending upon the personality pattern of the families, as well as the degree of neglect involved. Some children played truant from school and slept under porches rather than return to homes where they felt unwanted. Others merely complained that they never saw their mothers and fathers at one time, since the parents were working on different shifts and consequently had different sleeping, eating, and recreational habits. One three-year-old girl placed in a day nursery constantly wailed that "My Mommy doesn't love me." Another three-year-old developed feeding problems and other behavior difficulties after her mother went to work in a factory. A six-year-old boy expressed fear of Germans and Japanese bombers as a result of his basic apprehension after his mother went to work. A nine-year-old developed fears of the dark and of being left alone in the house when his mother took a war job. A six-year-old so lost his joy of living that he showed immediate signs of malnutrition and extreme nervousness when left with his older sister instead of his mother.[44]

The theme recurring again and again through these abbreviated case histories is anxiety at the possibility of neglect and frustration at its realization. The physical routine of the child was interrupted by the employment of the mother, but his mental stability was even more seriously threatened. Many such children experienced a "psychic trauma" upon separation from their mothers and the familiar environment of the home. Until the child was able to reestablish this emotional harmony with his new environment, his personality often disintegrated in the shape of various regressions to more infantile forms of behavior. These patterns included thumb sucking, bed wetting, whining, or other regressions, the continuance of which may indicate a serious personality disorganization in the neglected child.[45]

It was impossible for the infant or preschool child to understand the desirability of increasing war production by using every possible able-bodied worker in certain congested production areas—including his own mother. The child often unconsciously interpreted this absence as a sign of abandonment and betrayal, since to his mind his mother would not leave him unless she deliberately willed it so. In the solipsistic universe of the little child, his own emotional security outweighed any real or putative considerations of total war. He felt dimly that if his mother loved him enough she would stay with him and take care of him. Since she had not done so, she must not love him. In his dawning consciousness, it was as simple as that.

Children in Broken Families

A third major form of wartime change in social circumstance with an impact upon the personality of the child was the absence of the father. Such a situation was by no means new to the wartime family and the children composing it; desertion, divorce, and death have long brought about the disorganization of the normal family group, leaving the mother to carry on as best she could without the complementary role of the father. Until recent years, this problem was generally the result either of death or desertion of the wife and family by the husband and father. In recent decades, however, the physical disorganization of the family has been increasingly brought about by divorce.[46] The accelerated rate of social change in World War II certainly increased the number of families separated by the death of the father; it probably increased the number separated by desertion; and it also increased the number broken by divorce.

The war brought about another change of social circumstance whose repercussions upon the child were unprecedented in scope and duration. That change was the widespread and continued absence on military service of large numbers of fathers, a situation unique in the history of this country. The exact number of children involved in this mass deprivation is not known, but estimates have been made from various sources. The Bureau of the Census estimated, on the basis of its Monthly Report of the Labor Force, that in February, 1944 there were 1,250,000 women with children under 14 years of age whose husbands were in the armed forces.[47] This did not indicate the number of children involved, but only the number of family groups with young children broken by the war. The Office of Dependency Benefits of the Army Service Forces was sending dependency checks to some 1,738,897 children as of June 30, 1944,[48] a number which should be augmented by corresponding figures from the United States Navy, the Marines, and the Coast Guard to give a complete picture of the extent of the problem as a whole. Finally, neither the Bureau of the Census nor the Office of Dependency Benefit figures included the large numbers of children in families temporarily broken by the induction of fathers after February, 1944 and June 30, 1944 respectively. The exact extent of these separations may never be known. We only know that they were without precedent both in extent and duration.

The national character of the problem rendered it unique in the history of family bereavement. Family difficulties arising out of desertion, divorce, and death have hitherto been personal in character, a break in social relationships on an individual rather than a national scale. Depending on the nature of the bereavement, the members of the family have traditionally taken their personal deprivation with resignation, grief, or shame. These emotions were complicated in wartime by personal and family pride, particularly on the part of the children, as the absent father became a hero glorified by public opinion and the instruction of the mother. When millions of families were sharing the same general experience, considerable *esprit de corps* was generated which was lacking in former cases of family bereavement, particularly those involving desertion and divorce. The mother could interpret the situation in terms of patriotism and communicate this definition to the children in a manner impossible when the tragedy was personal and involved some element of shame or moral turpitude. This sense of participation in a great national enterprise tended to mitigate certain elements of personality disorganization customarily present when a peacetime family is broken.

This feeling of participation by no means solved the problem completely. Even though glorified through the heroic symbols of national service, the functional pattern of normal family life was still unmistakably broken. We have considered some of the effects of this break upon the relationships of husband and wife. The child also suffered, although in a less articulate fashion, the tensions and anxieties present in the war-broken home. In many cases, indeed, he seemed to react only indifferently to the enlistment of his father and survived the immediate shock with no perceptible emotional disturbance. In the early part of the war, the majority of the children referred to the Judge Baker Guidance Center did not experience any accentuation of the problems for which they were originally referred to the Center because of the enlistment or induction of their fathers and brothers. With but one exception, none of a group of 49 cases was referred to the Center for guidance and treatment solely because of emotional disturbances growing out of the enlistment of a family member.[49]

In another study, a number of cases were selected from the Bureau of Child Welfare of the City of New York, involving children whose

fathers were in the armed forces and who had manifested certain undesirable behavior after the enlistment or induction of the father. The
maladjustment of the children in most of these cases appeared to be
largely an accentuation of certain difficulties already present before
the father left. Some imbalance in the internal relationships of the
family seemed to be a prerequisite for the majority of instances of subsequent maladjustment of the child. The study therefore concludes
that "although the problems . . . created were new, where serious
behavior deviation is now reported we can recognize the existence of
latent forces of family breakdown within the family relationship."[50]
Furthermore, where children indicated undue emotional strain or excessive anxiety at the possibility of separation from the parent or presented general behavior difficulties, "they had previously shown symptoms of maladjustment or had come from unstable family groups."[51]
At this early level of behavior, the emotional unsettlement resulting
from the war was apparently an acceleration of previous symptoms.

Generalizations concerning the incidence of emotional maladjustment under such circumstances are difficult, however, both because
of the absence of national data and the prolonged incubation period
of such difficulties. Children apparently making an adequate adjustment to the prolonged absence of their father may have been living
in a world of fantasies and distorted father images which will distort
the structure of their personalities in years to come. Furthermore, the
emotional difficulties experienced by such children were not of the
type which would bring them into contact with clinics and child
guidance centers unless there were some accompanying behavior difficulty. Children would normally have to run away, play truant, be
incorrigible in school, or be referred to the Juvenile Court before they
would come to the attention of the average clinic. The emotional
disturbances generated by the separation of father and children would
not usually be such as to bring about this overtly antisocial behavior.
This does not deny the ultimate importance of these disturbances.
They are among the delayed psychic wounds of World War II, for
which no Purple Heart was awarded.

In terms of the American culture pattern, a family without a father
is an abnormal group. The emotional relationships within this broken
group are therefore atypical. "With the father absent from home life,"
as one psychiatrist puts it, "the family constellation is changed from
the normal triangle of mother, father, child (and siblings) to the

truncated home of mother, or mother substitute, and children. . . . It is similar to the situation of a home in which the father has died, where the child reaches a solution through an image of a father rather than through the experience of a real presence. This often creates distorted identifications or too great Oedipus guilt. From these spring many neurotic symptom formations, with warped adult characters."[52] One need not subscribe fully to all the implications of the Freudian position to realize that the prolonged absence of the father may produce mixed emotions in the child, both male and female. These emotions may take the form of an excessive mother fixation when the male child identifies himself too closely with the absent father in his relationships with the mother. It may also involve feelings of guilt arising from the absence of the possible rival for the undivided affections of the mother. This paternal absence may mean the failure of the boy to develop normally in the traditional male patterns without the example ordinarily set by the father.[53]

In other cases, the emotional difficulties of the child were intensified by those of the mother. Some women were incapable of bearing the additional burden imposed by the absence of the father, either because they were emotionally too young to assume the added responsibilities of motherhood or because they lacked the psychic energy to carry on in both maternal and quasi-paternal roles. Under peacetime conditions, these women would probably never have been called upon to face these additional uncertainties, since their husbands would always be on hand to assume the burdens themselves. The enlistment or induction of the husband left many women alone with small children and in a state of psychological demoralization. In one instance known to the writer, the young mother was committed to an institution for the mentally deranged after she broke down under the additional war-induced strain. The effects of such neurotic or psychotic parental symptoms upon the life organization of the child are not salutary. The child cannot easily escape the pathological effects of such domestic chaos. Mothers and children in this category were also casualties of total war, since without the war-broken home they might never have suffered such psychic damage.[54]

When the family is considered as a "unity of interacting personalities," the deprivation of the war years becomes even clearer. The personality of the child evolves under the play of these interacting personalities, each of which (mother, father, and siblings) has a unique role.

The family with the absent father was an incomplete relationship, since there was no one to play the male role in the lives of the growing children. This disadvantage of the conjugal family is mitigated in the consanguine family, where the child may have several social fathers in the person of his mother's brothers, each of whom is perfectly capable of playing the paternal role.[55] This role involves imitation and instruction by the father in all the behavior patterns, beliefs, and attitudes defined by the society as characteristically male. Everyone is conscious of this process when they consider how small children, especially boys, consciously and unconsciously ape their fathers and attempt to pattern their conduct upon the paternal example.

In the more intangible field of attitudes and values, the father has an equally important role in determining the beliefs and behavior of his children. When he is absent for any length of time, there is no one to take his place. The mother may do her best and even partially succeed in playing the dual role of father and mother. The very nature of the sexual division of labor makes complete success in this attempt impossible. The mother may try to bridge the gap between child and father by evoking the image of the father and instructing the child in his memory. The child thus responds to what is essentially a figment of the mother's imagination, since one cannot completely reconstruct the personality of another. Given the circumstances, this was the natural course for mothers to follow, but this shadowy paternal figure was at best an inadequate surrogate for the real thing.

We began this study with the general hypothesis that World War II intensified, but did not substantially modify, the nature of social problems. The presence of three or four million temporarily broken families gives us pause, however, for here was a situation with no peacetime parallel in terms of scope and effect. The impact of this situation upon the relationships within the family, especially those involving young children, constituted a new social problem resulting from the war and not a familiar problem merely accentuated thereby. This massive separation of the family is the first important evidence that our initial hypothesis may not explain all the repercussions of World War II upon social problems. Three to four million families, faced with a new experience of such universality and importance, cannot be ignored. We will have to modify our hypothesis if many more facts of this nature come to light.

CHAPTER FOUR

WAR AND ADOLESCENCE

The Nature of Adolescence

Adolescence has traditionally been a period of storm and stress in our society, a period marked by emotional conflicts, physiological disturbances, and minor personal maladjustments. The adolescent is in a transitional stage of development between childhood and manhood, during which he must adjust to the adult world at the same time that he is plagued with various physical and emotional changes in himself. Primary and secondary sex characteristics begin to manifest themselves during this awkward age, bringing with them adjustments complicated by the mores of a society in which sexual repression plays an important role. The adolescent boy is concerned with the role he will take in the economic world when he finishes high school; day and night he thinks the long, long thoughts of youth. The adolescent girl is bemused with fantasies of love and romance, the sort of man she will marry, the home she will have, and the problems of motherhood she will shortly encounter. Boy and girl alike wonder whether they will measure up to the expectations of parents, friends, and themselves, expectations which will soon be faced in actual experience in a world which whirls along at an ever-increasing pace. While old age is the time to dream dreams, adolescence is the time to see visions.[1]

The object of these visions is not always clear to the adolescent, faced with the immensity of choice in the modern world and perplexed by a variety of patterns of conduct. In a society marked by fixed and feudal relationships, the personal vistas open to the average boy or girl are relatively few and the choices comparatively simple. The adolescent in the feudal world was not beset with a bewildering variety of options of conduct and definitions of the situation. The way was already preordained, both in terms of his future place in the social order and the beliefs which defined this place. Similarly, the adolescent in the society of contemporary preliterate peoples is faced with an adjustment to a culture already established by custom and relatively unchanging. His choice of activitiy is already made for him in the simple division of labor which characterizes most primitive peoples. His religious, moral, and ethical beliefs are those of his group and are reverently handed down from generation to generation with a minimum of change. Definitions of right and wrong, morality and immorality, virtue and vice do not trouble the mind of the average primitive adolescent any more than that of the peasant boy of medieval Europe. Under these conditions, adolescence is reached and passed with a minimum of storm and stress.

Not so in modern American society. Here adolescence is marked by social alarums and excursions, doubts and self-questionings, and the abrupt passage from childhood to adult manhood or womanhood. The years of adolescence are superficially years of personal stability on the part of the young person in our society, supported as he customarily is in the bosom of his family and nurtured by its affection. This alleged state of blissful unconcern with the practical affairs of life is a fiction, however, in view of the transition facing the average boy or girl when they finish high school and take their place in the adult world. Among primitive peoples, boys and girls participate in the life of the group from the time they are able to toddle about, each performing certain chores which contribute to the general welfare. The transition from the world of the child to that of the adult is not abrupt, since the child and adolescent do many of the same things as the grown person. An economic system based upon a simple division of labor does not offer any such variety of choice of vocation as concerns the American adolescent during his formative years. In spite of the symbolic rites of passage marking the transition from childhood to manhood among many primitive groups, the actual transition, in terms of social participation, is seldom as pronounced as it is with us.[2]

Many of the growing pains of adolescence are social in nature, rather than primarily physiological. Difficulties traditionally considered inherent in the process of physical maturation itself are now seen to be largely cultural in origin, differing from one society to another and reaching perhaps their most difficult manifestation in our highly complex and dynamic social order. Anthropological researches among primitive peoples have conclusively demonstrated the cultural genesis of many adolescent adjustment problems; in a number of these groups, the problems besetting our own young people are largely nonexistent.

Certain sexual maladjustments, which play such a major part in the *sturm und drang* of our own adolescents, are not found among many primitive groups. Among the Samoans, for example, sex is considered a normal process and is surrounded with none of the fascinated shame that invests it in our society. Samoans are accustomed to the sight of sex behavior at an early age; by the time they reach puberty, the relationship has become part of their own normal business of living and is defined as such. The mystery, shame, and much of the maladjustment centered about this central urge are absent under these conditions. The period of adolescence among the Samoans is thereby made correspondingly smoother. The mores of our society make impossible such a placid acceptance of the visceral urges, with considerable resultant maladjustment among the adolescents beginning to experience these desires.[3]

These two general factors—the complexity of the society and the abruptness of the transition—render the adjustment of the adolescent doubly difficult with us. Adolescence is the period when the integration of the personality takes shape, when the individual first begins to orient himself to a world whose variety and rate of change are both increasing by geometric progression. The boy or girl continues to mature physiologically at a relatively early age; the arrival at economic and social maturity has, in peacetime at least, been delayed many years. The boy is physically prepared to take his place in the world at a time when he has not yet accumulated enough of its knowledge and skills to allow him to do so. He is defined as a child, or at least not an adult, at a time when he is equipped for sexual relations, parenthood, and the other physical obligations of adult status.

"In terms of growth, strength, fecundity, and mental capacity," as one observer puts it, "full maturity tends to be attained only a short time after puberty; but socially the adolescent still has a long way to go, in most cases, before full status is reached."[4] The later years of adolescence are years of preparation for an experience of whose exact nature the adolescent is unsure. The rapidity of social change is so great that the experience of the older generation offers less guidance than has traditionally been the case. The adolescent is thus faced with an uncertain future, bereft of many of the comforting moral solutions which are the natural heritage of the young in a simpler society.

In this brief discussion, we cannot explore the many ramifications —emotional, psychological, and social—of the complex process which we call adolescence. We can only examine, in the general context of social change, the impact of World War II upon the millions of young men and women in the age groups defined as constituting adolescence. This definition has here been made somewhat arbitrarily for two reasons: *one,* the exact age limits of adolescence are in dispute even among psychologists; *two,* most of the statistical data on the changing status of adolescence are confined to particular sets of age groupings. We shall therefore define adolescence for most purposes as the period from the fourteenth *through* the seventeenth year. In so doing, we are mindful not only of the variations between individuals, but those between social groups and classes in the relative rapidity with which physical and social maturity is reached. The years of adolescence are those in which the majority of children are in high school, groping to become men or women in this best of all possible worlds. The upper limit of this group was, symbolically enough, the minimum age of induction into the armed forces, the age at which millions of young men reached maturity in the fiery crucible of war, the age at which they definitely "put away childish things."

The 1940 Census showed 12,303,000 young persons of both sexes in the group 14–18 years of age. Of this number, 6,185,000 were male and 6,119,000 female. This total represented an increase from the 11,708,000 young persons of the same age enumerated by the 1930 Census; the estimated total of 10,529,000 for 1950 was considerably smaller. The figure of 12,303,000 young people is the most accurate available estimate of the number of adolescents in the population at the beginning of the defense period in 1940, the base point for any study of the impact of World War II. A substantial minority of the population, therefore, was involved in the changes in adolescent circumstances which accompanied this global conflict. Many of the changes experienced by the adolescent group took the same form as with other special segments of the population; other changes were unique in their impingement upon this age group alone. The following discussion will outline certain of the social changes and the accompanying modifications in behavior undergone by these 12 million.[5]

War and Adolescence

War is a great accelerator of social change. Adolescence is the time when the individual is painstakingly attempting to integrate his personality in terms of the social environment in which he lives. Other things being equal, the more rapid the social change, the greater the difficulty of such integration. The emotional ramifications of this adolescent difficulty were not completely apparent during the war, even as they were similarly delayed for the wartime child. Many of the effects of these failures and semifailures of personal integration will not be evident for years or even decades in the behavior patterns of those who were adolescent during the war. We are reasonably certain that some such changes took place, however, in view of the close reciprocal relationship between the adolescent personality and the social order in which it unfolds. Much objective evidence exists of the changes in adolescent status which accompanied wartime changes. While we can only infer many of the corresponding modifications in personality, we are on solid ground when we enumerate the changes in social circumstance.

The peacetime world between the two wars presented many problems of adjustment. The depression colored the lives of the children, with the fear of economic insecurity very real for millions of families. During these years, the traditional dependence of the child upon the family was paralleled by the dependence of millions of families upon the federal government. The adjustment to these conditions of dependence involved one of the most massive changes in attitude the nation ever experienced. Accompanying this insecurity was the mobility of a large minority of the population, as the unemployed ranged the country in search of work. These and other domestic problems made the lot of an extensive marginal group extremely difficult. In addition, an indelible imprint was left upon the personalities of the depression children, who were to become the war adolescents.

World War II intensified many of these aspects of social change and at the same time introduced certain new elements into the national life. The migrations of the depression years were accelerated during the defense and war periods, under different economic conditions but with many of the same effects upon the individuals and families concerned. The billions of dollars pumped into the national economy by the Federal Government resulted in a rapid increase in the national income and a change for many families from poverty to comparative affluence. The threat of unemployment was effectively removed for the duration, as millions of new workers entered the civilian labor force.

Adolescents formed an important part of this labor force. Some of the young people did part-time work while still remaining in school and others obtained full-time employment in war industries, service and retail activities, and agriculture. Modifications in the structure and functions of the family accompanied these broad economic changes and were thereby communicated to the adolescent. Families were broken by migration and induction, sometimes temporarily and sometimes permanently. These and many other changes in the social structure faced the adolescent boy or girl during the war, changes overshadowed for the older boys by the imminence of induction and for the older girls by the possibility of a wartime marriage. The psychological adjustments to these changes in social situation were more difficult to determine. Nevertheless, such adjustments were there.[6]

The most striking result of these adolescent adjustments to wartime change was the sudden maturity of the young people concerned. The boy who was inducted on his eighteenth birthday, spent several months in this country in basic training, and then went into battle on the western front before his nineteenth birthday underwent the most drastic form of maturation. For the majority of boys and girls, the process was neither so sudden nor so cataclysmic. The ability to adjust to new problems and situations is a characteristic of full maturity, when the individual is presumably equipped with sufficient knowledge and skills to solve whatever problems he may face. In this sense, maturity came early to many adolescents on the home front, as they entered industry as responsible adults, assumed the care of the younger brothers and sisters while their parents were in war plants and the armed forces, and generally took upon themselves adult roles in a wartime society.

Economic dependence of the adolescent was artificially prolonged during the depression years by the shortage of employment opportunities whereby the young man might get a job, marry, and assume a responsible position in the community. Almost overnight this situation changed and the adolescent was somersaulted into the adult world with unprecedented rapidity. From a source of embarrassment to society because it could find no jobs for him, the adolescent was forthwith subjected to all manner of interesting and lucrative proposals. His participation in the adult world was eagerly solicited and his elders called him the hope of the world. This change in status from a "social problem" to a responsible part of a nation at war was a heady experience. Such a wholehearted acceptance was the most significant contribution of the war to the emotional well-being of the adolescent generation.[7]

"There can be no doubt," states one observer, "that, leaving out of account the physical sacrifice entailed, war is far better for adolescents than depression; for it does meet that one great need, the need of youth to count in the world of men, the need to belong, the need to serve."[8] The degree of this service was amply demonstrated by the figures for adolescent participation in total war. In April, 1944, 2,900,000 persons from 14 through 17 years of age were employed in civilian jobs, of whom 1,400,000 were attending school at the same time and 1,350,000 were in full-time gainful activity. This may be compared to approximately 1,000,000 boys and girls in the same age group who were employed in 1940.[9] If the age limit for adolescence be momentarily lifted to include the 18- and 19-year-olds, the figures for gainful employment shot upward to 4,610,000, of whom 1,430,000 were part-time students and 3,180,000 were in full-time employment. In 1940, the number in the 14–19 age group employed in civilian jobs was 1,705,000; the wartime increase amounted to 2,905,000 persons. Still considering the 14–19 age group as adolescent, we find more than one and one-half million such young men in the armed forces in 1944, representing a tremendous increase from the 66,000 in the same group in 1940.[10]

In the figures representing the civilian employment of the 14–17- and 14–19-year-old groups, we can see the changes in this form of adolescent participation over the four years. In the changes in the military enrollment of the 14–19-year-old group, an even more direct participation in the total conflict is evident. These figures effectively summarize the causes for the sudden maturity, the increased feeling of service, and the sense of emotional well-being which accompanied this change of adolescent status. The youth of the nation responded generously and unhesitatingly to the call. The pity is that only a total war is considered sufficiently important to warrant the complete use of the nation's human and industrial resources. With the nation in imminent danger from outside aggression, hardly a voice was raised in Congress or elsewhere against a wartime budget running more than one hundred billion dollars. When the nation was in equally mortal danger from a prolonged depression, the sense of national peril was confined to a much smaller group of persons, both within and without the Congress. World War II saw a nationwide call go out to every able-bodied man, woman, and child to participate in a great collective enterprise. The decade of the 1930's saw a large minority of the population deprived of any opportunity to participate in the economic life of the nation.

A sense of increased freedom tends to accompany maturity. The adolescents of the war years experienced an increase in freedom which took a number of forms. With 3,180,000 young persons in the 14–19 age group employed full-time and another 1,430,000 combining school with part-time employment, the number of adolescents and postadolescents wholly or partially independent was probably greater than at any time in our history. This independence assumed a number of forms, some salutary to the adolescent and others not. The enhancement of the ego as the young person experienced freedom for the first time through his own unaided efforts was one aspect of the new maturity. This ebullience was often accompanied by an irresponsibility in the matter of casually shifting jobs in an economy where jobs were temporarily plentiful. The subsequent postwar readjustment to a situation where opportunities for employment are no longer so abundant will present certain obvious difficulties.[11]

Excessive self-assertion in the field of personal conduct was another facet of this wartime freedom. A certain amount of this behavior is desirable during the adolescent period, when the young person is gradually weaning himself away from his childish dependence upon his family. War further encourages the self-assertion of the individual by placing a premium on personal and national aggression. When carried to an extreme among the wartime adolescent population, however, this aggression sometimes took the form of behavior defined by society as delinquent. A balance between too much and too little adolescent aggression was even more difficult to maintain during World War II than during the troubled years immediately preceding it.[12]

The precocious maturity of the wartime adolescent also took the form of an emancipation from conventional sexual mores on the part of large numbers of girls in the 14–18-year-old group. This problem will be considered in more detail below, but mention should be made in this context of the attempt by young girls to play an adult role in the great wartime drama before their eyes. Their older sisters were marrying soldiers and sailors and many of them were becoming mothers in their late teens or early twenties. Other still unmarried older sisters were entertaining the members of the armed forces in various ways, from dating and dancing to secondary forms of sexual expression.

Adolescent girls in their middle teens, endowed with a precocious physical maturity and enjoying a social maturity enhanced by the times, often undertook to carry into reality their still childish fantasies about sex. In this way, they attempted to demonstrate to themselves, their friends, and their parents that they were already adult women, with all the prerogatives presumably pertaining to this advanced status. Commenting upon this situation, one social worker points out that ". . . these fantasies themselves lead them to seek this type of fulfillment in a world stimulated by war . . . their fantasy life is transformed into reality through the war situation before they are emotionally and psychologically equipped to handle it."[13] As long as these fantasies remained purely on the psychological level, they did not involve the adolescent girl in any relationships considered a social problem. When translated on a large scale to the level of overt activity, however, the behavior ceased to be an individual and became a social concern.

Adolescent conflict is "normal" in American society where the physiological and psychological changes characteristic of this stage are aggravated by the changes in status and role which accompany the adolescent years. These "normal" phases were further complicated by the social changes incidental to World War II, in which many adolescent drives and conflicts were colored by the most dramatic fact of our day. The revolt against authority apparent during the years of adolescence is ordinarily accompanied by an increasing interest in sex; in wartime, these elements combined to produce the "precocious adolescence" mentioned above. Evidences of this condition were apparent in case studies of wartime adolescent girls. Among the symptoms were ". . . ambivalence toward parental authority . . . conflict over religion . . . escape through excessive daydreaming . . . suicide attempts . . . fear of the opinions of her peers . . . desire to grow up fast, a marked lag between her emotional capacity and intellectual and physical development, and arousal of interest and curiosity in regard to sex (still in an undifferentiated stage and without any serious interest in, or capacity for, marriage)."[14] This desire to experience life before their time was apparent during the war among boys and girls alike. In many cases, the wish was eventually answered for the boys by combat participation. The expression took other forms among the girls.

Precocious wartime maturity thus involved many girls in situations they were not equipped to handle. The economic freedom was not limited to boys; hundreds of thousands of young girls were wholly or partially self-sufficient during the war. An important concomitant of such self-sufficiency was the desire to assume other freedoms which they normally would not encounter until they had matured considerably and acquired more knowledge of the world. Many precocious adolescent girls associated with girls slightly older than themselves, whose greater maturity and experience with boys made them objects of youthful veneration. These friendships between adolescent and postadolescent girls led both age groups into conflict with the mores and often with the law. The adolescent in wartime revolted against parental authority, the revolt often taking the form of flouting the sex mores in the name of individual expression, wartime freedom, or contribution to the morale of the armed forces. The result in many such instances was the involvement of girls in their middle teens in a pattern of behavior not conducive to an integrated personality in later life.[15]

War and Changed Social Circumstances

World War II brought about drastic changes in the social circumstances of adolescents, as it did those of a majority of the population. Two aspects of these changes may be differentiated, the one tangible and the other intangible. The first comprises those actions the adolescent was actually performing during the war years and the modifications which these functional roles underwent. Included in this category were the decline in the number of adolescents attending school, the increase in those playing either a part-time or full-time role in industry, the numbers with mothers working outside the home, the migration of families as a group and adolescents as individuals, and finally the tremendous increase in the number of adolescents in active military service.

The second category of changes was closely related to the first, but involved less tangible considerations. This comprised the changes in what has been called the "social climate" of the nation—the subtle cultural cross-currents in the attitudes and behavior patterns of the adolescent which determine his conduct in a thousand different ways. The greater financial independence and the sense of immediate participation in a great national enterprise made up part of this change in the social climate. The loosening of family ties and the widening of the psychological gap between generations were other aspects. Finally, the feeling of uncertainty as to what the next few years would bring, the emotional insecurity, and the ambivalent feelings of apprehension and adventure made up a complex emotional mélange which unsettled many an adolescent.

The marginal role of the wartime adolescent further contributed to the unsettlement which normally accompanies this period in our culture. No longer a child, the wartime adolescent was ordinarily unable to assume active service; on the other hand, he soon faced this probability as the war continued, a probability which he viewed with mixed feelings. The ambiguity of this position was characterized as follows: "The uncertainty of his social position, the inconsistencies it presents, the emotional conflicts it encourages, are increased by the fact that there is, going along with his changing status, a terrific inner physical disturbance of endocrine origin . . . [therefore] it can be safely assumed that most adolescents will react to war conditions more violently than either children or adults."[16] The immediate wartime present was difficult enough; the proximate future was even more difficult. We shall outline the most important changes in social circumstance of the adolescent generation during the war, indicating some of the resultant modifications in social climate.

1. *School attendance.* In 1940, the number of boys and girls in the 14–19 age group attending school was estimated at 9,159,000. In 1944, this figure had shrunk to 7,930,000, a decrease of 1,229,000. Over the same interval, the number not attending school increased by 559,000 —from 5,471,000 to 6,070,000. This country has traditionally set great store by education and has considered universal education one of the bases of democratic government. The increasing proportion of young people in the primary and secondary schools before World War II was pointed to with pride as a significant index of increasing public participation in the benefits of democracy.

A change in social circumstance in which the percentage of young people 14–19 attending school decreased from 62 (in 1940) to 56 (in 1944) represented an important modification in the social structure. The bulk of the million and a quarter differential in attendance was accounted for by the increased number of adolescents and postadolescents in industry and the armed forces. The total population in this age group also declined by some 630,000 during the period, a factor which accounted for some of the decrease in school attendance. The educational situation was defined, however, in different terms over the four-year period, both by the adolescents themselves and by the nation as a whole. A substantial number of young persons in their formative years were considered more important to the general welfare in industry and the armed forces than in the schoolroom.[17]

The changing definition of education was also indicated by the increased number of youths attending school and working at the same time. In 1940, only 212,000 adolescents were combining education and employment, while in 1944 the number had increased by 1,218,000 to 1,430,000, even in the face of a decline of 1,229,000 in the total number attending school. Student-workers comprised one-third of all civilian workers in the 14–19 age group in 1944. As might be expected, an inverse relationship existed between age and school attendance, with approximately two-thirds of the 14–15-year-old workers attending school, as compared with one-tenth of those in the 18-19-year-old group. The average number of hours worked per week by the student-workers was approximately 20, as compared to 45 hours for workers of the same age groups not attending school. When the hours of school attendance were taken into consideration, the *total* work week of the student-workers was estimated at 48 hours, three hours greater than those employed full-time.[18]

When the adolescent spends four or five hours per day at some form of agricultural, industrial, or service activity, he seldom derives as much benefit from his schoolwork as under more normal conditions of attendance. Many forms of part-time activity were beyond the strength and physical endurance of the young workers, already fatigued from a full day in the classroom. A survey of the outside employment of adolescent boys and girls in an eastern industrial state indicated that large numbers were working at occupations varying in difficulty and necessary physical stamina from setting pins in bowling alleys to fabricating sheet metal in aircraft factories. Boys of 16 and 17 years were working on the graveyard shift and coming directly to school from work; girls were working the shift from 3 to 11 P.M., after attending school the early part of the day. With such a combination of education and employment, education came off a poor second.[19]

2. *Full-time employment.* The number of out-of-school youths in the 14–19 age group employed full-time in industry increased from

1,493,000 in 1940 to 3,180,000 in 1944, an increase of 1,687,000 persons. This represented a change in social circumstance which was almost as complete as active service in the armed forces. This form of adolescent participation in the war effort will be considered below. Suffice it to point out here that more than one-third of the 3 million out-of-school youthful workers were employed in manufacturing and approximately one-quarter in farm work. Trade and service industries were important additional sources of employment, particularly among younger girls who had left school to participate in the war program. Many older girls were employed in manufacturing activities directly related to the war, such as the metal, chemical, and rubber industries. This change in social circumstance will be permanent for most of the generation involved. The majority of those who left school to enter industry or join the armed forces did not return. Reductions in the number of young persons in the postwar out-of-school labor force will probably take the form of a resumption of prewar trends toward longer education rather than large-scale withdrawals from the labor force itself.[20]

The accompanying change in social climate was immediate and pronounced. The generation which had been adolescent during the depression was now in the armed forces. The generation which was adolescent during World War II lived in a world which not only differed economically, politically, and militarily from that of their immediate predecessors, but psychologically as well. Even those boys and girls who ordinarily would have difficulty in finding and keeping a job because of mental deficiency, difficult personality, or other psychological and temperamental drawbacks were able to command good wartime wages at responsible positions. The sellers' market in labor power of all sorts and descriptions gave the adolescent generation a sense of its own value and importance to the national interest. Conflicts arose between parents and children, as the former saw their authority undermined by the financial independence of their teen-age offspring. The extent of these conflicts may have been overemphasized because of the spectacular form some of them took. Indeed, Ernest R. Groves commented upon the comparatively small number of adolescents who emancipated themselves completely from their families. The good sense and cohesiveness of the average American family were both evident in this crisis. The modification in social climate was great, but the ties of family solidarity were even greater.[21]

3. *Employment of parents.* A third change in the social situation of wartime adolescents was the increase in the number of working mothers with children. The number of married women aged 18–64 in the labor force increased from 4,671,000 in 1940 to 6,700,000 in 1944. Of this group, 833,000 in 1940 had children under ten, and by 1944 the number with children under ten had grown to 1,470,000. The number of employed married women *without* children under ten increased from 2,838,000 to 5,230,000, of whom an indeterminate number *did* have children in the adolescent age group. While we have no exact figure on working mothers with adolescent children, the number was considerable and represented an important change in social circumstance for a substantial segment of the population.[22]

Emphasis was placed during the war upon the effect of this employment on the emotional security of the infant and child.[23] Without gainsaying the importance of the mother's presence in the home during these early crucial years, it is also true that the adolescent is greatly in need of a settled family environment, in which he is sure of receiving the sympathetic attention of his mother during the many emotional crises which mark the adolescent years. Children who came home from junior high school during the war and found their mother at work were deprived of intangible but important emotional benefits. In one sense, the presence of the maternal parent is even more important to the adolescent than to his younger brothers and sisters. The capacity for independent locomotion of the adolescent is greater than that of a younger child and his range of possible social contacts is correspondingly wider. Opportunities for getting into trouble are thus compounded during the adolescent years, particularly when intensified by the cultural changes characteristic of our society. With more money in their pockets than ever before and with the opportunity to channel normal sexual desires into co-operation with the armed forces, wartime adolescents needed their mothers even more than before. The successful functioning of the family requires the presence of all its members in the home. In our society, the mother is the parent who maintains this stability by her constant physical presence; here she is on call twenty-four hours of the day to infants, children, and adolescents. When the mother was at work in a war plant, such supervision was impossible.

4. *Migration of families.* Another change in the social circumstances of the wartime adolescent was the increase in family mobility. During the depression and the early defense period, the majority of migrants

were single men, who either had no families or temporarily left them to shift for themselves. As the demand for workers and soldiers increased, more families were stimulated into mobility, often with adolescent children. While there are no precise figures for the numbers of adolescents involved in these wartime movements, it has been estimated that 17 per cent of the population migrating into the Congested Production Areas of the country were under 15 years of age.[24] A large number of families with adolescent or near-adolescent children came into areas congested by war production, where they were obliged to make whatever adjustment they could to the new environment.

Many permanent residents of the congested areas viewed the wartime migrants with suspicion, partly because of the hostility to strangers and partly because the new migrants were considered threats to the jobs of the residents once the war boom was over. Many of these migrant families lived both physically and socially on the fringe of the new community and the adolescents were isolated from their fellows. Adolescence is the period of individual development when the greatest importance is attached to making contacts outside the family group; this marginal position made it difficult for the sons and daughters of the migrant families. Adolescents whose only home was a trailer, a tent, or a crowded flat in an urban slum lacked the security of a settled home that is so important to the favorable growth of personality. The strangeness of the social environment of hundreds of thousands of families of defense workers contributed to the difficulty of adjustment. In these and many other ways, the migrant adolescent underwent a change in social circumstance which partially isolated him from his contemporaries during an important epoch in his life.[25]

A related change of social circumstance for a number of wartime adolescents was the complete break in their family relationships brought about by running away. During the depression, thousands of boys and a smaller number of girls were on the road in search of employment. During the war years, the employment was there for the asking, and large numbers of young persons of both sexes left home to take jobs in war industries. A variety of social problems grew out of this migration, including the housing of the young people in the industrial centers, the recreational facilities offered to them, the community attitude toward them, the counseling services available to them, and the postwar arrangements for those who became stranded far from home. During the height of the war boom, the only major adjustment problem *not* facing this group was that of employment at fairly high wages. The other difficulties growing out of social mobility were conspicuously present.[26]

5. *Imminence of personal change.* Perhaps the most important change in social circumstances of wartime adolescents was one which had not yet happened but which was nevertheless imminent and hence conditioned their thoughts and actions. This impending event was the immediate prospect of induction on or shortly after their eighteenth birthday for the boys and the more remote but equally important changes in their own lives which the girls anticipated. The extent of this military participation may be seen from the presence in the armed forces in April, 1944, of some 1,680,000 young persons in the 14–19-year age group, the overwhelming majority of whom were 18 and 19 years old.[27] These boys experienced the transition from adolescence to manhood in a few months. Younger brothers and friends could identify themselves with those already in the armed forces, which made the service seem more personal and less a process imposed by a bureaucratic government. This military identification of the adolescent not yet 18 helped to make his imminent service a desirable experience, one which he would choose for himself and would not under any circumstance be deprived of.[28]

Filled with the anticipation of service, many boys found it difficult to concentrate on their studies, their chores, or their jobs. Preparation for college seemed to many an irrelevant way of spending their time, in the face of the real possibility that they would never live to go to college. The imminence of induction also served as a convenient rationalization for many boys with no particular desire to apply themselves to their school work. Likewise, many boys felt that their employment, whatever its nature, was a temporary stop-gap until they entered the service and that it would not engage their attention when the war was over. Establishment of a good employment record was therefore not considered so important as under peacetime conditions, when the young person might hope to find permanent employment where he was then engaged. These transitory phases of the wartime social climate should not, of course, be overemphasized; the majority of boys and girls applied themselves with reasonable competence to whatever task was assigned them, even though they were faced with an uncertain future.

The problem of the adolescent girl differed from that of her brothers and boy friends. With no conscription of young women and a comparatively small number of girls serving in the armed forces, the average girl could expect no such uniformity of experience as the average boy. Her adjustment to the uncertain future had to be made on an individual basis. She might get a job, stay home and help with the housework, or marry in the immediate future. In any of these three possibilities, however, she would be acting as an individual and not as a member of a large group undergoing the same basic experience.

The desire to participate in the great experience of her generation caused many young girls to assume, as we have seen, a precocious maturity, one of whose manifestations was the establishment of a sexual liaison with some member or members of the armed forces. The prevalence of such behavior should not be exaggerated, as the figures for this form of juvenile delinquency were so small as to represent but a tiny minority. Many more girls, it is true, indulged in this behavior than were ever apprehended and brought before the juvenile courts. Even with this increased violation of the traditional sexual code, however, the majority of adolescent girls conducted themselves in conformity with the mores. The possibility of such emancipation, however, was ever-present in the fantasy life of many girls whose adherence to the conventions was maintained by strict family control. Behavior of this kind was part of the social climate of the times, whether or not the majority of girls were directly affected thereby.[29]

Adolescent and Family Relations

The acceleration of social change weakened the ties between many families and their adolescent children. With mothers at work, fathers in the armed forces or away from home, and the economic opportunities open to youth to participate actively in the war effort, family bonds in many cases were interrupted and attenuated. Both generations were placed in novel situations during the war, situations which the parents had not experienced when *they* were adolescents. This change still further widened the gap between generations. Even under peacetime circumstances this hiatus is very wide, as the rate of social change continually increases. In time of total war, the divergent experiences of each of the generations became even more difficult for the other to comprehend. Fathers and mothers long accustomed to the decrease in adolescent employment and the accompanying increase in the length of dependency were faced with the widespread employment of their teen-age sons and daughters and the corresponding increase in their independence. One result of this change was an increase in parent-child conflict. "Sociologically speaking," remarks one observer, "war is a complex of social changes involving the entire societal pattern; one phase of this is to break the cultural continuities between generations, with an inevitable increase of conflicts between them."[30]

One of the concomitants of this increased adolescent independence was the comparison made by many adolescents of their own earning power and that of their parents during the depression. Many adolescents remembered vividly that their fathers were unable to find work ten years before. Others remembered that their parents worked at lower wages than they (the children) were earning during World War II. The economic reasons for this abnormal situation were not apparent to the majority of young people who imputed, consciously or unconsciously, an inferiority to the father and by comparison a certain superiority to themselves. The traditional pattern of American family life still implies a residue of subordination by the young people to the father. This relationship was often difficult to maintain during the war, when the adolescent members flaunted their new independence, with open or tacit reference to the erstwhile parental incompetence to provide for the family.[31]

Another corollary of this new status of wartime youth was the dilemma of many parents in dealing with their children. Some parents were encouraged to give greater independence to the 16-year-old daughter who might soon be married or the 16-year-old son holding down a responsible job in a war plant and who in two years might be in the western Pacific. Many youngsters in their middle teens were not emotionally or intellectually prepared for such increased responsibility. Beneath their sophisticated exteriors, they were still little boys and girls, bewildered by a rush of events they could not fully understand and secretly appalled at the responsibility suddenly thrust upon them. Many parents, sensing this bewilderment, attempted to protect their children and in so doing unduly retarded them. The choice between leaving the adolescent to his own devices and maintaining an oversolicitous restriction brought about many parent-child conflicts. Some girls ran wild with soldiers and sailors, while their parents looked on indulgently or were preoccupied with their own wartime problems. Others left home because their parents would not let them have harmless dates with their friends in the armed forces. The wartime parental role was a difficult one, with a delicate and not always perceptible line dividing excessive liberty from unwise over-protection.[32]

"There are," suggested Margaret Mead, "two aspects in which the usual processes of identification and forward projection of the self into the future are being interrupted for adolescents . . . the influence of parents, conceived of as different from the self; and the influence of age-mates and those just older, conceived of as the same as the self."[33] Both of these models, Miss Mead continued, were broken by the war, with results upon the personality of the adolescent not immediately apparent. The wartime changes in the family interfered with the proper identification of young people with their parents. This interruption took place in two aspects of family life—the employment of the mother and the absence of the father in war work or military service. The adolescent girl lost the intimate identification with her mother when the latter was home only a few waking hours during the day. The adolescent boy was deprived of close identification with his father when this parent was absent for periods ranging up to several years. Lacking either or both of these parental identifications, the adolescent child lost emotional stability and self-confidence, which was often not completely restored by his own participation in war work or war service.[34]

The images of the mother and father play a basic role in the development of adolescent personality. These images tended to become distorted during World War II. The forces bringing about this distortion were certain large and impersonal changes in the social structure. Commenting upon this interference with adolescent-parental identification, a psychiatrist remarked: "During a war period . . . this process of identification is likely to be impeded by the fact that parents spend less time with their children, because of the migration of fathers to war-industry communities, or the preoccupation of both fathers and mothers with the new economic opportunities that are becoming available or with voluntary activities of a war-connected nature."[35] Difficulties and delays in transportation combined with the exacting character of wartime living to decrease the amount and adequacy of parental supervision. The interest of many parents in their own recreation, intensified because of the previous years of depression when such facilities were not financially available, also contributed to parental neglect. The result of these various deprivations was often a lack in the emotional life of the adolescent, at a time when the world was complicated enough without any added complications in his own home.[36]

War and Adolescent Participation

The most prominent effect of the war upon the adolescent population was the increase in its employment. World War II reversed the trends of recent decades, during which the employment of boys and girls had shown a steady decrease. In the period from 1920 to 1940, the number of boys and girls 14–18 years of age in the labor force decreased from approximately 2,500,000 to 1,000,000. In the four years from 1940 to 1944, the number increased from 1,000,000 to approximately 2,900,000, an expansion of 190 per cent. The number of employed boys in the 14–18 age group rose from 733,000 in 1940 to 1,950,000 in 1944, an increase of 169 per cent. While not so great numerically, the percentage increase in the participation of girls was even more impressive. In 1940, some 271,000 girls were listed as gainfully employed; by April, 1944, this number had swelled to 950,000, an increase of 243 per cent.

The social factors which combined to bring about this overall increase in the participation of American youth were summarized as follows: ". . . urgent demands for workers of all ages, especially in war production centers, the opening up of new job opportunities for children and young persons, high wartime wages, patriotic pressures, and social restlessness . . . pushed the numbers of employed boys and girls of this age group up to unprecedented levels."[37] In 1944, there were approximately 9,200,000 young people in the age group 14–18 years of age, of whom roughly 30 per cent were employed. This figure compares with approximately 10 per cent of the same age group employed in 1940, according to the decennial census taken in that year.[38] This increased level of participation was a new experience for large segments of the adolescent population, particularly in urban areas where the nature of the economic environment made such aid difficult. Total war had thus set in motion other modifications in the social structure whose eventual results were incalculable.

The bulk of the employed youth was concentrated in four general industry groups. The 2,900,000 adolescents in the labor force on April 1, 1944 (including approximately 100,000 in the labor force but not at work when the sample census was taken) were distributed as follows:

Agriculture	800,000
Wholesale and retail trade	800,000
Manufacturing	650,000
Domestic and personal service	250,000
Total, four main groups	2,500,000

Another 300,000 youths were engaged in "other" activities, a miscellaneous group composed of such diverse functions as forestry and fishing, mining, construction, transportation, commerce, public utilities, finance, insurance, real estate, amusement and recreation, and government. Since the census was taken in April, 1944, the large number of young people engaged in farm labor is not fully shown; in July, 1944, the Bureau of the Census estimated the number of youths aged 14–18 in agriculture at 1,555,000, nearly twice the number in April.[39]

A significant aspect of the increased wartime participation of young persons was the proportion of the different age groups involved. The largest increase between 1940 and 1944 took place among the 14–15-year-olds, with a more than threefold increase over the four-year period. The numerical increase during these years was from 225,000 to 850,000. The number of young girls 14–15 years of age showed the most spectacular single increase, from 45,000 in 1940 to 200,000 in 1944; boys in this age group increased from 179,000 to 650,000, an increase of approximately 275 per cent. In the 16- and 17-year-old group, the number of boys rose from 553,000 in 1940 to 1,300,000 in 1944, while the number of girls increased from 225,000 to 750,000.[40]

The demand for labor brought about by the vast governmental expenditures for all-out war production brought millions of new workers into the market. A number of these workers would not ordinarily have been gainfully employed outside the home and hence constituted an excess over what would "normally" have been expected. This excess over the normal labor supply was estimated in April, 1944, at 6,700,000 persons, of whom 3,700,000 were male and 3,000,000 female.[41] The adolescent contribution to this reservoir of manpower was large; over one-fourth of the total, or 1,730,000, was made up of boys and girls from 14-18 years of age. Teen-agers in the 18- and

19-year-old groups contributed an additional 1,030,000 of the 6,700,000; of this late teen-age group, 600,000 were boys and 430,000 girls. Inasmuch as there were over 1,500,000 boys in the age group 14–19 (of whom the majority were 18 and 19 years of age) in the armed forces, the relative impact of the war upon the 18- and 19-year-olds was especially apparent. The large number of boys in this group in the armed forces further explained why the male contribution to the 18- and 19-year-old civilian labor force (600,000) was not much larger than the female (430,000). In and out of the armed forces, the war laid a heavy hand upon the young men at the end of their teens.[42]

War and work were the two principal forms of participation of the adolescent boys. Work and wedlock were the principal forms of participation of girls of the same age. Many nubile maids who ordinarily would not have married for several years did so under the emotional and patriotic compulsions of a wartime society. Other young girls made their supreme sacrifice to the morale of the armed forces in less formal ways. Much of the adolescent delinquency in the field of sex behavior was an outgrowth of some such conception of patriotic duty among large numbers of young girls in all parts of the country, notably those living in close propinquity to army camps, war industry centers, and ports of embarkation. Many of these young girls believed, in their confused way, that by catering to the sex impulses of transient members of the armed forces, particularly those about to go overseas or who had just returned from there, they were thereby making a unique contribution to the war effort. This was their special form of participation.

World War II interrupted a secular trend toward a decrease in youthful employment. Child labor (more strictly, adolescent labor) was on the decline until the war established a temporarily unlimited demand for young persons in the armed forces and industry. During the peacetime decade of the thirties, the general level of employment was so low that the number of 14–15-year-olds gainfully employed shrank from 431,790 in 1930 to 209,347 in 1940; in the same period, the number of 16–17-year-olds declined from 1,478,841 to 662,967.[43] In many cases, adults could be hired at equal wages to do the work children had previously done; public opinion and the surplus of available workers thus reduced the participation of the adolescent in the years immediately prior to the defense period. Humanitarian efforts made considerable headway during the years when it was economically unnecessary to employ children in many occupations.

As the nation mobilized for total war, social welfare definitions were largely superseded by those favoring maximum production no matter what the human cost. Social welfare was thus a partial war casualty, sacrificed to the desire to end the war with maximum speed. One of the principal means to this end was the utilization of every available source of labor—young married women with children, old and retired male workers, female workers who had never worked before, and adolescent children. The results of this adolescent participation were summarized by the Children's Bureau in the following terms: "Children are working long hours, at night, at tasks beyond their strength, and often under conditions morally unsafe."[44]

All along the line, efforts to increase the labor supply by lowering standards for adolescent and child labor were intensified. These efforts took various forms. Compulsory school attendance requirements were modified in some states, permitting children to attend school for shorter periods and work for longer periods during the year. Special permits were issued in other states, granting emergency privileges for underage children to work at certain activities previously forbidden under the Fair Labor Standards Act. In other states, legal prohibitions were relaxed against employment of minors under 16 at night work, while in others minors were permitted to evade the requirements for physical examination. Still other states reduced the age from 18 to 16 for employment in certain hazardous occupations and made it possible for boys in their middle teens to drive fuel trucks, work in rolling mills, act as helpers in blast furnaces, operate high-speed wire-stitching machinery, run certain types of lifts and hoisting machinery, work at railroad track repairing, participate as full-time members of threshing crews, and work at a variety of other activities whose physical effects were undesirable.

"Even though," comments the Children's Bureau in this connection, "some of the modifications may have been justified in the light of prevailing labor needs and of existing high standards, much of the action seems to have been taken without weighing the cost to children and to the Nation against the gain to the labor market. Also, in some cases the relaxation has not been limited to the war period, nor has machinery been provided to safeguard the modification."[45] The Bureau concludes gravely that "These trends give warning of danger of permanent loss to the Nation through denial of adequate child-labor protection and educational opportunity for its youth."[46]

The majority of employment problems incidental to the participation of adolescents in the labor force were temporary. The young people who formed the adolescent labor force during the war soon reached the age when they would have sought employment in any event. Their age group will not be replaced in the labor force in anything like the numbers present during the war. Most of the young people in the postwar adolescent generation will remain in school longer than their older brothers and sisters, whose adolescence was spent in the frenetic atmosphere of World War II. Their numbers will partially depend upon the trends in the business cycle, with more employment opportunities for young people in times of prosperity and fewer in depression.

We have seen that, during the two decades prior to World War II, the trend was toward longer periods of schooling and less adolescent participation in the labor market. This trend was interrupted by the large-scale adolescent participation in gainful employment during the war. The changes in this field thus represented something new; they were not mere continuations and accentuations of problems apparent in a peacetime society. A drastic, although temporary, reversal of a secular trend was evident in child and adolescent labor during the war. Our hypothesis of war as an accelerating but not a modifying force in social problems is again called into question.

CHAPTER FIVE

WAR AND SEX OFFENSES

The Nature of Sex Offenses

One of the most powerful prohibitions in the cultural tradition of Europe and America has accompanied the attempt to confine primary sex expression to persons joined in lawful monogamous wedlock. So firmly has this attitude been incorporated in Christian civilization that sexual transgressions have been among the most bitterly punished of all lapses from the mores. Indeed, so close has the relationship between sex and morality been that the word "immoral" is customarily applied exclusively to departures from traditional sex customs, even though many other actions constitute equally abrupt digressions from the behavior subsumed under the mores. The mores of our society have tended to condemn any and all sexual manifestations outside marriage with a unique virulence. While the scarlet "A" of the adulteress is no longer literally branded upon the bosom of the female transgressor, the belief in the importance of the traditional sex mores is still a basic tenet of our social structure. Persons—particularly young and underprivileged girls—who take this moral law into their own hands do so at their own peril.

Satisfaction of the sex impulse outside marriage is thus defined as a social problem of the most serious kind. Persons who engage in such behavior—whether spontaneously and freely or deliberately and commercially—are defined as individual problems that combine to make up the social problem. It will be remembered that a social problem is said to arise when "there is an *awareness* among a given people that a particular *social situation* is a threat to certain *group values* which they cherish and that this situation can be removed or corrected only by *collective*. action."[1] The social situation in this case is the undeniable increase in premarital and extramarital sex expression in recent decades. Some of the most cherished of our social values are endangered or believed to be endangered by this situation. Collective action is clearly

97

necessary to change this behavior and render it more in accord with traditional values. The alternative is to modify the values, a course which would be highly distasteful to a large number of persons, including many of those who clandestinely violate the mores while maintaining lip-service to them.

Transgressions of the moral code are defined as undesirable not only by the majority who rigorously observe these codes. Most men and women in our culture who violate the sex mores do so with an accompanying sense of guilt, either conscious or unconscious. The vagaries of the double standard of morality cast much of the stigma upon the female member of this clearly collaborative relationship, whether she be an impetuous adolescent or a hardened prostitute. Persons who commit sex offenses also define themselves as sex offenders, with a corresponding decline in their own self-esteem. Few men or women can flaunt the conventional moral standards and substitute their own standards of behavior. In the eyes of both the group and themselves, the majority of sex offenders are just that. They are offending against one of the most powerful social standards and their collective responsibility constitutes a grave social problem.

This problem has two aspects, which merge imperceptibly as one type of behavior becomes indistinguishable from the other. These two aspects of sex offenses are known as "promiscuity not for hire" and "promiscuity for hire," the latter better known as prostitution. The first form of behavior is relatively new in our moral experience, at least to the extent to which it is now practiced. The increasing knowledge of contraception and new medical discoveries in venereal disease treatment are among the proximate causes. The underlying social causes of this trend toward sexual freedom emerge directly from our changing culture. The American Social Hygiene Association, the most authoritative source of information in this controversial field, characterizes this changing behavior as follows: "It seems apparent that the causes of this kind of behavior are deeply imbedded in our whole social structure, that they stem from the whole environment of the individual, and are extremely complex."[2] Sexual freedom, one phase of changing sex behavior, is a manifestation of a rapidly changing society. Sexual promiscuity for hire, the other phase of sex behavior, is allegedly the world's oldest profession.

The Committee on Sex Delinquency Among Young Girls, appointed by the American Social Hygiene Association, has defined sexual

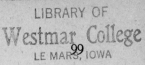
LIBRARY OF
Westmar College
LE MARS, IOWA

promiscuity in the following terms: "Promiscuity as differentiated from prostitution (although it may at times border upon it) is sex delinquency of a non-commercial character. A girl may receive a meal, a gift, or even money, but this does not constitute her conscious or primary reason for resorting to sexual promiscuity. A more basic motive in her sex hunger is adventure and sociability, but she does not confine her attention to one or two male friends."[3] Such behavior reflects the breakdown of the class structure of a stratified society, in which men traditionally consorted with women of a lower social class for purposes of sexual pleasure. The contemporary promiscuous girl as often as not enjoys an equal social status with her consort; there is no assumption of social inferiority in this relationship. She is a companion who exchanges her person for entertainment, sustenance, or for no tangible reward at all. The promiscuous girl is, in a sense, exercising a prerogative traditionally confined to the male—that of seeking sexual companionship without waiting for the advances of the other sex. The fundamental motive is social rather than pecuniary, a characteristic in which the promiscuous girl differs from the prostitute. A considerable degree of choice also characterizes her sexual relationships, in contrast to her commercial sister who must, in theory at least, accept each and every comer.

Sexual promiscuity is an increasingly important factor in the total problem of extramarital sex relationships. The source of these relationships (and the consequent venereal infection) was formerly the prostitute, but in recent years the emphasis has shifted to the promiscuous girl or woman. In a study of 1,402 girls and women brought before the Separate Women's Court in San Francisco, 751 (53.5 per cent) were defined as promiscuous and only 311 (22.2 per cent) as prostitutes. The line of demarcation is often difficult, if not impossible, to draw. Many women accordingly represent themselves as promiscuous (i.e., as sexually delinquent in a noncommercial way) rather than as prostitutes because of the greater moral stigma attaching to the latter behavior. A generation or more ago, such relationships would have been on a more commercial level and women engaged in promiscuous behavior for noncommercial reasons would have been rare. The changing times, especially in the congested wartime communities, have complicated both the problem of maintaining the traditional sex mores and of keeping the community free from veneral disease.[4]

The sex offender is often a young girl from an underprivileged

14966

home who is seeking friendship, attention, and entertainment in the only form she knows. "By and large," suggests Eliot Ness, "the promiscuous girl is not criminally motivated, nor is she beyond reclamation as is the hardened prostitute. She is more likely to be a casual, fun-seeking girl, wanting male companionship; a young experimenter, somewhat lonely, easing her conscience by quixotic references to 'patriotism'; immature in her judgment and, perhaps more important, dissociated from the stabilizing forces of family, the church, or any significant group which strengthens the individual's integrity and belief in herself."[5]

The adolescent girl furthermore is often too young to have her instinctual sex impulses fully awakened. This physiological fact does not, however, prevent her from becoming an adequate sexual companion. Sex hunger as such is probably no more instrumental in this form of behavior than in inducing young girls to enter prostitution. Young girls away from home, bewildered and frightened by their failure to find work, and lonely without their husbands or their erstwhile boy friends may easily fall into quasi-promiscuity as they drift about in the half-world of a large city. Other young girls living at home, with mothers in war plants and fathers indifferent or unable to help them, may seek sexual adventure in the dingy amusement sections of the community. Other girls, working in the service trades at substandard wages, may come in contact with the transient public, with resulting behavior defined as immoral. Still others, living in hall bedrooms with another and more venturesome girl, may make it a practice to spend their evenings hanging around places of refreshment and entertainment, waiting for something to happen. The first adventure may lead to others and the young girl may find herself hardened in spirit, debauched in mind, and diseased in body. What price, she may ask bitterly, adventure?

The sexually delinquent girl is often one whose mental capacities are below normal and whose judgment is correspondingly incapable of regulating her impulses. A study of 500 venereally infected females admitted to the Midwestern Medical Center in St. Louis during wartime (February–August, 1944) revealed the subnormal mentality of this sizeable sample of sex delinquents. The mental ability of both the white and the Negro women was found to be considerably below normal. For the 340 white cases, the median intelligence quotient was 84, while for the 160 Negro girls it was approximately 70. A large

proportion of both racial groups showed a level of intelligence sufficiently low to warrant mental care at the institutional level. Girls
whose mental processes operate on this subnormal plane often do not
understand the dangers of venereal disease, either to themselves or
society as a whole, nor do they understand the desirability of consistent medical treatment. Many chronic sex offenders come from this
mentally retarded group, where they present a constant danger to social
welfare.[6]

"Sex offender" is a general term and the types of girls who engage
in this practice are very different. The offenses themselves superficially
assume a depressing similarity, but the motives which precipitate them
are by no means as simple. The Referee of the Girls' Division of a
Court of Domestic Relations makes the following classification of
motives and personalities of sexually delinquent girls: (1) The uninhibited girl with normal sex desire who is expressing the normal desire
to love and be loved, only in a fashion of which society disapproves;
(2) The girl with no sex instruction who fails to find the answers to
her questions from parents, church, or school and seeks to satisfy
her curiosity with a succession of male companions; (3) The girl
discouraged with life who fails to see any reason for not indulging in
illicit sex behavior in a world which has consistently treated her shab-
bily; (4) The girl with conflicting desires who alternates between religious expression and intellectual interest on the one hand and
drunkenness and indiscriminate sex activity on the other; (5) The girl
who turns from sex deliquency to prostitution and becomes correspondingly more difficult to rehabilitate; (6) The girl who is starved for the
affection which she fails to get at home and eagerly falls into the
arms of the first man who appears to offer a reasonable facsimile
thereof; (7) The girl with some form of glandular disorder that
provides a physiological stimulus for sexual delinquency. These categories might be supplemented by others; each covers a variety of girls
whose only similarity lies in the definition which society places upon
their behavior.[7]

The weakening of many of the taboos against unconventional sex
behavior has been a product of the social changes taking place in recent
decades. The new freedom, which too often becomes license, was not
uniquely a product of World War II. The evidence, statistical and
otherwise, indicates that unconventional sex relationships were rapidly
increasing during the decades between wars.[8] Men seeking sex adven-

ture are no longer forced to resort to the prostitute or the quasi-prostitute, whom society has always stigmatized by placing on the lowest social level. The male in search of sexual excitement can now find it with girls of his own class and often his immediate group. This trend toward changing sex behavior was clearly apparent prior to World War II. The intensified rate of social change attending that struggle had a profound influence upon the problem of the sexual offender.

War and Sex Offenses

The social disorganization of World War II probably accelerated the rate of departure from conventional sex behavior. The indices clearly point to such a trend, although the difficulty of completely adequate measurement is obvious. The loosening of the bonds of an ordered society which insists upon sex relationships only within marriage would bring about a corresponding increase in the behavior previously prohibited. The agencies which have historically played the most important part in inculcating the patterns of sex behavior were precisely those most seriously weakened by the wartime social changes. The family is the chief social relationship wherein are transmitted, by precept and example, the patterns of behavior sanctioned by society. When the forms of millions of these individual relationships were weakened and disrupted by the war, their influence upon the younger members was correspondingly lessened.

The influence of the family in maintaining the traditional sexual codes is supplemented by the informal pressure of neighborhood opinion. The force of this opinion varies in general from the small rural community to the large metropolitan center. The neighborhood exerts its most profound influence upon those persons who have lived in the same location over a long period and have been consistently exposed to this informal public opinion. Social mobility tends to vitiate this opinion by removing the person from its influence and depositing him in a community where he is unknown.

Social mobility was a characteristic of our society long before World War II.[9] The movement of population during wartime, as we have seen, was even greater. Counting both civilian and military migration, more than 27,500,000 persons experienced at least one wartime change of residence that removed them from one set of social influences and often failed to substitute similar influences.[10] Deprived of these informal social controls, which are especially strong in the field of sex behavior, many persons entered into unconventional sex relationships. The combined number of these unsanctioned actions constituted a social problem.

"In war time," declared the late Willard Waller, "there is a decay of all the established moralities, which tend to be replaced by hedonistic life adjustments on a short-term basis. In a word, the mores decline, and vices spread and become respectable."[11] This situation was evident during World War II in the increase in unorthodox sex behavior. Other changes in the mores took place with even greater vehemence during this struggle (the prohibition against killing, for example) but such moral adjustments were sanctioned by the nature of the war emergency and hence were censured only by a small minority.

Hedonistic life adjustments in sex relationships, however, were viewed with alarm by many civilians and were only grudgingly condoned by the military authorities as a concession to the frailty of its enlisted personnel. A considerable proportion of the youthful population engaged in sex conduct during the war ordinarily defined as contrary to the mores. There is usually a noticeable lag between changes in behavior and changes in social definition. The greater sexual laxity of the generation in their teens and twenties during the war may eventually lead to modifications in the definitions of sexual conduct. Any such modification in the conception of sexual delinquency as a social problem was not apparent during World War II, however. The wartime increase in extramarital sex relationships continued in violation of the mores.

Another element in the social climate of a world at war which contributed to the increase in sex offenses was the widespread uncertainty and corresponding decline in moral responsibility. For the millions of adolescents about to be inducted and the millions only slightly older already in uniform, the immediate future was uncertain at best. The future of millions of young women was equally problematical, particularly those interested in a man in service. Young married women with soldier husbands were even more uncertain, and their behavior was often keyed to a correspondingly hedonistic level. For untold numbers of persons, young and old alike, plans for future conduct were impossible to make or carry out with any certainty. Adherence to the mores is in part a matter of adjusting to future expectations;

if the proximate future is uncertain, the present is equally so. From such indecision comes a decline in the force of the mores.[12]

War is the most exciting time the average person experiences. For millions of young people, World War II was the supremely exciting period of their lives and their subsequent experience was one long anticlimax. Even for the civilian, the progress of the war was a constant mental and emotional stimulus. As the citizens of the United States roused themselves from the shocked aftermath of Pearl Harbor and plunged vicariously into the Battle for the Solomons, the invasion of North Africa, the campaigns in Italy, the supreme moment of the invasion of Western Europe, the subsequent campaigns in France and Germany, the tempered enthusiasm of V-E Day, and the final culmination in the surrender of Japan—as the country experienced this succession of crises, its emotional tempo rose accordingly. The social climate of wartime living was suffused with excitement and emotion, a circumstance which brings about departures from conventional behavior. World War II saw this sense of emotional participation extended to a greater extent than ever before in history. The advances in communication and transportation mobilized the nation as a single psychological unit and brought the war vividly home to every individual.

The desire of the adolescent girl for individual participation in the common adventure probably contributed to the rise of sexual delinquency as much as any other factor. Teen-age boys could identify themselves with the national effort in the most direct manner. If they were still underage they could identify themselves with their friends and brothers already in service and could realize that soon they would be participating in the common cause. Adolescent girls had no such possibility of identification. To many of them, their only resource was their sex, a resource which, in some curious fashion, appeared to aid the war effort and at the same time provided excitement, recreation, and prestige. With the vigorous repression of prostitution, sexual participation offered an unequaled opportunity for large numbers of adolescent girls to gain these social ends.[13]

This desire for participation was both a result of the precocious adolescence of the war and a cause for further precocity. As young men neared the age of 18, they were faced with an abrupt transition from adolescence to manhood, whereby they encountered situations of an elemental nature. Except in connection with military matters, these young men were relatively independent. In terms of the prerogatives of sexual behavior, they were adults. Thousands of young girls from 14-18 years of age entertained similar illusions concerning their own adult status.[14] The only way many of them could prove to themselves and their friends that they had reached adulthood was to engage in sex relationships with men in the armed forces. These adolescents were emotionally immature and unable to experience or communicate the nuances of sentiment possible for older and more mature girls. The average relationship with a soldier or sailor was not, however, one that called for many of the sentimental niceties, but was an abrupt and rather ugly affair with very little psychological subtlety. As Groves points out in connection with these adolescent courtesans, "Although in most ways immature and distant from adult experience, they are not necessarily, so far as structure is concerned, handicapped as sex partners."[15] Especially, he might have added, in terms of the equally immature standards of their male companions.

Changes in social situation as well as social climate had a significant effect upon the participation of young persons in wartime sex offenses. These changes were canvassed in the previous chapter, insofar as they modified the wartime way of life of large numbers of people. The widespread mobility of individuals and families, the unsettlement of the family group, the employment of hundreds of thousands of adolescents, the lack of recreational facilities bringing young people together under adequate chaperonage, boredom with school in wartime—these and other factors combined to change the way of life of an adolescent generation so that an increase in sexual offenses resulted. These psychological factors have been summarized as follows: "Certainly, the physical and emotional turbulence of normal adolescents is heightened by the atmosphere of wartime living, which is characterized by restlessness and excitement, breakdown in social and normal standards, pressures upon adolescents to assume adult roles and their own desire to be adult, the glamour of the men in uniform, and the girls' romantic notions about 'service' to servicemen."[16] To these psychological changes certain material manifestations were added, such as "school programs that are dull and uninspiring, failing to satisfy the need for adventure; widespread employment of youth, often under conditions that put a strain upon physical and social well-being; the preponderance of commercial recreation, some of which is definitely harmful; and the lack of basic services to reinforce the home and assist young people in finding an outlet for energies generated by the heightened tempo of wartime society."[17]

The Measurement of Wartime Sex Offenses

It is one thing to say that sex offenses became an increasingly important social problem during World War II. It is another to document this categorical statement with facts and figures.[18] The Director of Social Protection, Office of Community War Services, Federal Security Agency was presumably as familiar as anyone in the country with wartime trends in this field. In a paper read before the National Conference of Social Work in 1944, however, he stated that "no accurate figures are available to indicate the total volume of sex delinquency on a nation-wide basis, or the rate of increase caused by wartime conditions."[19] He pointed out that police figures from a number of communities indicated that from 50 to 75 per cent of all women detained for sex offenses were under 21 years of age. In one state, he continued, 41.5 per cent of all cases of venereal infection in hospitals were those of young girls under 19 years of age. Venereal infection among girls of adolescent age, furthermore, increased at a more rapid rate than among the population as a whole.

While this admittedly does not illuminate the extent of wartime sex delinquency as a whole, it does indicate that the problem was increasingly that of the young and promiscuous girl rather than the older and more experienced prostitute. Additional evidence for this general point of view comes from such varied sources as the commonsense observations of the man (and woman) on the street, who saw hundreds of young girls swarming about the entertainment centers of every large city, many still in their early teens; the trained observations of social workers in all parts of the country; studies made of individual communities, cities, or metropolitan areas; statements by the Army and Navy of the venereal infection of its personnel coming from sexually promiscuous adolescents, as contrasted with prostitutes; and finally the increasing numbers of girls brought before the juvenile courts on charges of sex delinquency during the years of defense, mobilization, and total war. Roughly in the order named, these sources become more accurately indicative of conditions as a whole.[20]

But even these data were indicative rather than conclusive. The rate of girls' cases disposed of by the juvenile courts, for example, indicates the trends in the numbers of juvenile delinquents brought to the formal attention of the authorities. The majority of these girls come from underprivileged homes, or they would not be in the courts. The cases of girls from middle and upper-class families are ordinarily handled "unofficially," either by the courts or by private agencies, presupposing that the case receives any official attention at all. Such girls rarely swell the figures for juvenile court commitments. Moreover, the country is not completely covered by the juvenile courts, and many communities are without such institutional arrangements. In spite of the rapid increase in the number of such institutions in recent years, only 399 courts reported in 1943, serving areas including 37 per cent of the total population of the United States.[21]

A final consideration in determining the extent of wartime sexual delinquency is that the nature of the behavior itself precludes measurement in the ordinary sense. Sexual behavior does not lend itself to statistical generalizations in the same fashion as births, deaths, marriages, or morbidity, not to mention such prosaic phenomena as freight-car loadings, bank clearings, and security transactions. Sex behavior is private behavior, rendered so by the prohibitions against extramarital and premarital relationships. Strong moral and religious taboos resist the compilation of adequate information on this form of behavior, either in peace or war, so that direct efforts to pierce the veil of secrecy are doomed before they start. Such evidence as we have, however, suggests that sex delinquency increased during World War II.

The Extent of Wartime Sex Offenses

Approximately 60 per cent of all girls' cases disposed of by the juvenile courts fall in the categories of "running away," "being ungovernable," and "sex offense." These offenses form a pattern of which sex behavior is ordinarily the core; ungovernable behavior and running away are often euphemisms used in the official records to avoid the morally damning statement of sex offense. The majority of girls who actually are ungovernable and run away do so because of some conflict over sex behavior, which may vary from an innocent date to promiscuous relationships. The sex factor is an important determinant of adolescent behavior and motivates many of the conflicts experienced by girls in these impressionable years.[22]

In the year 1943, a total of 23,965 girls were referred to 399 courts reporting to the Children's Bureau. Of this number, 4,843 (22 per cent) were referred for "running away," 4,923 (22 per cent) for "being ungovernable," and 3,772 (17 per cent) for "sex offense." Comparable statistics for boys throw an interesting sidelight upon the survival value of the double standard. Only 6 per cent of the boys were referred because of "running away," 5 per cent for "being ungovernable," and 3 per cent for "sex offense." Sex behavior is clearly not considered as reprehensible for boys as for girls. This definition is consistent with the condemnation of the prostitute and the condonation of her partner.[23]

In a preliminary compilation of figures released by the Children's Bureau for 1944, some additional information was provided on the general trends in juvenile delinquency among boys and girls during the war period. This subject will be considered at length in a later chapter. We are interested here in the overall figures only insofar as they indicate the general trends in delinquency divided according to sex and intensified by World War II. In 1943, boys' cases in the reporting 69 courts increased by 34 per cent over 1942, whereas girls' cases increased by 27 per cent over the same year. By 1944 the boys' and girls' cases both showed a decline from 1943 of 3 and 4 per cent respectively. Even with this slight decline in 1944, however, the numbers for both sexes showed large increases over 1939. Since the outbreak of the European phase of the war, boys' cases increased by 51 per cent and girls' cases by 82 per cent. The year-to-year changes in the 69 courts were as follows:

Table VI

Percentage Increase from 1938 to 1944 in Cases Disposed of in 69 Juvenile Courts*

Year	Total Cases	Boys' Cases	Girls' Cases
1939	9	10	1
1940	5	4	8
1941	13	11	23
1942	21	16	49
1943	60	55	89
1944	56	51	82

* Preliminary Statement—*Juvenile-Court Statistics, 1944,* Division of Statistical Research, Children's Bureau, Washington, (February 24, 1945).

After the defense program had begun, the percentage increase in girls' cases was consistently higher than boys', although the absolute numbers of boys' cases remained several times higher than girls' cases.

The social maladjustments brought about or intensified by World War II apparently caused more serious repercussions for girls than for boys, at least to the extent that this conduct came to the attention of the juvenile courts. In view of the high percentage of the girls' cases that involve sex behavior, the effect of the war upon the sexual life of adolescent girls was disproportionately great.

The great majority of sex offenses do not occur under circumstances which could even remotely be defined as rape. Under that offense is classified all attempts at forced intercourse, successful or unsuccessful, as well as statutory rape, in which no force is used but the victim is merely under the age of consent.[24] Nevertheless, the annual trends in such offenses are of some interest in exploring another phase of the complex problem of antisocial sex behavior. Statistics gathered by the Federal Bureau of Investigation for offenses known to the police in 318 cities with a 1940 population of 45,062,198 show the following trends for rape: the average for 1939–1941 was 4,286 yearly cases, which figure increased to 4,764 in 1942, to 5,224 in 1943, and 5,443 in 1944. This was a percentage increase of 27.0 over the average prewar year and offers an index to one phase of sex offenses.

Regional trends in rape are revealing, insofar as they reflect population movements from certain regions and into others where military installations and war industry centers were an important source of new population. Decreases over the five-year period were apparent in the New England states and the Middle Atlantic states, whereas in the East North Central, the West North Central, the South Atlantic, the East South Central, the West South Central, the Mountain, and the Pacific states the number of cases was higher in 1944 than in the average prewar years. With minor fluctuations, the trends for rape were consistently upward during the war years, with striking increases in 1944 over 1943 in the West North Central (29.0 per cent) and the South Atlantic states (24.5 per cent).[25]

Seasonal trends for rape suggest the nature of the offense as well as the factors which bring it about. The rate reaches a high point during the summer months, when persons of the opposite sex are more apt to come together under conditions facilitating sexual relationships, either voluntary or forced. The suggestion that hot weather "inflames the passions" or otherwise physically stimulates the predatory male to commit acts of sexual aggression has little validity compared to the social factors involved in the seasonal fluctuations. The summer months are characterized by the increasing mobility of young persons in out-door places of amusement and under other conditions stimulating heterosexual activity. In somewhat similar fashion, the increased mobility of World War II stimulated the movement of individuals from communities where they were restrained by neighborhood opinion to others where they were not. Within the community itself, the heightened mobility during the warm months intensifies the anonymity of a different urban environment. Offenses against the person—such as rape, murder, and aggravated assault—all tend to increase during the summer months when people mingle in close and anonymous physical intimacy.[26] Such intimacy increased during the war years, particularly in certain congested areas.

A further significant, although still indirect, indication of the trend in undesirable sex behavior was the increase in the arrests of young girls under 21 whose records were examined by the Federal Bureau of Investigation. Although the specific offense is not tabulated in this enumeration, the preponderance of sex offenses in the arrests of girls under 21 gives the figure some significance as an index to such behavior. A comparison of 1941 and 1944 data reveals that arrests of girls under 18 increased from 2,662 in 1941 to 5,798 in 1944, an increase of 117.8 per cent; the number in the 18–20 age group increased from 7,013 to 16,838, or 140.0 per cent; the total under 21, derived from adding the two groups, increased from 9,675 in 1941 to 22,636 in 1944, an overall increase of 134.0 per cent.[27] The difficulty of drawing definitive conclusions from these figures should be stressed. Many local police, in a zealous effort to stamp out prostitution, made it a practice during the war to arrest girls whose only offense was that they happened to be in places suspected of being centers of commercialized vice. An indeterminate number of the 22,636 girls enumerated above were thus merely present in a roadhouse, café, or dance hall at the time of a police dragnet raid.[28] These girls were clearly not all prostitutes or sexually promiscuous. The precise nature of their past, present, or future sex behavior is not known.

The determination of wartime sex offenses was also difficult on a national scale because of the different experiences of the various communities, metropolitan areas, and geographic regions. The figures for rape declined in New England and the Middle Atlantic states and increased in regions where the mobile population, either civilian or military, brought together large numbers of strangers. Differences between one metropolitan area and another were even more striking, as some areas showed a substantial increase in population brought about by the war, whereas others showed a decrease, presumably brought about by the same factors. Investigations by the Children's Bureau for the years 1940-41-42 indicate that the percentage increase in juvenile delinquency in areas which increased in population was greater than in those which decreased in population. The Bureau suggests that "As it is probable that variations in the child population were insignificant compared with the increases in juvenile-delinquency cases, this analysis of the reports from 83 courts indicates that in the growing war-production centers delinquency was accentuated by wartime conditions."[29] In both the areas of declining population and those of increasing population, the increase in girls' cases was greater than boys' cases, indicating the presence of sexual unrest in the metropolitan centers. The rate of increase for girls' cases in the centers with increasing population was 40 per cent, as compared with 30 per cent for the areas where the population decreased. Sex behavior was clearly accentuated by the social changes of a wartime community.[30]

Wartime Trends in Illegitimacy

The most tangible manifestation of an offense against the sex mores is an illegitimate child. This does not mean that illegitimate parenthood is an indication of a greater defiance of the moral code than many other forms of behavior. The unmarried mother is often a young and unprotected girl who gets into trouble because of ignorance, impulse, or innocence. The fact of her unmarried parenthood, however, is incontrovertible evidence of her transgression and carries a corresponding social stigma in a society which is often more concerned with concealing illicit sexual relationships than in refraining from them. "Her 'fatherless' child," comments one study, "is . . . the outward and visible sign of an inward and spiritual fall from grace. Upon her defenseless head are vented all the outraged sentiments of the community, whose members may be concealing their own transgressions in their haste to cast the first stone at this modern Hester Prynne."[31] In these days of widespread knowledge of contraceptive devices, the extent of illicit sexual relationships far exceeds the number of illegitimate births annually recorded. The unmarried mother pays more than her share.

Unmarried mothers are only partially representative of the different types of adolescent girls and young women who contract extra-marital sex relationships. The different types of unmarried mothers have been described as follows: "(1) The mentally subnormal girl, who is an easy prey to sex advances; (2) the young and unprotected girl who gets into trouble because of ignorance or force; (3) the older girl of good character who yields to a sudden impulse or to false promises; (4) the 'really delinquent' girl or woman whose illegitimate maturity is an incident to repeated illicit adventures . . . (5) In addition there is the 'intellectually emancipated' group of brave feminists who defy social conventions because they desire a child first and foremost . . ."[32] Unmarried mothers are young, with a considerably higher proportion under 20 than among married mothers. The lack of age and experience in normal times leads approximately 75,000 young girls every year into motherhood without visible benefit of clergy. In 1937, there were 74,938 illegitimate live births and 5,348 stillbirths, as compared with 1,786,931 legitimate live births and 57,357 legitimate stillbirths.[33]

The majority of unmarried mothers are of the same social class as most sex offenders. This does not imply any monopoly of "moral turpitude" on the part of the daughters of the underprivileged but rather that the average girl in such an environment has greater opportunities for illicit sexual behavior and less financial assistance to conceal a possible lapse. Parental neglect, sophisticated companions, employment at an early age in occupations bringing them into contact with the opposite sex under conditions unfavorable for virtue—these are among the factors causing a girl to become sexually delinquent in the sense of being brought to a juvenile court, arrested for prostitution, or becoming the mother of an illegitimate child. Knowledge of birth control is found to a greater extent in the upper income groups, as well as the knowledge and resources to terminate an illegitimate pregnancy. A large although indeterminate number of the 600,000 to 2,000,000 abortions variously estimated as taking place yearly in the United States keep this form of the birth rate down.[34]

In a study of the psychological implications of unmarried motherhood, it has been suggested that this behavior may be partially attributed to certain common adolescent fantasies, defined as fantasies of rape, prostitution, and immaculate conception. These aberrations are entertained in one form or another by many adolescents. The meaning of the first two is clear in relation to the promiscuous sex behavior which often culminates in unwanted motherhood. The basis of the immaculate conception fantasy is said to be the unconscious feeling that the girl can bring about conception and birth by her own unaided efforts, since she is socially both father and mother of the illegitimate child. The suggestion is further made that "Unmarried motherhood in our culture represents a distorted and unrealistic way out of inner difficulties and is thus comparable to neurotic symptoms on the one hand and deliquent behavior on the other. The choice of unmarried motherhood as a way out or a solution of unconscious conflicts depends on external environmental factors, including the girl's childhood reality relationship with her parents . . ."[35] Whether or not such inner conflicts were increased or decreased by World War II is difficult to ascertain, although it is a reasonable assumption that they were.

The social circumstances of large numbers of young people during World War II made for an increase in sex relationships outside of marriage. Much of this increase took place among very young girls, hardly past their middle teens and often with little or no previous experience. The youth and inexperience of these girls, plus the casual view taken of such relationships by many members of the armed forces, would seem to point to an abrupt increase in illegitimacy. The increased mobility of millions of young men would appear to contribute further to this end result; stationed in one section for a few months, then in another, the tendency would presumably be to acquire a new wife in every landlocked port. Such relationships were often entered in mutual good faith, with the men promising marriage and often meaning it at the time. In many instances, when the soldier was moved to another camp or overseas, his sweetheart was left with a child on the way. Under peacetime conditions, many of these relationships would have culminated in marriage, but with social pressures relaxed in a strange community, there was often no marriage ceremony to legitimatize the child. The result would thus be an increase in the number and rate of illegitimate births during World War II.

This plausible theory did not correspond to the facts. The number of illegitimate births did increase between 1941 and 1944, but not as spectacularly as expected. In 1944 there were 87,001 illegitimate live births reported from 38 states and the District of Columbia, as compared to 81,488 for 1941. The figures for 1942 and 1943 were 81,954 and 82,586 respectively. Although these two middle years showed slight increases over the prewar year 1941, the ratio of illegitimate live births to total live births actually *decreased* because of the large wartime increase in the total number of births. The situation in the early war years differed so much from expectations that the Bureau of the Census expressed mild surprise. "The problem of illegitimate births," commented the Bureau, "is one of considerable public concern, particularly during war-time. Much publicity has . . . been given to the increasing magnitude of this social problem and it is somewhat surprising that the ratio of illegitimate live births to total live births has not increased but actually decreased in the first year of war."[36]

The next year another decline in the illegitimacy ratio occurred. The ratio of illegitimate live births to total live births decreased from 37.8 in 1942 to 36.5 in 1943.[37] No adequate explanation has been advanced to explain the failure of the illegitimacy ratio to follow the probable increase in extramarital sex contacts during the first two years of the war. One possible explanation is the education of all members of the armed forces in methods of birth control and prophylaxis against venereal disease. Many young men who in peacetime would have carried on relationships resulting in illegitimate children were thus exempt from some of the consequences of their behavior.

The year 1944 saw the first large wartime increase both in the number of illegitimate births and in the illegitimacy ratio. The number increased from 82,586 in 1943 to 87,001 in 1944, while the ratio rose from 36.5 to 40.4. This sudden increase in the third year of American participation in World War II may have represented the cumulative effects of the extramarital sex behavior presumably present during this period. Such an explanation, however, would largely nullify the effects of the aforementioned birth control knowledge among members of the armed forces who were responsible for much, although by no means all, of the increased sexual contacts. The 1944 increase in the ratio of illegitimate births was especially apparent among white females aged 20 to 29. The figure for the white group as a whole rose from 16.3 per 1,000 live births in 1943 to 19.6 in 1944. Comparatively little change was noted among nonwhite women during the same period, although the latter provide the bulk of the illegitimate births.[38]

The following table indicates the trends for illegitimate births by white and nonwhite groups during the period 1941–1944:

Table VII

Illegitimate Live Birth Ratios per 1,000
Total Live Births, by Race: 1941–1944*

Year	Total	White	Nonwhite
1941	41.4	18.8	176.4
1942	37.8	16.9	171.2
1943	36.5	16.3	165.2
1944	40.4	19.6	166.1

* Adapted from Federal Security Agency, Vital Statistics—Special Reports, *Illegitimate Births By Race: United States and Each State, 1944*, Vol. 25, No. 14 (October 31, 1946).

The differences in ratios by race arise from the depressed social condition of a considerable majority of Negroes, further evidenced by such indices as venereal disease, homicide, and per capita annual income. The explanation for such differences is social rather than "racial" in character and reflects the way of life of the Negro people rather than any innate predisposition to antisocial conduct.

Illegitimacy is also a reflection of youth and inexperience. In 1944, approximately 75 per cent of all illegitimate births occurred to mothers between 15 and 25 years of age. In the lowest age group reporting, that between 10 and 14 years of age, 43 per cent of all the white and 76 per cent of all the nonwhite live births were illegitimate. The actual number of births in this age group was not large, but the proportion of illegitimacies was very high. The most important age groups in point of illegitimacy were those 15–19 and 20–24 years. Girls in the first group reported 39.2 per cent of the total illegitimate births in 1944, while the percentage of the total for mothers 20–24 was 37.7. The presence among girls in the second half of their teens of nearly 40 per cent of the total number of illegitimacies is a significant commentary on the youth and inexperience of this group.[39]

The degree to which the eighty-odd thousand illegitimate births annually recorded actually represents the true situation is not precisely known. The registration is presumably very incomplete in some areas, less so in others. The tendency of the average unmarried mother is to conceal the fact as vigorously as possible, both for her own sake and that of her "fatherless" child. There has been considerable discussion among the various states concerning the desirability of reporting illegitimacy on the birth certificate at all, since many officials believe that nothing is to be gained by so stigmatizing the mother and child. In recent years, California, Colorado, Connecticut, Maryland, Massachusetts, Nebraska, New Hampshire, New Mexico, New York, and Wyoming have removed this leading question from their birth certificates. In these states the bar sinister will not further complicate the already difficult life of the illegitimate child.[40]

The Family and the Wartime Sex Offender

The family background of the adolescent is perhaps the most important single factor in determining whether or not she will ultimately engage in sex practices which society considers delinquent. The primary institutional mechanism for the inculcation of traditional sexual attitudes is the family group composed of father, mother, and children. World War II brought the physical disruption of millions of families, as the father migrated to a war industry area or was inducted into the armed forces and the mother entered a factory. Only one of these factors—the induction of large numbers of fathers and their subsequent absence from home—was a novel outcome of the war emergency. The industrial mobility of many fathers and the presence of hundreds of thousands of mothers in industry existed in prewar society and were merely accentuated by the wartime changes. The combined modifications in the physical structure of the group constituted such a change for large numbers of families that the customary transmission of the moral heritage was seriously interrupted. The effects of these changes were evident in many wartime social problems.

Such fragmentary information on local conditions as we have indicates the importance of the wartime home in producing sexual delinquency. A study of 1,402 women brought before the Separate Women's Court in San Francisco on charges of sexual delinquency, vagrancy, or prostitution showed that 794 (56.7 per cent) came from broken homes or homes in which there was "an unhappy background." These conditions resulted from the breakdown of the family from the following causes: "(1) death of one or both parents when the child was 18 years of age or under; (2) divorce or separation of the parents; (3) removal of the child from home, i.e., placed in boarding school, work home, foster home, et cetera; and (4) illegitimate child of mother."[41] More than half (52.9 per cent) of these girls and women were first offenders, an indication of the conditions brought about by wartime changes, of which the breakdown of the solidarity of the family formed an important part. Many of these young girls appearing before the Separate Women's Court for the first time were wartime casualties of a broken home.

The mere fact of a physically broken home—through divorce, desertion, temporary separation, or service in the armed forces—was not in itself sufficient to bring about a departure from the moral codes by the adolescent children. Many homes in which the father was still present and the mother devoted herself singlemindedly to the children nevertheless produced young girls who became sexually promiscuous in wartime. Similarly, the mere fact that a family was obliged to exist on considerably less than what we are pleased to call the American standard of living did not imply the eventual transgression of its adolescents. Other factors than physical disintegration and financial instability combined to make the family a partial or complete failure in successfully indoctrinating its young people with the traditional mores. Wartime failures at social control were also the product of a complex pattern of social-psychological factors within the family itself.

A variety of factors produced an unsatisfactory adjustment of the sexual delinquent to her family relationships. Girls residing with parents other than their own, whether stepmother or stepfather, were often dissatisfied with their environment and hostile to one or both parents. Other girls resented the presence of half- or stepbrothers and sisters or were themselves in such a position and felt unwanted. Other girls in their early teens were obliged by the employment of their mothers to take the responsibility for the maintenance of the home and the care of younger children. Other girls were ashamed of their family and home surroundings because of the moral turpitude of the parents or their unfamiliarity with American customs. Still others resented the failure of their parents to provide a sufficiently luxurious home to measure up to the dreams derived from the motion pictures. Finally, some parents were so indifferent to the welfare of their children that the latter felt repulsed and spent more time in the streets as a result.[42]

Such domestic situations led to the dissatisfaction of the girl with her home and family. Several forms of behavior followed. Some girls withdrew from the intimacy of the family group and brooded by themselves. Others deliberately disobeyed parental discipline and flaunted the moral standards which parents attempted (with signal lack of success) to instill in them. This disobedience took different forms—from staying out later than the family curfew with girl friends at the neighborhood movie to staying for several days with a succession of sailors in cheap hotels. For girls with even a modicum of sex appeal, such parental defiance often led to involvements with members of the armed forces who were not much more sophisticated than their bobby-socked companions. A third form of reaction was less deliberate but in the end had the same results. The adolescent girl by almost imperceptible stages found herself staying out later and later, accepting the attentions first of high school boy friends and then of complete strangers, frequenting places of recreation of an increasingly dubious nature, and finally becoming sexually delinquent at the end of a long series of unpremeditated steps.

At any stage in these events, certain parents reacted by still further rejecting the girl and becoming either indifferent or resigned to her continued misconduct. In such instances, the confusion was worse confounded and the family conflict was increased by geometric progression. The relationship between parents and girl may have reached a complete impasse which was only resolved by the girl's leaving home permanently. This step often meant cutting her off permanently from any social influence which would so present the traditional moral codes that she would follow them. To society, her family, and herself, she became a thoroughly disorganized person, a lost lady. The case records of every social agency are full of such cases in peacetime. The confusion of wartime did not reduce the case load.[43]

"The girl who hangs around the street hoping to be picked up is the girl who has not found in her family relations the love, attention, and admiration—in other words, the emotional satisfactions—she is looking for. She is the kind who is susceptible to the blandishments and sweet words of the man looking for a 'pick-up,' be he soldier or civilian."[44] In this way is the importance of affection and admiration in the family defined by one authority. Conditions leading to such negation of affection toward the adolescent girl were by no means unique to World War II. Many of the temperamental differences which lead to this denial are found no matter what the general conditions may be. Even under utopian conditions, such temperamental difficulties would continue to mar the happiness of the family. However, many of the emotional conflicts in the family group are reflections of the larger world with which adults and adolescents live in reciprocal interaction. When the state of the world makes other demands upon the emotional resources of the family, the lack of these sentiments may intensify the conflicts already latent. Although statistical evidence for this hypothesis is lacking, other evidence suggests that this was the case.

The School and the Sex Offender

Case histories of sexually delinquent girls show a consistent record of truancy prior to their initial appearance in the Juvenile Court or other formal involvement with the authorities. Truancy is often the first step in a long process of personal maladjustment which starts innocently and culminates in sexual promiscuity and other delinquent behavior. In many cases, the pattern is unfamiliar to the girl when she begins her truancies, since it constitutes activity which must be learned through experience and instruction. The girl does not take "naturally" to sexually delinquent behavior, particularly if she has received prior training in traditional sexual morality. When this earlier training is directed toward maintaining sexual integrity before marriage, the related attitudes must be unlearned or replaced by attitudes justifying irregular conduct. The pattern of sexual delinquency and the corresponding social attitudes are often acquired during the stolen hours of truancy.[45]

Like the majority of other delinquency-conditioning factors, truancy was not a new phenomenon brought about solely by the excitement of wartime living. The routine of school seems dull and unnecessary to many boys and girls in peacetime, who are either anxious to start the "real" business of living or are mentally or temperamentally unable to adjust to school attendance. Even under normal conditions, many boys and girls not yet out of high school wish to get a job; obliged by their parents or the state to remain in school, these malcontents vent their animal spirits in playing truant. Truancy is closely related to the attitudes of millions of young persons toward regular school attendance. The war changed that definition drastically and caused a considerable decrease in the number of adolescents attending primary and secondary schools.

The outbreak of the European war in 1939 did not initially change the policy of the United States toward education as compared to work. In 1940, before the country had been shaken by the fall of France, there were 9,159,000 young persons in the 14–19 age group attending school.

In 1944, with the nation at the height of its industrial and military mobilization, this number had declined to 7,930,000, a decrease of 1,229,000. In percentage terms, the end of the "phony war" in Europe found the United States with 62 per cent of its young people in the 14–19 age group in school, while the European invasion in 1944 found only 56 per cent of the same group similarly occupied. The crisis of the war thus modified the definition of school attendance in the minds of large numbers of young persons. The ethical desirability of the changing definition is not at issue. The point is that education as such was found less important than noneducation to a considerable segment of the youthful population.[46]

We do not know whether a proportionate increase in the national truancy rate accompanied this change in the definition of education. It is reasonable to suppose that such a change did take place, although there are no figures to prove it. The heightened excitement of the war, plus the desire of large numbers of adolescent girls to contribute to the morale of the armed forces at all times and places, undoubtedly increased the disinterest in school of thousands of restless and nubile maidens. In spite of the nationwide efforts to maintain the interest of young persons in school and induce them to return thereto, such theoretical arguments often had little effect upon a girl who had experienced the initial delights of playing truant and going to an afternoon movie with a sailor. The conclusion of this innocent diversion was often an experience which the adolescent girl did not expect. The final result of such affairs was sometimes a moral breakdown which changed the course of her life.

The school is the one community institution which touches the lives of all young persons, delinquents and nondelinquents alike. In spite of considerable lip-service to the paramount value of education in a democracy, many members of the community do not define it as basically important, when it must be bought at the price of increased taxes or interference with war activities. During the war, hundreds of thousands of teachers left the schools to accept better-paid positions in war industry or related service occupations. Although this exodus was bewailed by educators and many enlightened members of the general public, it was not considered sufficiently important to motivate the most obvious step in increasing the efficiency of the schools, namely, substantially increasing the salaries of teachers.

This loss of vital personnel, which more than counterbalanced the decrease in wartime enrollment in the secondary schools, meant that the school systems of many war centers were wholly inadequate either to handle the increased load or make their activities sufficiently vital to keep many young persons in school. The Committee on Sex Delinquency Among Young Girls, with this general problem in mind, recommended that "the situation in the schools would be improved by a conscious and unremitting effort on the part of the teachers to appeal to the pupils' admiration for the strong and to their desire for personal accomplishment such as is valued in a normal community."[47] Such an effort, particularly in wartime, was easier suggested than done.

Many adolescent girls became truants because the school was unable to hold their attention. Some were bored. Others wished to take a more active part in the war effort. Still others took to truancy because they were denied recognition by their fellows or the school authorities. This lack of recognition stemmed in some cases from personality difficulties, in others from the emotional failure of the family, in still others from the inability of the parents to provide the requisite social background. The war contributed to some of these difficulties, particularly in areas where the mobile family was unable to provide a home to which their daughter could bring her friends. In other cases, the absence of the mother from the home made that traditional refuge unsatisfactory. When the home was inadequate, the girl often turned to her teachers or her associates. When this recognition was denied, many girls sought it elsewhere.[48]

In the field of promiscuity not for hire, World War II did not substantially modify the general pattern apparent in the preceding decades. Evidence accumulated in the period between the wars pointed to an increase in extramarital sex behavior on the part of girls who acted without mercenary motives. Behavior of this general nature apparently increased during the war. The members of the armed forces were the principal recipients of the favors of those young girls who wished to participate in the war effort in this unsanctioned fashion. The resulting social problem can be explained in terms of the general hypothesis of war as primarily a catalytic agent in social change and social maladjustment. No further modification of the original hypothesis is necessary in this connection.

CHAPTER SIX

WAR AND PROSTITUTION

The Nature of Prostitution

Prostitution has been defined as "illicit sex union on a promiscuous and mercenary basis with accompanying emotional indifference."[1] Following the pattern developed in the previous chapter, in which sex offenses were considered as "promiscuity not for hire," prostitution may also be defined as "promiscuity for hire." In a number of marginal cases, wherein the girl exchanges her sexual favors on a promiscuous basis in exchange for food, lodging, or entertainment, the dividing line becomes very fine. In the majority of instances, however, the behavior and the motives of the female participants fall rather clearly into one category or the other. The sexually promiscuous girl who does not exchange her person on an habitual cash basis is distinguished from one who barters her person for money as the major or sole source of her financial support. Many of the social characteristics which formerly distinguished the prostitute from the rest of organized society are fast disappearing as sex behavior in general becomes more uninhibited. The social definitions, however, as formally incorporated in law and informally established in the mores, still distinguish sharply between these two forms of behavior, although both constitute serious encroachments upon social values and hence are considered social problems.

World War II saw a decline in prostitution and an increase in sexual promiscuity. The reasons for this change were various, but of primary importance was undoubtedly the fact that prostitution was a military as well as a civilian problem. In times of peace, prostitution is considered undesirable and sporadic efforts are made by local and federal authorities to eradicate it. The combined forces of these agencies are often insufficient to overcome both the inertia of public opinion and the vested interests of vice. Considerations advanced in peacetime are couched largely in terms of social welfare and are not such as to galvanize many law-enforcement agencies and private citizens into action.

When the situation becomes defined in terms of winning the war, a powerful element of social control is added. Venereal disease is then considered in terms of the number of divisions of infantry or naval task-force complements put out of action, instead of the number of private individuals and families incapacitated and disorganized. Prostitution is thus clearly a menace to the military operations of the nation at war.[2] Sexual promiscuity on a not-for-hire basis, on the other hand, is not so vividly defined nor are the mechanisms for eradicating it so well organized. Public opinion refuses to consider the latter in the same terms as prostitution. As a result, prostitution declines and noncommercial promiscuity flourishes.

The causes of prostitution are rooted deep in the society of the western world. The reasons for the entrance of thousands of girls into prostitution every year involve diverse social and psychological factors. For our present purposes, however, a comparatively simple statement of the etiology of prostitution will suffice. These causal factors may be summed up in the statement that "previous sex experience together with low resources and differential response to the trade or to girls practicing the trade constitutes the syndrome of factors most frequently associated with girls entering prostitution in the United States."[3] In simpler terms, "the girl . . . who enters the racket is most likely to be a girl with previous sex experience who lacks resources and responds to prostitution as a vocational opportunity by way of suggestion or help of prostitutes."[4] This dearth of personal resources in turn includes such matters as inadequate education, limited vocational skills, unsatisfactory family background, and poor personal judgment (often involving subnormal mentality). When such a girl comes in contact with similar girls who have already entered prostitution and hence can provide instruction and business facilities, the end result may be another candidate for the oldest profession. Prostitution under these circumstances is not so much the forcible moral degradation of an innocent and sexually unsophisticated girl as it is a business opportunity and way of life for one with limited personal resources who has already had considerable sex experience.

If this hypothesis is valid, then the changes in social values, the rapid increase in social mobility, the induction of large numbers of young men into the armed forces, and the growing sexual laxity of World War II should have produced a substantial increase in prostitution. If prostitutes are recruited largely from girls with previous sex experience, then more girls with such experience should produce a bumper crop of prostitutes—other things being equal. But in World War II other things were not equal. The ferocious attacks of the military against commercialized vice as a breeder and disseminator of venereal disease, the vigorous co-operation of the local police authorities for the same reasons, and the increased number of sexually promiscuous adolescents *not* for hire—these were the ponderables which decreased the incidence of prostitution in World War II. More men were away from home with money in their pockets than ever before. Commercial recreation boomed, soft drink sales burgeoned, liquor dispensations soared, and sexual delinquency increased. But prostitution declined.

Social Types of Prostitutes

The line dividing the prostitute from the sexual delinquent is often a very fine one. The same girl may engage in either type of conduct, depending upon the circumstances in which she finds herself. An accidental encounter with an older or more experienced girl may change the sexual delinquent into a prostitute; without this contact, the line between promiscuity not for hire and promiscuity for hire may never be crossed. A group of girls held on one charge would not differ in many respects from a group held on the other. The overt behavior of the sexual delinquent often does not differ materially from that of the prostitute; the major distinction is one of motive and reward.

We shall examine a group of women charged with prostitution in World War II for some insight into the social backgrounds and personal motivations of persons engaging in such behavior. This group comprised the first 100 women committed to the Federal Reformatory for Women in Alderson, West Virginia, charged with violation of the May Act. This Act is a Federal statute prohibiting prostitution near military installations in the continental United States. Designed to safeguard the military from venereal infection, the Act was first invoked in the military areas surrounding Fort Bragg, North Carolina and Camp Forrest, Tennessee. The girls in this study were taken in the wholesale roundup of prostitutes which followed.

Contrary to the popular stereotype of the prostitute as an alluring, flashily dressed, and sophisticated young woman, these unfortunates were anything but alluring, flashy, and sophisticated. With but six exceptions (girls who followed their husbands or sweethearts to camp and became prostitutes when their funds were gone) the girls charged with prostitution were sad, bedraggled, and comparatively unattractive young women from the submarginal areas of the Middle South. "Under ordinary circumstances," commented the warden of the Women's Reformatory, "most of them would have spent their lives in poverty and obscurity; but the world upheaval has changed their destinies. They were ill equipped for the rapid whirl of soldiers, easy money, beer taverns, and freedom from drudgery, drabness, and monotony."[5] Prostitution offered a way of life and a means of livelihood.

These 100 girls were presumably a cross section of the young women entering prostitution in the Middle South—or at least of that group which got caught. A brief résumé of the facts of their personal and social backgrounds offers considerable insight into the forces which produce prostitution, particularly in time of war.

1. *Age.* As might be expected, the women offenders were predominantly young. Of the 100 prostitutes in the sample, 12 were under 18, 25 were 18–20, 31 were 21–25, and 22 were from 26–35. Only 10 were over 35. Prostitution is obviously a way of life adopted by young girls and women who have sufficient physical attractiveness to beguile male custom.

2. *Educational achievement.* The educational attainments of these young women were low, reflecting the marginal educational standards of the regions from which they came. Fifteen of the women reported no schooling whatever, 25 less than sixth grade, 27 claimed to have finished the sixth grade, and 25 said that they had finished the eighth grade. Only 8 had even entered high school; one claimed the distinction of being a high school graduate.

3. *Family backgrounds.* The case histories of these girls were full of family difficulties. Forty-three came from homes broken in one way or another, and in many others there was evidence of immorality, cruelty, drunkenness, and various forms of delinquency. Sexual promiscuity of the mother was a familiar part of the family background. At an early level, many of the girls were initiated into sexual behavior not in accordance with the mores.

4. *Economic background.* Almost two-thirds of the girls came from submarginal homes, where economic conditions were inadequate to insure even the minimum standards of health and decency.

Practically all of them were reared in rural or small town environments, which suggests that the allurement of urban society is not the only milieu in which sexual delinquency flourishes. The allegedly higher moral standards of the rural areas were not, in these cases, sufficient to maintain conventional sexual behavior, particularly when combined with poverty, degradation, and immorality.

5. *Marital status.* More than half (53 per cent) of the girls reported that they were or had been married. Of this number, 31 declared themselves divorced or separated. During the course of their sexual history, some 31 illegitimate children were reported among the group; two more girls were pregnant at the time of examination, with the paternity unknown. In addition to the 53 girls reporting previous marriage, the majority of the others undoubtedly had previous sexual experience before they entered prostitution.

6. *Work history.* In spite of the widespread employment opportunities open during the defense program and the early war years, the majority of the girls apparently had very slight work experience. A few represented themselves as formerly employed in textile factories or laundries and a considerable number (18) had previously worked as domestic servants. Fifteen reported work experience as "waitresses," an occupation which apparently often led to or combined with prostitution. Serving in taverns, tourist camps, bars, and dance halls, they had ample opportunity to meet the mobile male population.

7. *Arrest history.* These girls were not criminals in the accepted sense of the word, even though a number of them (64) had been previously arrested. Most of the charges were for vagrancy, disorderly conduct, drunkenness, solicitation, prostitution—all offenses against the moral code but only misdemeanors in the eyes of the law. Furthermore, most of these misdemeanors were related either to a pathetic attempt to enjoy themselves or to make a livelihood through trading on their dubious sexual attractions. Prostitution had imperceptibly become a "normal" way of life like any other, and many were bewildered that their conduct had brought them into conflict with the Federal Government.

8. *Prostitution history.* Although some of the young women had histories of prostitution stretching over a number of years, the

majority apparently entered promiscuity for hire as a direct result of the war. It appears that "participation in sex activities on a commercial basis had its beginnings with the construction of military camps in the areas of residence." The sudden introduction of thousands of young men with plenty of money into areas with limited recreational resources was too much for the none-too-strong moral standards of the young women. Many of these women were sexually promiscuous for hire only on occasions, but were apprehended with soldiers under the May Act and hence classified as prostitutes.

9. *Alcoholism.* Of the hundred women in the sample, 35 reported themselves as moderate or occasional drinkers, while 56 admitted excessive drinking. Only nine said that they never indulged in alcoholic beverages. Many claimed that they became sexually promiscuous only when under the influence of alcohol (and hence were presumably not "morally" responsible for their actions). If their stories of excessive indulgence were true, their behavior was probably motivated by certain basic psychological maladjustments of whose nature they were unaware. Alcoholism was thus a symptom of more fundamental personal disorganization.

10. *Methods of prostitution.* Only 24 of these women operated in organized houses of prostitution, with the elaborate complex of procurers, "madams," and the other traditional professional appurtenances. The majority operated either independently or with one or two other girls, taking their clients to hotels, trailers, tourist camps, parked automobiles, taxicabs, abandoned buildings, barns, or open fields. The illicit activities were essentially unorganized and represented the spontaneous adjustment of the individual girl to the total war situation. For the most part, these young women drifted into prostitution without any prior plan and with little direction other than that supplied by a friend in the business. As a way of life, prostitution was adopted by these young women in the lower social groups who had previous sex experience and very few personal resources to tide them over the changes brought by the war.[6]

Numerous other studies were made during World War II of women charged with prostitution. In San Antonio,[7] Tacoma,[8] and San Francisco,[9] the findings were generally much the same, although the social background of the women differed in some respects between regions. In the northern areas, the educational achievement of the average girl was considerably more advanced, reflecting higher regional standards. The economic foundation of the home was also somewhat higher, since the average family income was considerably greater in these regions than among the sharecroppers and tenant farmers of the Middle South, who furnished the majority of candidates in the May Act study. But for the most part, the picture was strikingly similar over the country—young girls from a background of broken homes, with inadequate personal and vocational resources, indulging in excessive alcoholism, and making whatever adjustment they could to a situation clearly beyond both their comprehension and their control.

War and Prostitution

War traditionally modifies the old situation and renders the mores inapplicable to the new. War increases the mobility of millions of persons and cuts them off from the restraining moral force of neighborhood opinion. War dissolves many families and causes their isolated members to seek sexual satisfaction in extramarital channels. War brings large numbers of industrial workers together in congested areas, where recreational facilities are not only limited but tend to encourage sexual irregularity as well. War increases the cash income of workers and provides increased financial basis for sexual irregularity for hire. War places several million young men in the most vigorous age groups in uniform and encourages the same psychological releases which have in the past increased sexual irregularity. War should, therefore, bring a substantial increase in prostitution. This was apparently the case with every war except the last one. World War II was virtually unique in curtailing the *commercial* sexual license which has distinguished warfare since the beginning of time.[10]

The emphasis throughout this study has consistently been upon civilian rather than military problems and upon the effects of World War II upon the individuals, institutions, and relationships of civilian society. The complex world of the military has largely been left to other analysts. In the case of prostitution, this limitation is abandoned on the obvious grounds that the problem is both a military and a civilian one. Many of the wartime patrons of prostitution were men in uniform and much of the conduct took place in areas adjacent to military camps, leave centers, and ports of embarkation. With 12 million young men in the armed forces, it is no reflection upon them to suggest that prostitution became deeply tinged with the olive drab of the Army and the blue of the Navy. The wartime interaction between the civilian and the military population was interaction in the most literal sense; the two elements met in a relationship fraught with problems of a military as well as a civilian character. Finally, it is impossible to speak realistically of wartime prostitution without considering its military aspects because the situation was universally defined in military terms, the repressive measures were established either directly by the military or at their urgent request, and the emphasis in repression shifted from individual morality and social welfare to military efficiency and wartime necessity.

The gravity of the problem was appreciated by the military and those civilians professionally concerned with such matters long before the outbreak of hostilities involving this country. Selective Service called hundreds of thousands of young men into camps and military installations all over the nation long before Pearl Harbor. Other hundreds of thousands of civilians were flocking to isolated areas where additional facilities were in process of construction. Still others were moving into congested production areas as the industrial program went into high gear. The effect of this concentration of manpower upon those engaged in prostitution or who entertained vague notions of so doing was instantaneous. Prostitution was firmly entrenched in various communities, many of which were in the same areas receiving the largest influx of men for training. Broadly speaking, prostitution in pre-Pearl Harbor days flourished not so much in the metropolitan centers of the north and east as in the smaller cities of the south and far west. The worst conditions generally prevailed in the South Atlantic, East South Central, West South Central, Mountain, and Pacific Coast regions. These were precisely the regions immediately deluged with servicemen in training or about to embark for overseas.[11] In these centers, "The congregation of millions of American youths into army camps has acted like a blood transfusion to a profession suffering in recent years from serious competition from non-professional sources. Prostitution has heard the distant clarion call, and stands ready and willing to serve our youth, who, removed from the usual restraints of home life, offer a fertile soil for the implantation of the venereal diseases."[12]

Such a community was El Paso, Texas, a city of 100,000 situated on the Mexican border adjacent to Juarez, a Mexican city of 50,000. An investigation carried on in the early days of the war by the American Social Hygiene Association disclosed some important aspects of the prostitution situation. Within a short distance of the El Paso city limits was Fort Bliss, a military cantonment with about 25,000 troops at the time of the investigation. In March, 1941, at least nine large houses of prostitution were operating in El Paso under police sur- veillance, plus large numbers of individual prostitutes operating more or less clandestinely. Efforts were made by the military, in conjunction with the local authorities, to close the houses in El Paso and make the facilities in Juarez unavailable to the enlisted personnel by closing the International Bridge across the Rio Grande. The measures demon- strated conclusively that houses of prostitution, even those where the inmates were periodically "inspected" by the local health authorities, played an important role in the dissemination of venereal disease. When a policy of repression was followed in the El Paso area, a de- crease in venereal infection was quickly apparent. As the commercial prostitute was made less available, the venereal rate took an immediate change for the better. This general policy was the one adopted by the armed forces during World War II, with generally satisfactory results.[13]

The changing role of prostitution during the war may be further seen from a brief case study of another community. The community was a flourishing center of commercialized vice long before the mobil- ization. During the early years of the war, it was a leave center and playground for thousands of members of the armed forces.[14] The fol- lowing excerpts are taken from a series of studies made over a two- year period in 1942 and 1943.

March 1942. "Many soldiers go into this town every day. . . . It is generally known that there are always an abundance of women, that there are many inmates in brothels, that 'hustlers' and 'come-on' girls can be had in many taverns and 'call girls' in many hotels. . . .

July 1942. "At the instigation of the Federal and State authorities, the municipal authorities were persuaded to repress prostitution.

October 1942. "Regardless of whether or not a man is in uniform, law enforcement has reached the stage where it is difficult to find any prostitutes.

January 1943. "It is exceedingly difficult to find any white prostitutes. A few brothels, camouflaged as massage parlors, are found to be operating very cautiously. Some 'hustlers' are found in 'Nite Clubs.' Prices are high. Girls have to be 'sneaked' into a hotel room.

June 1943. "Some former 'hot spots' are found to be padlocked. Getting girls is mighty expensive business. Bellboys will not help and neither will cab-drivers. 'Go-betweens' receive stiff jail sentences which act as a deterrent to others. The vast majority have abandoned the practice.

September 1943. "Some former brothels are being 'held down' by caretakers for the duration in the hope that during the postwar period erstwhile operators will be able to resume business. The police are found to be checking up closely. White commercialized prostitution has been reduced to a minimum. Police started an intensive drive against Negro prostitutes who 'switched' their activities from white trade to their own race. Many were arrested. ... However, the grapevine has it that 'as soon as the war is over the heat will be turned off.' "[15]

In this community long accustomed to the large-scale practice of commercialized vice, the war came as a great (although temporary) redefining agent. An activity which had formerly been a source of considerable profit to many persons—either directly related to prostitution or indirectly profiting therefrom—came to be defined in terms detrimental to the national interest. Individual morality and social welfare were temporarily obscured by wartime necessity. The Federal and State authorities were the first to act, since they were most directly interested in the prosecution of the war and also had no financial interests in the complex. By July 1942—only six months after Pearl Harbor—the State and Federal pressure was such as to close the brothels in this community, an action followed by progressively more drastic enforcement of the statutes against prostitution, that had formerly been allowed to languish. By midsummer 1943, the local commercialization of sexual relationships had been almost completely curtailed, insofar as it was within the power of the authorities to do so. The negative wartime definition of promiscuity for hire had reached its most effective manifestation. Vice operatives had resigned themselves to hanging on grimly until the war was over, the evangelistic fervor subsided, and the situation again defined in terms of the good old days.

By the end of 1944, much progress had been made in the majority of communities throughout the country and prostitution had been completely eradicated in others. In summary, the American Social Hygiene Association stated in its 1944 report that "Through the efforts of law enforcement officials throughout the country, the nature of the problem . . . has changed considerably since 1939. Then there were many communities in which commercialized prostitution had sprung up and was being openly tolerated and permitted to flourish; now such conditions are exceptional. By the end of 1944 most communities had closed any brothels that existed and cracked down on facilitators of prostitution of all sorts."[16] Promiscuity for hire continued to exist, particularly the unorganized variety typified by the young women apprehended under the May Act. Promiscuity not for hire continued to be a difficult problem for both military and civilian personnel and a progressively greater percentage of venereal infections originated in such relationships. But for perhaps the first time in the history of a nation at war, prostitution became less rather than more serious during the conflict itself.

"Since Pearl Harbor," stated an official of the Federal Bureau of Investigation, "organized prostitution has been greatly reduced throughout the United States. Spurred by patriotism and backed up by public opinion, law enforcement officials have hit hard at the 'business' wherever it has tried to set up shop, and the results may be seen in 'red-light districts' closed in more than 650 communities, and in the fact that today a low proportion of venereal disease infections among the armed forces may be considered chargeable to prostitutes."[17] This work of enforcement was carried on by such agencies as the Federal Bureau of Investigation, the Social Protection Division of the Federal Security Agency, the International Association of Chiefs of Police, the National Advisory Police Committee on Social Protection, the National Sheriff's Association, the National Association of Taxicab Owners, the American Hotel Association, the National Probation Association, and many other public and private organizations operating on a local as well as a national scale. Their combined efforts are proof of what can be done in the field of social control when there is unanimity on the definition of the problem.

The wartime trend toward a decreasing incidence of prostitution was further shown by a series of investigations conducted by the American Social Hygiene Association between January 1, 1940 and March 31, 1945. Some 1,912 studies were carried on in communities near which members of the armed forces were stationed and where prostitution therefore constituted a direct military menace. A community was defined as "good" if there were no brothels or houses of prostitution with resident prostitutes. A community was said to be "bad" when it had black marks on the following counts: solicitation of customers by prostitutes on the streets or in public places; work as "go-betweens" by bellboys, bartenders, taxicab drivers, or other groups to bring customers and prostitutes together; and finally acquiescence by hotels, taverns, rooming houses, and similar establishments to the presence and operation of prostitutes on their premises.[18] The percentages of communities found to be good and bad in this sense during the five-year period were as follows:

Table VIII

An Analysis of 1,912 Studies Made by the American Social Hygiene Association, January 1, 1940 to March 31, 1945, in Communities Adjacent to Military Installations.*

Year	Percentage "Good"	Percentage "Bad"
1940 (82 Communities)	36.6	32.9
1941 (364 Communities)	44.5	24.2
1942 (517 Communities)	44.7	12.7
1943 (401 Communities)	47.4	9.0
1944 (415 Communities)	46.8	6.2
1945 (First Quarter, 133 Communities)	47.3	3.8

* "Social Protection—A Summing Up," *Journal of Social Hygiene*, 31: 303-307 (May, 1945).

Although the definitions of good, fair, poor, and bad communities were based upon subjective evaluations, the general trend was clear and pointed conclusively toward a substantial decrease of prostitution during most of World War II. The percentage of "good" communities increased from 36.6 in 1940 to 47.3 in 1945. The most striking change, however, was the decrease in the percentage of "bad" communities. The steady decline in such communities from 32.9 per cent in 1940 to 3.8 per cent in the first quarter of 1945 represents a triumph for social control backed by aroused public opinion. Prostitution has long been considered a social problem threatening the values of a large majority of the population. In spite of this virtual unanimity upon the theoretical dangers of prostitution, previous efforts at social control have encountered considerable opposition and, above all, a vast public apathy.

The war galvanized the nation into action on this problem to an extent never before believed possible.

Another index to the wartime trends in prostitution was furnished by the yearly number of arrests for prostitution and commercialized vice. This offense is defined as including "sex offenses of a commercialized nature, or attempts to commit the same, such as prostitution, keeping bawdy house, procuring, transporting or detaining women for immoral purposes."[19] These data were compiled by the Federal Bureau of Investigation and were limited to arrests for violations of State laws and Municipal ordinances. They do not include arrests for violation of Federal statutes nor do they include all persons arrested for prostitution, since an unknown number taken into custody in the local communities do not have fingerprint cards sent to Washington. Finally, the number of persons arrested does not coincide with the number of offenses committed, since two or more persons may be arrested for the same offense; conversely, a single person may be arrested and charged with the commission of more than one crime.[20]

With these reservations, the figures indicate the extent of wartime arrests for promiscuity for hire, as compared with the peacetime year 1939.

Table IX

Trend of Arrests for Prostitution and Commercialized Vice*

Year	Total	Male	Female
1939	6,928	1,427	5,501
1940	8,987	2,494	6,493
1941	9,273	2,429	6,844
1942	9,031	2,508	6,523
1943	9,263	2,483	6,780
1944	10,787	3,155	7,632
1945	10,959	3,138	7,821

* Compiled from *Uniform Crime Reports*, 1939–1945, *loc. cit.*; Also *Uniform Crime Reports*, Annual Bulletin 1945, *loc. cit.*, p. 113.

These figures indicate a considerable increase in arrests for prostitution and commercialized vice in 1940 as compared to 1939. This figure may have reflected an increase in prostitution arising partially from higher wages and the beginning of military mobilization. The increases in 1940 and 1941 may also have reflected the growing solicitude of the local police in enforcing the existing statutes against commercialized vice. The desire for military security through minimizing prostitution and venereal disease may have resulted in the increase in arrests. There were no significant changes in 1942 and 1943, but the year 1944 saw another increase from 9,263 in 1943 to 10,787 in 1944. In the year 1945, there were 10,959 arrests, a slight increase over 1944. The comparatively small number of persons involved in these arrests suggests that prostitution played a relatively small role in the sexual life of the nation during wartime. Even with the admitted desire of the local officials to stamp out a practice deleterious to the physical prosecution of the war, these minions of the law were able to arrest no more than 10,959 persons at the height of the campaign.

Venereal Disease and the Military

The military is not primarily interested in morality or social welfare but rather in maximum efficiency for the successful prosecution of a war. This does not mean that morality or welfare are not considered in time of war; every effort consistent with military efficiency is made to promote the morality of the individual soldier or sailor and the general welfare of the population. The armed forces, however, exist for the primary purpose of prosecuting a war as efficiently as possible. The problems of prostitution and venereal disease are viewed in these terms. The basic tenets of the Army may be summarized as follows:

1. *Continence.* The most desirable method of maintaining traditional morality and avoiding venereal infection is by sexual continence.

2. *Individual sex habits.* The sex habits of the "civilian in uniform" have largely been established before entering the service. Men promiscuous in civilian life will tend to continue their promiscuity in the Army.

3. *Individual exposure.* Certain members of the armed forces will expose themselves to infection in spite of formal efforts to promote continence. To withhold prophylactic instruction from these men would increase the incidence of venereal disease, a practice contrary either to medical or military policy.

4. *Mass instruction.* It is impossible for the Army to decide which of its members need instruction because of their propensity for promiscuity and which, because of continence, do not. Hence instructions must be given to everyone.

5. *Nature of instruction.* Instruction should be presented in an unemotional manner and without any attempt at fright, since fear of

infection is not an adequate deterrent to exposure. This instruction should be given on a level understandable to the lower half of military mentality. Men on the lower levels of the intelligence quotient brackets are often those who have had a minimum of education and hence are most in need of simple instruction.[21]

The point of view of the Navy is substantially that of the Army. Individual instruction by the responsible authorities is used to inculcate the principles of traditional morality and, failing that, of ordinary care in the maintenance of health. Emphasis throughout the educational program of the Navy is placed upon the average boy in the service, the stages of training through which he will pass, the different social and moral conditions at his stations at home and abroad, and the situations he will meet which involve the possibility of venereal infection. Naval forces afloat have higher rates than those stationed ashore, while those on foreign duty either afloat or ashore ordinarily have higher rates than within the continental United States. The Navy encounters different types of situations, each with their own problems of prostitution and infection. The training and treatment program of the Navy is geared to these different situations.[22]

Both Services agree that the enlisted man shall not render himself unfit for military service through activities not connected thereto. The emphasis is placed first upon continence, second upon prevention and prophylaxis, and third upon treatment. Every effort is made to avoid infection; once infected, the emphasis shifts to prompt notification so that the individual may first be rendered noninfectious and then cured. Discretion is customarily vested in the commanding officer concerning the penalty if the individual becomes infected and fails to report his condition. The offender may be subject to loss of pay during his incapacitation or other penalties may be imposed upon him for his disregard of the prime military consideration to remain physically fit. The mechanics of this program do not concern us here; the important consideration is the attitude of the armed forces and the general implementing policies.[23]

Wartime trends in venereal disease in the armed forces reflected the wisdom of this approach. Broadly speaking, rates for both the armed forces during World War II were the lowest for any army and navy in history. Rates were substantially lower for World War II than for World War I. Certain fluctuations were evident over the entire progress of the second war, as its characteristics changed and a larger proportion of men were serving overseas. The infection rate for venereal disease was generally higher among soldiers stationed within the continental United States than among those stationed in foreign countries. The degree of social control exercised upon military personnel under foreign conditions was greater than that possible at home. Both of the services indicated an increase in the rate of infection among troops returning to the United States from foreign service. This infection was acquired *after* and not *before* their arrival in this country.[24]

The year 1944 saw an increase in the Army venereal disease rate for the continental United States from 26.3 per 1,000 men for 1943 to 36 per 1,000 in 1944. This increase was found to be due entirely to gonorrhea, with an astounding 40 per cent increase in the Army rate for this infection. In the same period, the Army syphilis rate declined by approximately 20 per cent. The reservoir of infection for both diseases for the majority of troops stationed in the country in 1944 was the civilian population, with a considerable increase in gonorrhea among this group, and presumably a decrease in syphilis. A great deal of unrecorded and untreated gonorrhea in the civilian population was a menace to the health of the civilian and military population alike. The difficulty of control of gonorrhea is indicated by this experience, while the comparative success of the syphilis program is similarly suggested.[25]

A significant factor was the increase in the infection rate of units after they returned to the continental United States. The military authorities cannot effect such a rigid control upon their personnel within the United States as in foreign theaters of operation. Furthermore, while men with long overseas service distrusted foreign girls and took adequate prophylactic precautions with them, they were less suspicious of American girls. The feeling was, apparently, that American girls were miraculously free of infection and hence no precautions were necessary. With the subsequent influx of returning soldiers, this situation was presumably duplicated on an even larger scale, with a corresponding increase in venereal infection.[26]

The Navy had somewhat the same experience in the closing years of the war. Rates for men stationed within the continental United States showed an increase from 24.5 per 1,000 in 1943 to 30.4 for the first eleven months of 1944. This was an overall increase of approximately 24 per cent over the preceding year. A partial explanation for this increase was suggested by a Navy medical spokesman early in

1945: "The pressures pulling and hauling at our young people in and out of the armed services are well beyond our comprehension, at least in emotional terms. . . . The lengthening of the war, the increasing disruption of normal home life, the heightening transiency of our population, the experiences which the men and women of the services are undergoing—all these and others too enter into the picture."[27] An increasing number of servicemen returning from overseas service, their pockets full of back pay, and the smile of an American girl before them—these were some of the factors which increased the rate of venereal infection during the closing years of the war.

Civilian Trends in Venereal Disease

Venereal disease is a civilian as well as a military problem, as the two groups infect and reinfect each other to their mutual disadvantage. The majority of the uniformed personnel returned to civilian status; and the habits they acquired, as well as the physical infections they suffered, will continue with them in their postwar careers. The trends in venereal disease among the civilian population during the war reflected the precautions taken by the military, first in their campaign against commercialized prostitution, second in their educational program against venereal disease among their own personnel, and finally in the medical treatment of the armed forces so that they ceased to be infectious to the civilian population. The problems of prostitution and venereal disease were clearly those of the entire population, whether in or out of uniform. Particularly during the early years of the war, when the majority of troops were still quartered in the continental United States, the problems were physically and socially inseparable.

The period of national defense beginning in 1940 provided the first large-scale opportunity for accurate measurement of venereal disease in the civilian population. Every man who enlisted or was inducted into the armed forces from 1940 on was given a serological test for syphilis. Results of the first two million examinations indicated a high prevalence of syphilis in the population, despite the campaign undertaken some years before by the United States Public Health Service. The syphilis rate for males aged 21–35 in this group of 2,000,000 men was 47.7 per 1,000 for 44 states and the District of Columbia. The rate for white persons was 23.5 and that for Negores 272.0, or more than ten times as high. In general, "incidence and prevalence rates among whites are higher for men than women; higher for the colored race than for white; and higher in the South than in other sections . . . chances of infection are in an inverse ratio to income . . ."[28] Diagnostic tests of similar accuracy for gonorrhea were lacking during this examination of the nation's manpower, so the peacetime incidence of this disease is not fully known. It is estimated, however, that gonorrhea is at least three times as prevalent as syphilis.[29]

Civilian trends in venereal disease may best be measured by changes in the number of cases reported over the years to state health departments. In the six-year period from 1939 through 1944, the number of cases of syphilis so reported decreased from 485,967 in 1939 to 473,993 in 1944, a decrease of 2.5 per cent. Over the same period, the number of cases of gonorrhea similarly reported increased from 184,679 in 1939 to 311,795 in 1944, an increase of 68.8 per cent. Annual trends in the syphilis rate were as follows:

Table X

Annual Trends in Cases of Syphilis Reported to
State Health Departments*

Year	Number	Percentage Increase Over Previous Year
1939	485,967	
1940	487,464	0.3
1941	494,813	1.5
1942	489,172	−1.1
1943	579,147	18.4
1944	473,993	−18.2

* Walter Clarke, "Postwar Social Hygiene Problems and Strategy," *Journal of Social Hygiene,* 31:4-15 (January, 1945), Table p. 8.

The reasons for the abrupt increase of 18.4 per cent in 1943 over 1942 are not precisely known. Part of the increase may have resulted from the cumulative effects of social congestion, which had become intense by January, 1943. In its 1943 report, the American Social Hygiene Association suggested that "War production needs and the location of large military establishments had by January, 1943 caused great concentrations of population and created boom towns unprepared to meet emergency social hygiene needs."[30] The failure to fill these needs, particularly in public health and disease prevention, may have been partially responsible for the substantial increase in new syphilis cases during 1943. By 1944, with more men overseas, the situation was apparently better in hand, with that year showing an equally abrupt decline of 18.2 per cent in the new case rate over 1943.

The annual trends in the cases of gonorrhea reported to the state health departments were as follows:

Table XI

Annual Trends in Cases of Gonorrhea Reported to
State Health Departments*

Year	Number	Percentage Increase Over Previous Year
1939	184,679	
1940	180,383	−3.3
1941	198,432	10.0
1942	220,432	11.1
1943	281,980	27.9
1944	311,795	10.6

* Walter Clarke, "Postwar Social Hygiene Problems and Strategy," *loc. cit.*

The overall increase of 68.8 per cent from 1939–44 was an indication of the continued seriousness of the problem, but it did not necessarily mean a corresponding increase in the actual number of cases. As Dr. Parran, Surgeon General, United States Public Health Service, pointed out, the increase in reported cases may have arisen from the fact that many more patients suffering from gonorrhea came to the attention of physicians during than before the war. Until 1938 there was no miraculous drug which could cure this disease. Since that time, greater public knowledge of the disease, an increase in the number and distribution of clinics, and the new methods of treatment all contributed to the increased number of reported cases, many of which would have remained unreported under former conditions. A change in public awareness, both on the level of those infected and those curing the disease, thus led to an apparent increase which in turn reflected the changing definition. This does not mean that gonorrhea did *not* increase during the war years. In all probability, the mobility and sexual promiscuity of the war years brought about a net increase in this form of venereal infection. The extent of this increase, however, is complicated by the changing social definition.[31]

Trends in appropriations for the prevention and cure of venereal disease were closely related to the changes in their reported incidence.

In 1938, the Venereal Disease Control Act, sponsored by Senator Robert M. LaFollette and Representative Alfred L. Bulwinkle, went into effect. This Act provided that Federal funds be given to the states in the form of grants-in-aid, to be used for trained personnel, new clinical facilities, and medical supplies for the treatment of venereal disease. These appropriations increased during the war from the initial sum of three million dollars in 1939 to $12,500,000 in 1945. The yearly trends in these appropriations for the fiscal years ending June 30 were as follows:

Table XII

Annual Appropriations under the Venereal
Disease Control Act*

Year	Appropriation
1939	$3,000,000
1940	$5,000,000
1941	$6,200,000
1942	$8,750,000
1943	$12,500,000
1944	$12,500,000
1945	$12,500,000

* Walter Clarke, "Postwar Social Hygiene Problems and Strategy," *loc. cit.,* Table p. 9.

These Federal funds were supplemented by state and local appropriations, which increased from $4,342,329 in 1939 to $9,300,275 in 1944, or 114.2 per cent. The problem was defined throughout the emergency as one primarily of national defense and the efficiency of the entire population in the conduct of the war. Considerable danger exists that a postwar wave of economy may curtail or eliminate these funds altogether because of the end of the national emergency.

Evidence of these expenditures was found in the increased number of clinics treating venereal disease, the number of admissions for the two principal diseases, and the drugs administered in treatment. Clinics increased from 2,080 in 1939 to 3,707 in 1944, a growth of 78.2 per cent. Admissions to clinic service for syphilis rose from 249,464 in 1939 to 413,222 in 1944, an increase of 80.2 per cent. Admissions for gonorrhea rose 134.4 per cent from 62,835 in 1939 to 147,267 in 1944. Individual treatments in clinics for syphilis rose from 6,667,798 in 1939 to 11,388,312 in 1944, an increase of 72.2 per cent. Similar figures for gonorrhea showed a decrease from 881,875 to 726,093 from 1939 to

1944, probably reflecting the changes in treatment for this disease from clinic to home. This supposition is reinforced by the figures for the distribution of sulfonamide tablets by the state health departments, which had an astronomical rise from 3,332,450 in 1939 to 18,524,376 in 1944, an increase of 455.9 per cent.[32]

These figures are not completely indicative of the trends in venereal disease among the civilian population during World War II. They indicate only the number of such cases for which treatment was sought. The increase in the number of clinics where such diseases are treated, the publicity campaign waged by the Public Health Service and the military, the new forms of treatment which were formerly either painful and/or difficult to administer, and public consciousness of the necessity for keeping fit in wartime—these were some of the factors which increased the number of cases brought for treatment during the war. When the emergency was over and venereal disease became once more merely an individual and welfare problem, instead of a manifestly patriotic one, many of the wartime gains were threatened.

Prostitution and Social Control

A social problem by definition questions or infringes upon a social value held by a large number of persons. In attempting to defend these values, various agencies of social control are set in motion, ranging in formality from public opinion to the mechanisms of government. Prostitution has traditionally been one of the most perplexing of all social problems because of the conflict between social values and sexual impulses. The majority of persons—including those who make use of the facilities of prostitution as well as those who profit by them—are convinced of its undesirability and unite in its moral condemnation. So strong and pervasive are the desires of many persons for extramarital sex relationships, however, that they continue to patronize the oldest profession while at the same time condemning their partner and even themselves. Motives for this conduct are more complex than mere hypocrisy and their complexity makes doubly difficult any realistic social activity dealing with prostitution.

Social control is therefore difficult in peacetime, since it involves the right of the individual to indulge his own weakness, as well as the somewhat nebulous value (in our individualistic society) of social welfare. In wartime, however, the problem quickly transcends in-

dividual and welfare conceptions and becomes one of national efficiency. New and powerful forces exert social control. Other forces,
hitherto indifferent, take a hand: the local police, for example, become
convinced of the desirability of eliminating commercialized vice. The
problem then becomes defined in other terms, often with spectacular
results. The agencies of social control in wartime increase in efficiency.

These agencies are extremely complex, even on the single level of
prostitution.[33] The United States Army is the largest single instru-
mentality directly concerned with the wartime control of prostitution
and venereal disease. The administrative units within the Personnel
Division of the Army intrusted with carrying out this policy during
World War II were the Medical Department, the Morale Branch, the
Corps of Chaplains, and the Provost Marshall General.[34] The organization of the United States Navy with respect to these problems
is in general similar to that of the Army. The same general functions
are carried on in the Navy by the various officers in charge of social
hygiene, morale activities, religious and moral instruction, and self-
education.[35]

Among the civilian agencies, the Venereal Disease Division of the
United States Public Health Service is intimately concerned with the
discovery, treatment, and prevention of venereal infections in the
civilian population.[36] The Social Protection Division of the Office
of Community War Services of the Federal Security Agency was
interested in the social control of prostitution during World War II.[37]
Working directly with the local police authorities, field representatives
of the Social Protection Division furnished information and assistance
leading to the closing of red light districts in some 650 communities
throughout the country.[38]

The Department of Justice was the third major civilian agency
enlisted in the wartime fight against prostitution and venereal disease.
The Department is intrusted with the enforcement of federal statutes
concerning the suppression of prostitution and all behavior which
might lead thereto.[39] In addition to the enforcement of the federal
laws, the Federal Bureau of Investigation of the Department of
Justice co-operates with state and local officials in the suppression of
delinquent and criminal behavior relating to the commercialization
of sexual vice.[40]

The American Social Hygiene Association is the principal voluntary
agency concerned with these related problems. The Association co-

operates with Federal, State, and local agencies and supplements their efforts toward eradicating prostitution and venereal disease. During World War II, as noted above, the Association became the central clearinghouse for information on the extent of prostitution and the trends in its suppression. Information obtained by the fieldworkers of the Association is published in *The Journal of Social Hygiene* and constitutes the most authoritative material available to the general public. The Association brings its findings to the attention of interested and influential persons and thus influences and directs public opinion. Because of these and many other functions, the Association is the most important voluntary agency in the discovery, treatment, and prevention of prostitution and venereal disease.[41]

In the decrease in prostitution in the continental United States demonstrated above, we have another striking evidence of the differential effect of World War II upon social problems. Change in this particular situation largely resulted from the danger presented by prostitution to the health of the armed forces. This danger introduced a new social element into a problem which has traditionally involved definitions of morality and social welfare, considerations important in themselves but nevertheless not ordinarily powerful enough to bring about the eradication of prostitution. War introduced a new element of social control, which was limited to the duration of the conflict but which nevertheless functioned with unusual efficiency during our active participation therein. In this instance, instead of intensifying a former social problem, World War II had precisely the opposite effect, albeit a strictly temporary one. A further modification in our hypothesis will be in order when we come to the end of the road.

CHAPTER SEVEN

WAR AND DELINQUENCY

The Nature of Delinquency

During the course of World War II, the general public continually professed concern about the prevalence of juvenile delinquency. In the midst of a war to preserve the dignity of the common man—and by implication the common child—it was considered particularly unfortunate that large numbers of young people on the home front were engaging in conduct believed deleterious both to themselves and the community. This situation was a threat to certain fundamental values of the democratic heritage, which presupposes that the youth of the nation will have an equal opportunity for development to productive manhood and womanhood. A large and apparently increasing number of boys and girls were obviously not receiving this opportunity during World War II. It was generally agreed that something must be done about this situation, which threatened many of the reasons for which the war was being fought. Only by collective action could this situation be eliminated, or at least mitigated. In other words, delinquency in World War II was a social problem.[1]

It may come as a surprise to many persons, therefore, that juvenile delinquency was not exclusively or even largely the product of total war. For many years prior to this crisis, approximately a quarter of a million young people under 18 had annually come into formal contact with the law, and thousands of others had received "informal" treatment from various public and private agencies. Hundreds of thousands of married women with young children took wartime employment in war plants and service industries, but other hundreds of thousands of working mothers, with similar responsibilities, had been leaving their infants and adolescent children for many years before World War II. The adolescent girls who cast themselves into the arms of the armed forces brought forth many horrified expressions of disapproval during the years of the great mobilization. These same righteous people were comfortably unaware that in any peacetime year other thousands of young girls take similar action for hire or not for hire. The children in congested war production areas forced to play in the streets were equaled in peacetime by those in under-privileged areas who sought the streets, the pool halls, the dance halls, and the vacant lots for want of a better place. In short, delinquency did not spring full-blown from the dislocations of total war, but was all too familiar to some people long before World War II.

Like many other perennial problems, juvenile delinquency was either accelerated by World War II, brought suddenly to public attention, or both. The majority of social problems previously considered fall in one or both of these wartime categories; others like adult crime and family separation were more drastically modified by the war. Many situations defined as social problems were changed from the concern of the private citizen or social welfare worker to that of the nation as a whole. The storm and stress of adolescence, the sex behavior of the promiscuous girl with venereal disease, the family whose extreme mobility makes them inefficient workers, the inadequate housing and other utilities in congested production areas, the working mother with small children, and finally the boy or girl whose truancy, larceny, or promiscuity bring them into contact with the law—these problems were present in peacetime but did not come to the public attention.

Juvenile delinquency is a social problem no matter what the state of the nation; nevertheless, delinquency became a more serious problem during World War II because the matter was brought for the first time to the attention of many people. World War II accentuated the rate of change in an already dynamic society, thereby aggravating many social problems. The war also brought to public attention certain chronic conditions of whose scope and even existence many people had hitherto been only vaguely aware. Juvenile delinquency was one of these conditions. In this connection, therefore, the role of war was that suggested in the initial hypothesis—namely, one of intensifying former social problems without fundamentally modifying their nature.

Social behavior is not inherently delinquent, but is merely behavior which a particular society at a particular time defines as delinquent. As William I. Thomas has so eloquently pointed out, any behavior must be invested with moral flavor by the group before it can be adjudged good or bad, desirable or undesirable, delinquent or nondelinquent.[2] Social definitions undergo rapid change in a dynamic society, as witnessed by many of the modifications in social attitudes and values in the period between the two world wars. The change is even more rapid during the war itself, when situations formerly considered private concerns suddenly become grave matters of public policy. At the same time, actions normally evoking little interest from the majority of persons become emotionally involved with the national welfare.

This change in social definition complicates the analysis of wartime social trends, since it is sometimes difficult to discover whether a particular practice has actually increased during wartime (as indicated by the statistical evidence) or whether public attention has merely been directed toward behavior prevalent in peacetime but not then considered a social problem. When behavior is defined as socially undesirable, the agencies of social control attempt to eliminate or mitigate it; when no such definition exists, the agencies ignore the behavior and it does not appear in the formal records.[3]

The definition of juvenile delinquency is therefore highly elastic, depending upon the legal structure of different regions, urban areas, and local communities, as well as upon the social values of various groups in the local population. Broadly speaking, the juvenile delinquent is a young person (usually under 16 or 18) whose conduct is in some way opposed to existing laws, ordinances, or mores.[4] Delinquency is usually considered as involving conduct contrary to statute, although this is not necessarily so. Indeed, as the Children's Bureau points out: "Because in the juvenile-court laws delinquency is so loosely defined that it covers the whole gamut of undesirable behavior, many of the acts for which children are referred to juvenile courts are obviously of a very different character from what is usually considered lawbreaking. Reasons for referral may range from ungovernable behavior to assault; from using obscene language to stealing large sums of money; from hitching on street cars to unlawful entry; from riding a bicycle on the sidewalk to robbery."[5]

In his study of *Delinquency Control*, Professor L. J. Carr has pointed out the varying contexts in which the term "delinquent" is used and the variety of behavior to which it is applied. He indicates at least six possible meanings of the term and suggests a less ambiguous phrase for each.

1. *Juvenile deviants.* All children showing socially deviant behavior, whether or not the behavior is actually antisocial.

2. *Legal delinquents.* All deviants who in addition commit antisocial acts as defined under the law.

3. *Detected delinquents.* All antisocial deviants detected by the police or social agency in the commission of their acts.

4. *Agency delinquents.* All detected antisocial deviants who have been brought to the formal attention of the police, the school, or other agency dealing with delinquents.

5. *Alleged delinquents.* All apprehended antisocial deviants brought to the attention of a juvenile court where they become court cases and hence subject to statistical enumeration.

6. *Adjudged delinquents.* All court antisocial deviants whom the courts have adjudged to be legally delinquent. This group constitutes from 75 to 90 per cent of all alleged delinquents.[6]

It is clear that accurate information is not available on many of the possible forms of delinquent behavior so defined. When the phrase "juvenile delinquent" is used, the referent is usually a case disposed of by a juvenile court—in other words, an alleged delinquent. Trends in juvenile delinquency ordinarily refer to trends in the numbers of alleged delinquents coming to the attention of certain groups of courts throughout the country which report to the Children's Bureau. The exigencies of fact-finding confine the study of wartime (and peacetime) juvenile delinquency to two general sources: the publications of the Children's Bureau of the Department of Labor and the *Uniform Crime Reports* of the Federal Bureau of Investigation of the Department of Justice. The former agency publishes yearly statistics on cases of juvenile delinquency disposed of by representative groups of juvenile courts throughout the country. The latter agency publishes certain data compiled from fingerprint records of persons arrested throughout the country—broken down by age and sex, as well as by other categories—giving information on the numbers of young persons of different age groups arrested for violations of state laws and municipal ordinances. Data on disposals of the juvenile courts (i.e., alleged delinquents), however, are the most complete and hence comprise the standard criteria for determining the nature and extent of delinquency. The working definition of delinquency here employed, therefore, will be a case disposed of by the juvenile court and enumerated by the reporting courts.

War and Delinquency

The central question is whether the social changes attendant upon World War II brought about a net increase in the number of activities defined as delinquent, brought before the juvenile courts, and so disposed of. The answer to this question is an unqualified "yes." Delinquency involves social behavior and depends upon social definitions of that behavior. Any drastic change in the social structure—boom, depression, or war—affects the rate of delinquent behavior. The impact of World War II has been noted above, both in general terms and in various individual contexts. These modifications in the conduct of millions of individual men, women, and children present uniformities and hence constitute social trends.

It has been suggested that delinquency and crime "arise from an attempt on the part of the individual to satisfy one or a combination of his fundamental wants and needs; that an individual who does not acquire satisfactions through socially acceptable behavior, seeks and finds gratification of his needs through conduct which is against the established mores of the community."[7] These needs include emotional security, prestige, physical protection, and adventure, some of which may be encouraged by war and others thwarted by the same means. Therefore, "in any study of the effects of war on delinquency and crime we should consider how wartime conditions and situations influence the offender's attitudes and feelings about himself and others, and the way he responds to situations and circumstances which confront him."[8] The essence of the wartime change lies in the attitudes and values of millions of individuals whose behavior does not deviate from the social norms, as well as the thousands of individuals whose behavior does deviate sufficiently to become a social problem. With the data at our disposal, however, we can only infer the changes in attitude as we note the overt changes in behavior. World War II brought about many significant changes which can be measured either directly or indirectly. It also brought about many changes which cannot be measured.

The general nature of the wartime changes which produce delinquency is outlined by the Children's Bureau as follows: "In war as in revolutions, depressions, and other periods of social upheaval," the Bureau points out, "people's ordinary, everyday way of life is disrupted. Standards of behavior are confused and social controls

weakened. Social and moral values are shaken. . . . It is to be expected
that with such social disorganization would come personal disorganization. Children and adolescents, as well as adults, reflect in their behavior the disturbances of the times. They are restless and excited and
do not know where to turn their energies. . . . They seek an outlet for
their restlessness, for their urge to do important things. But their
outlets are often few and sometimes their restlessness leads them into
difficulties."[9] We have seen how this restlessness was communicated
into the emotional difficulties of children and adolescents. For the boys,
socially approved outlets were provided through war work and by
the ultimate certainty of service in the armed forces when they were
18. For the girls, no such certainty of participation was open and they
were forced to seek prestige, security, and adventure as best they
could. This is one, although not the only, reason why delinquency
among girls increased more rapidly than among boys during World
War II.

World War II increased the differential rate of social change, brought
about disparities between actual and desirable conduct, and thereby
produced or intensified social problems. Most of the factors resulting in
wartime juvenile delinquency were present in the social structure long
before our actual participation in hostilities. Disturbances of family
life, mobility of family groups, bad housing conditions, inadequate
recreational facilities, overcrowding of schools and the consequent high
rate of truancy—these and many other delinquency-producing factors
were apparent in the society of a peacetime America. World War II
added several changes of its own, such as the prolonged separation of
millions of family groups, but a great deal of the social disorganization arising from the wartime situation was similar to that of the
"normal" world.[10]

The existence of a large number of young persons in formal contact
with the agencies of social control thus did not originate with the
chaotic conditions of World War II. Information is available from
28 juvenile courts in areas serving 100,000 persons or more from 1929
until the outbreak of the war. From 1929 to 1938, the number of
cases disposed of by these courts fluctuated between 28,000 and 31,000,
depending upon the state of the business cycle. This was presumably
typical of the trends in large urban communities during this period.
For our purposes, the nature of these minor prewar fluctuations is
unimportant. The basic consideration is that a great deal of juvenile

delinquency, represented only partially by these 28 courts, was continually present during the piping times of peace. The total annual number of such youthful offenders coming to the attention of all official and unofficial agencies was estimated at 200,000. The number of adolescents whose cases were disposed of by the juvenile courts during the war increased considerably over the prewar figure. This prewar figure, however, was by no means a negligible one.[11]

Social Factors in Wartime Delinquency

The factors which combine to bring about juvenile delinquency are highly complex.[12] In the present discussion, we cannot consider these factors in all of their ramifications. The following does not purport to be a complete consideration of all the social elements causing delinquent behavior. The discussion merely attempts to show how some of the causal factors in juvenile delinquency underwent certain modifications during World War II that were partially responsible for the increases in delinquency over the war years. Dislocations took place in several segments of the population closely related to juvenile behavior. The distribution of the population through social mobility; the resultant congestion in certain war industrial areas; the dislocation of many institutional relationships of the local community, such as the home, the school, and recreational institutions—these are some of the social factors that underwent demonstrable changes during the war, with repercussions upon adolescents and adults alike.

1. *Dislocation of population.* World War II brought about a great dislocation of population through an intensification of social mobility. We have previously considered the already high rate of mobility during the period 1935–1940,[13] as well as the interim movement from April, 1940 to November, 1943.[14] The over-all movement of population from Pearl Harbor to March, 1945, as we have seen, involved a minimum of 27,500,000 persons (including the military) who changed their place of residence at least once during the war period.[15] Whatever the approximate number of individuals and families whose lives were dislocated during the war, there is no question that this movement formed the basis for much juvenile delinquency.

The adolescent participants in these wartime migrations could not maintain intimate contact with the institutions of the community which normally regulate their conduct. The family tended to be more unstable under the conditions of this large-scale mobility. The connection of the child with the school was more tenuous and truancy often resulted from the failure to adjust to a series of new school situations. Adequate recreational facilities were often unavailable in the congested production areas, while living conditions in the 400 or more defense areas scattered over the country were often completely unsatisfactory to the mobile population forced to live in them. Under these conditions, the Children's Bureau remarks, "The strain of such difficult family life hardly makes for healthful physical or emotional development of a child and may well lead to maladjustments that find expression in delinquency."[16]

2. *Dislocation of community relationships.* Closely allied to the physical dislocations of population attendant upon World War II was the abrupt change in the psychological relationships within the local community, particularly those adjacent to army installations or experiencing a boom from war industry. Studies of communities within 50 miles of army camps disclosed a variety of conditions directly attributable to the mobilization. Among these conditions were the tendency of young persons to take less interest in their schoolwork, especially the young girls who were subject to the attentions of the soldiers on leave; the tendency of many such young people to condone or accept new standards of behavior, particularly in the field of sex relations; an inordinate increase in the social activities of young girls of high school age who were "drafted" by local committees for dances and other entertainments; and finally the interchange of venereal disease between the youth of the local community and the military personnel, with uniformly unfortunate results.[17]

The effect of such modifications in the customary relationships of young persons was most clearly evident with the girls. Many of the problems of sexual promiscuity on a nonremunerative basis were the most obvious results of the changed community relationships. Increases in the rates of juvenile delinquency during the war years were more pronounced for girls than boys; the bulk of these increases for girls were directly or indirectly related to sex behavior. Although prostitution declined throughout the country under the combined efforts of the civilian and military agencies, in many communities near military installations sexual relations for hire increased. As pointed out above, the May Act was invoked in two such areas; the conditions which led to its invocation were also present in many other communities where they were treated as local, rather than federal, offenses. As

one high school superintendent remarked, with commendable under-
statement, "I must say that the near-by camp for more than 30,000
men has made this a very undesirable place in which to bring up boys
and girls."[18]

3. *Dislocation of economic relationships.* It is popularly believed
that delinquency varies inversely with the business cycle, with a low
rate in periods of prosperity when employment and incomes are high
and economic conditions are generally favorable. By the same reasoning, it is assumed that periods of depression and economic insecurity
have an unsettling effect upon children which results in an increase in
juvenile delinquency. Like many popular assumptions concerning
social problems, this is not correct; on the contrary, the available
evidence indicates that delinquency increases in prosperity and decreases in depression.[19]

We are concerned here with trends in delinquency during World
War II rather than with a detailed discussion of juvenile delinquency
as such; consequently, it need only be stated that certain social concomitants of prosperity apparently have an adverse effect upon juvenile
behavior. "At such times," it is pointed out, "the less stable elements
of the community have unusual opportunity and temptation for
dissipation and irresponsible conduct. Consumption of alcohol soars,
divorces increase, and commercialized recreation flourishes. Increased
employment of women and irregular working hours tend to take
parents from the home and interfere with supervision of the children.
All these factors lead to family disorganization and neglect of children
and multiply situations that tempt youth to engage in delinquent
behavior."[20]

The United States was the only nation in the world which was able
to fight a total war and enjoy an internal economic boom at the same
time. Beginning in 1940, the Federal Government began to appropriate
billions of dollars for rearmament. The heightened industrial activity
arising from the defense program was accelerated as we entered the
war and the national income rose to unprecedented heights. Unemployment fell to an irreducible minimum and industrial production
and business activity rose to the highest levels in history. This artificial
wartime boom solved a number of social problems, but not juvenile
delinquency. It is impossible to segregate the increased prosperity of
the war years from the other factors making up the complex which
brought about the rise of delinquency. Nevertheless, it is clear that

many of the socially disorganizing aspects of peacetime prosperity were present in wartime and, combined with other factors growing out of the total situation, brought about an increase in delinquent behavior.[21]

This hypothesis was examined in the State of Michigan, where some of the most spectacular social dislocations took place during the war. In 1939 there were 5,500 cases disposed of by the 83 juvenile courts in the state; in 1943 the number had grown to 7,750, an all-time high. Much of this increase was attributed to the expansion of manufacturing activity, the rise in per capita income, and other evidences of a high rate of economic prosperity. In summarizing the delinquency situation in this war-prosperous state, a sociologist stated that "No recourse to a possible 'wartime breakdown of moral standards' is necessary to explain the nearly 7,800 delinquents in 1943. Population growth and the rapid expansion of business activity and employment alone are sufficient to account for the 40 per cent increase since 1939. . . . The admonition to 'watch your wallet when in a crowd' apparently applies to the hustle and bustle of a fully employed industrial economy."[22] Prosperity is not enough; man does not live by bread alone.

4. *Dislocation of employment relationships.* Closely related to the wartime boom was the increased employment of young persons. Tempted by high wages and unprecedented employment opportunities, hundreds of thousands of adolescents quit school to go to work. As indicated above, the labor force as a whole during the four years ending in April, 1944 exceeded normal expectations by 6,700,000 persons; almost seven million extra persons were called into gainful employment by the consuming demand for wartime labor. This group was composed of housewives and mothers of all ages, some with young children and some without; men who came out of retirement for the emergency and those who would have retired but for the emergency; and boys and girls who would under normal conditions have been in grammar school, high school, or college. The largest group of these "extra" workers was composed of 2,800,000 boys and girls from 14–19 years of age;[23] when children of this age group came into contact with the law in any way, the offense was generally defined as juvenile delinquency.

For many adolescents, these employment opportunities offered not only participation in the war effort and a substantial addition to the

family budget, but also the ability to be largely or wholly self-supporting
at an unusually early age. The majority of these opportunities in
industry, trade, or agriculture were under conditions which were
perfectly conducive to normal adolescent development. Some opportunities, however, were not so desirable from this point of view, while
still others were definitely detrimental. Setting pins in bowling alleys
until the early morning hours was not the most salutary activity for
boys of 11 or 12 years of age, nor was employment as waitresses in
all-night restaurants and hostesses in taverns and dance halls the most
desirable activity for 14- and 15-year-old girls. The wartime freedom
of thousands of adolescents employed at different activities, many not
inherently undesirable, was often too heady for these inexperienced
young people. Delinquent behavior was frequently the result of this
freedom.[24]

5. *Dislocation of educational opportunities.* The increase in child
labor accompanying the war was accompanied by a substantial, although
not necessarily equal, loss in education. Figures from the United States
Office of Education indicate a decrease of approximately one million
pupils enrolled in the high schools between the school year 1940–41
and the school year 1943–44. Some of this decrease was due to enlistment or induction into the armed forces and some to the decrease in
the population of high school age. The largest element reflected the
hundreds of thousands of young persons who left school—often in
the middle of a term—to go to work. In spite of a back-to-school campaign carried on during the last years of the war, a large segment
of this group never returned to complete their education. In thus
curtailing the educational opportunities of hundreds of thousands of
young persons, World War II reversed a dual trend toward an increase
in education and a decrease in child labor apparent for some time. In
the two decades from 1919–20 to 1940–41, the number of young people
in the high schools of the nation increased by nearly 5,000,000 to the
grand total of 7,244,000 the year before Pearl Harbor. The number
of working minors 14 through 17 years of age decreased from two
and one-half million in 1920 to approximately one million in 1940.[25]

The war brought other disruptions in the school experience of large
numbers of children. The closing of the schools in England in the
early months of the war was accompanied by a sharp increase in the
delinquency rate, which was only partially adjusted when the schools
reopened. While this drastic step was unnecessary in the United States,

nevertheless the individual cases of educational interruption were considerable. Particularly in many of the congested production areas, existing school facilities were inadequate to meet the increased enrollment. All manner of makeshifts were necessary, with some schools running on double shifts, others with classes in lunch rooms, basements, and abandoned temporary buildings, and still others forced to deny admission to children of migratory families. Other wartime changes involved the doubling-up of classes and the overcrowding of rooms to meet the shortage of teachers who left their profession to accept more lucrative employment in the war industries. Finally, school terms were cut and the school day curtailed so that pupils could put in a full working day after school.[26]

While the specific relationship between this disruption of normal educational experience and juvenile delinquency cannot be exactly demonstrated, its role in the delinquency pattern is universally admitted. Regular school attendance is one of the norms of adolescent life; when those norms are interrupted or broken, the child is out of step with his contemporaries and subject to other behavior aberrations. When the disruption takes the form of truancy, the first step down the road to delinquency has often been taken, and the end is not yet in sight. Furthermore, many of the psychological elements in the individual child which bring about delinquency can often be mitigated or eliminated entirely by the proper school attention. Children often get into serious trouble during persistent and wilful absence from school—girls in sexual adventures and boys in depredations involving property or physical assault. For this reason, truancy has been called "the kindergarten of crime," as children who become delinquents and criminals start their misbehavior by playing truant. The social modifications attending World War II were responsible for much of this educational disruption, with consequent changes in juvenile behavior.[27]

6. *Dislocation of family life.* The central institution in the life of the child, whether delinquent or nondelinquent, is the family. We have previously indicated some of the changes in this central relationship that took place during World War II. The "causal" relationships between the war, the family, and juvenile delinquency are difficult to isolate; however, we are justified in assuming that some relationship did exist between the wartime modifications in the structure, functions, and relationships of the family and the increase in juvenile delinquency

during the same period. The family is the chief institution in which conduct is defined and meaning attached to behavior. When thousands of families are unable to function with customary efficiency in defining desirable conduct, an increase in undesirable conduct may be expected.

Commenting upon the wartime decrease in the efficiency of many families and the attendant increase in delinquent behavior, one specialist has stated that "If in terms of our experience with children we consider the factors contributing to a wartime increase in delinquency, I think beyond any doubt we should list first the disruption of homes by the war, the departure of fathers into the armed forces or into defense work in other communities, and probably even more important, the full-time employment of mothers."[28] World War II introduced widespread knowledge of a new social phenomenon—"latchkey children," "doorkey children," and "eight-hour orphans,"[29] whose names are self-explanatory. The war also saw hundreds of thousands of fathers leave their families by enlistment, induction, or industrial migration. These influences have been discussed briefly insofar as their effects upon the structure of the family were concerned. We may indicate the principal changes more directly pertinent to juvenile delinquency.

In February, 1944, there were approximately 6,700,000 married women aged 18–64 in the civilian labor force, as compared to 3,671,000 in 1940. Some 1,470,000 of this wartime working force had children under ten, as compared to 833,000 with similar responsibilities in 1940. An indeterminate but considerable number of the 5,230,000 without children under 10 in 1944 *did* have children between ten and 18. From the standpoint of wartime behavior, as contrasted with postwar behavior, the groups with teen-age children were even more important than those with younger children. The teen-agers in the war years swelled the ranks of the delinquents, rather than the younger children, whatever the ultimate fate of the latter might be. It would be revealing to know even the approximate number of mothers with adolescent children in the civilian labor force absent from the home from eight to twelve hours every day. The group must have been large, since the immediate physical needs of adolescent children are less than those of children under ten. No such disparity exists between the emotional needs of the two age groups. Hence many mothers, induced to enter the labor force because of the superficial self-sufficiency of their adolescent children, failed to provide the necessary psychic security and guidance at a time when the adolescent boy or girl needed them most.[30]

In relative terms, the percentage of the total population in the age and sex group represented by working mothers offers a significant insight into the changes in the wartime population. In 1940, the married women age 18–64 with children under ten in the civilian labor force represented 7.8 per cent of the total population in that age and sex group. In 1944, the percentage had risen to 12.1. The percentage without children under ten rose from 17.7 per cent of the married female population age 18–64 years in 1940 to 30.0 per cent in 1944, an increase significantly greater than among women with younger children. While the increase within this working group was undoubtedly greater among women with no children whatever, it is probable that those with adolescent (and potentially delinquent) children answered the call for wartime labor more frequently than those with children under ten.[31]

The disruption of the family took place because of the military service of the father, as well as the industrial service of the mother. Of the 1,470,000 working mothers with children under ten, 280,000 also had absent husbands in the armed forces in February, 1944. Almost three hundred thousand families were thus doubly broken, first through the absence of the mother during the day and secondly through the absence of the father for years on end. The number of families with young children and soldier fathers increased through 1944, as the draft bit deeper into the reservoir of young married men with children. Of the 5,230,000 working married women without young children, some 1,080,000 had husbands in the armed forces. A considerable number of the 1,080,000 husbands in this age group were also fathers of adolescent children and were unable to lend their moral support during the trying teen-age years. To function with maximum efficiency, the family needs a father as well as a mother. When this relationship was broken by the absence of both mother and father, delinquent or antisocial behavior was a grave possibility.[32]

The figure of a million absent fathers represents only those families in which the mother was working. It fails to include those families in which the mother carried on as before but where her efforts were handicapped by the absence of her husband. Statements by the Bureau of the Census and the Bureau of Labor Statistics for the early spring of 1944 estimated the total number of broken families at that time at approximately three million. This included those families with no children and those with children under ten, as well as those with teen-age children which are the object of special interest here.[33] Added to these millions of service-broken families were the hundreds of thousands temporarily broken by the migration of the father to centers of war industry for periods ranging from a few months to the duration.

"Certain groups of children," according to the Children's Bureau, "are particularly susceptible to juvenile delinquency. As a result of war conditions, more children are subjected to situations conducive to delinquency than in pre-war days. Furthermore, many children whose stability would be sufficient to withstand ordinary pressures are unable to adjust satisfactorily to the strains inherent in war conditions."[34] We have indicated some of the principal factors growing out of World War II which subjected children to conditions conducive to delinquency. The dislocation of population, the breakdown of community relationships, the modifications in economic relationships, the increase in child labor, the curtailment of educational opportunities, the dislocation of family life through the employment of mothers with children, and finally the drastic break in family continuity through the military service of hundreds of thousands of fathers— these were among the tangible social changes reflected in increased juvenile delinquency. We are now in a position to inquire more precisely into the nature and extent of these increases.

Indices of Juvenile Delinquency

Writers of Sunday supplements and other professional viewers-with-alarm would have us believe that a "wave" of juvenile delinquency swept the country during World War II and engulfed the majority of the male and female adolescent population. It is desirable at the outset to place this form of socially disapproved conduct in its proper statistical setting by stating that wartime (or peacetime) delinquency did not involve a majority or even a large minority of the children of the country. The best estimates are that, in peacetime, the number of alleged delinquents (i.e., all apprehended antisocial deviants brought to court) comprise approximately 1 per cent of the total population of the country aged ten to 16.[35] Even if the total number of alleged delinquents doubled during World War II (which it apparently did not) the proportion of the nation's children involved would have been no more than 2 per cent. This by no means minimizes the magnitude of the problem presented by the thousands of adolescents who *do* pass through the juvenile courts of the nation and the thousands more comprising the other groups of social deviants. The problem is large enough in its own right. There is no reason to exaggerate it.[36]

The principal source of information on wartime trends in juvenile delinquency is the Children's Bureau publication, *Juvenile-Court Statistics*. The year 1944 showed a slight decrease in the number of cases disposed of for the first time since the war began. Preliminary figures for 1945, however, showed an over-all increase of 5 per cent over 1944. This represented a 7 per cent increase in boys' cases and a 4 per cent decrease in girls' cases. These figures do not "measure" the total amount of juvenile delinquency in the country, if by measurement is understood an enumeration of all behavior in conflict with the law or the mores. They measure only the volume of business transacted by a group of juvenile courts which submit to the Children's Bureau periodic reports on the nature and volume of their work.

Between the actual commission of the delinquent act and the appearance of the boy or girl in the juvenile court (where the case becomes a matter of public record) a variety of statistical hurdles must be surmounted. The act must first be discovered and then reported to an agency or official; the delinquent must next be apprehended and the decision made whether to refer the case to a court or handle it privately; the facts must then be determined as to the correctness or propriety of the petition; the court must then decide whether to handle the case privately and off the record or publicly and on the record; and finally the pressure of public opinion must be considered as to whether or not a particular child shall be judged by the court. Individual decisions must be made by different persons all along the line, decisions arising from personalities, policies, and pressures which differ from court to court and from time to time within a single court. Hence any investigation based upon juvenile-court statistics must start from the initial premise that "What we compare is not the behavior of children but the recorded activities of courts dealing with children's cases."[37]

Juvenile-court statistics therefore do not record the total amount of delinquent behavior, however defined, present in the country or even that occurring in the communities covered by the reporting courts. Many legally delinquent children are not apprehended in the first place and, even if apprehended, are handled by the school, the police, or by various public or private agencies dealing with youth. The juvenile court is only one of a number of social agencies professionally interested in the service of youth. The degree to which cases disposed of by the various courts actually represent the total amount of delinquent behavior in a given community is the result of many fortuitous circumstances. The cases disposed of by the courts furthermore range in severity all the way from a child riding a bicycle on the sidewalk to one who commits burglery. The mere enumeration of the total number of cases disposed of by a given group of courts is therefore not necessarily conclusive proof that serious delinquency is increasing; such an increase may merely mean that the police have become increasingly aware of a particular type of behavior and are charging adolescents therewith before referring them to the courts.[38]

A final limitation on juvenile-court statistics in determining trends in wartime delinquency grows out of the nature of the tabulations themselves. One set of figures represents 255 courts serving certain specified areas for 1943 and 1944. Another tabulation comprises 199 courts in various sections of the country for the period 1939–1945. Another involves a group of 77 courts serving large urban areas for the years 1943 and 1944. Other wartime trends are derived from the number of cases disposed of by a group of 69 courts serving areas with a population of 100,000 or more for the years 1938 through 1944. Certain more intensive figures are available for a group of 399 courts that reported on individual cases for the year 1943. These final tabulations contain more specialized information on the social characteristics of wartime delinquents.

The numbers of delinquents involved in the various tabulations range from a total of 108,662 in 1945 for the 199 courts serving specified areas, through 75,063 for 1944 in 69 courts serving areas with populations of 100,000 or more, to 25,793 for 1942 in 26 courts reporting on individual cases. These tabulations are admittedly incomplete and furnish neither a comprehensive nor a consistent picture of the extent or the nature of juvenile delinquency during the war years. Nevertheless, they are the best available. In the following analysis, we shall use different compilations for different purposes, based upon the extent to which they lend themselves to each purpose. This practice is not entirely satisfactory, since the numbers of delinquents naturally vary on the basis of the number of courts reporting. Under the circumstances there is no other choice.[39]

Wartime Trends in Delinquency

In 1938 the total number of cases of juvenile delinquency disposed of by 56 courts serving areas with populations of 100,000 or more was 47,816. In 1939 the figure increased to 52,800, while 1940 saw a slight decrease to 50,700. In 1941 the total resumed its upward climb, with 55,064 cases recorded for that year. In 1942 the number increased to 59,316, while 1943 saw a tremendous jump to 78,692. Figures for 1944 showed a slight decrease to 76,058 but the upward trend was resumed in 1945, when preliminary figures showed a total of 79,748. The increase from 47,816 cases in 1938 to 79,748 in 1945 was 67 per cent for all cases. In the same period, the boys' cases increased by 65 per cent and girls' cases by 79 per cent, despite a temporary decrease in both cases in 1944 over 1943. While boys' cases represent more than four-fifths of the total number disposed of in any one year, the percentage of increase in girls' cases was an even more significant indication of the changes in juvenile behavior during World War II. The figure of 67 per cent over-all increase from the days of peace to the middle of the war does not include the total change throughout the country. Nevertheless, this figure represents the largest number of courts for which continuous information is available during the entire period of the crisis. Something was clearly happening during World War II to the behavior of a substantial segment of the adolescent population, of which these figures were merely an index.

The complete figures for the period from 1938 through 1945, with the breakdown for boys' and girls' cases, are as follows:

Table XIII

Number of Juvenile Delinquency Cases Disposed of by 56 Courts Serving Areas with Populations of 100,000 or More, 1938–45*

Year	Total Cases	Boys' Cases	Girls' Cases
1938	47,816	40,149	7,667
1939	52,800	44,981	7,819
1940	50,700	42,355	8,345
1941	55,064	45,474	9,590
1942	59,316	47,675	11,641
1943	78,692	63,972	14,720
1944	76,058	61,813	14,245
1945	79,748	66,047	13,701

* U. S. Department of Labor, Children's Bureau, *Juvenile-Court Statistics, 1945* (Preliminary Statement), Division of Statistical Research, (March 8, 1946).

These figures may be partially compared with those for 255 courts in various sections of the country reporting to the Children's Bureau for 1943 and 1944. A drop of 5 per cent in boys' cases was registered from 1943 to 1944, with a total of 86,097 in the former year and 81,602 in the latter. Girls' cases showed a similar decline, from 20,340 in 1943 to 19,349 in 1944. The total for the two years was 106,437 cases disposed of in 1943 and 100,951 in 1944, a decline of 5 per cent. Comparable data are not available for these 225 courts for the whole period of the emergency, but the declines in 1944 similar to those in the 56 courts considered above indicate a similarity of experience in the two samples.[40]

The Federal Bureau of Investigation compiles figures for each calendar year on the number of persons arrested. These figures are broken down by age groups, so that we have here another index to the general trends in juvenile delinquency during the war. A comparison of these data for 1941 and 1944 discloses the following trends:

Table XIV

A Comparison of Juvenile Arrests Compiled by the Federal Bureau of Investigation for 1941 and 1944*

Age	Males			Females		
			Percentage			Percentage
	1941	1944	Change	1941	1944	Change
Under 18	34,408	40,892	18.8	2,662	5,798	117.8
18–20	66,689	44,234	−33.7	7,013	16,838	140.1
Under 21	101,097	85,126	−15.8	9,675	22,636	134.0

* Federal Bureau of Investigation, *Uniform Crime Reports,* Vol. 25, no. 2, (January, 1945), p. 94.

A "moderate" decrease in 1944 over 1943 was indicated in the interim figures for juvenile arrests as compiled by the Federal Bureau of Investigation. In spite of this decrease, approximately duplicated in the Children's Bureau statistics enumerated above, the trends from Pearl Harbor to the wartime climacteric of the European invasion showed a spectacular increase. The Federal Bureau of Investigation commented upon these trends in juvenile behavior as follows: "The foregoing figures indicate quite clearly that we have an abnormally high level of juvenile delinquency, that the moderate reduction in 1944 is in effect a 'leveling off' of a previously sharply ascending crime curve, and that the main job of reducing delinquency still remains to be accomplished. Until the amount of delinquency on the part of youths is reduced at least to pre-war levels, we will continue to have a situation constituting a grave threat to the future strength of our Nation."[41]

Other data for the defense period and the early years of the war clarify other aspects of the delinquency problem. For example, the impact of the war upon a particular area was often marked by a substantial increase in population resulting from industrial migration. During the defense and initial war periods, the character of this migration was largely adult male, so that the increase in population of juvenile age was not proportionate to that of the population as a whole. In general, the areas which increased in population during the years 1940–43 were those with greater than average wartime activity, such as shipyards, aircraft factories, munitions plants, various other forms of heavy industry, and military establishments.[42]

An indication of the specific impact of World War II upon conditions leading to juvenile delinquency may be obtained by comparing the number of cases disposed of by the courts serving areas which *decreased* in population during the 1940–43 period with those which *increased* during the same period. The Children's Bureau reported that the number of cases disposed of by 82 courts serving areas of 100,000 or more increased by 51 per cent from 1940 to 1943. The population showed a net decrease in 43 of these areas and an increase in 39. The number of cases in the 39 areas which *increased* in population rose by 55 per cent; those in the 43 areas with a *decreased* population rose only 44 per cent. The congested production areas with their teeming population, inadequate housing, heavy employment of married women, overworked public officials, burgeoning commercialized recreation, insufficient provision for new public utilities, and large numbers of mobile individuals in or out of uniform experienced an inordinately rapid rate of wartime social change. This change presumably increased the social disorganization in these expanding communities. The 44 per cent increase in juvenile delinquency between 1940 and 1943 in the areas with *decreasing* population indicated, however, that social disorganization was not confined to the expanding communities. Such factors as the departures of men from home to enter war industry or the armed forces, the increased employment of married women, the employment of young persons under undesirable conditions, the shortage of trained social workers and recreational leaders, and the anxieties and emotional stresses of wartime were not peculiar to areas of increasing population. These factors were the wartime heritage of the entire country.[43]

Analysis of Wartime Delinquents

The Children's Bureau has collected data from 399 courts reporting on individual cases for 1943 on such matters as race, age, sex, and reason for reference to the court. This sample involved some 125,488 boys and girls and hence constituted a representative cross section of the wartime delinquent population.

1. *Sex of child.* In the years before the war, the "normal" ratio of boys' to girls' cases was approximately six to one. By 1943 it had dropped to approximately five to one, with 101,523 boys and 23,965 girls in the 125,488 cases disposed of by 399 courts. In other words, 81 per cent of the cases were boys' and 19 per cent were girls'. The explanations for this wartime increase in girls' cases have been considered above.[44] The principal reasons for reference of young girls to juvenile courts—in peace or war—are sex offenses, ungovernable behavior, and running away. The last two are generally euphemisms for sex offenses when the courts do not wish to enter a sex charge on the official records. The rise in girls' cases may therefore have been the result of two general factors: (a) an actual increase in the above offenses; or (b) an increased interest on the part of the local authorities in the sex behavior of young girls, causing the former to be more solicitous in their enforcement of existing statues. It is probable that both factors were operative and combined to bring about the disproportionate rise in girls' cases. The evidence suggests a rapid increase in sexual promiscuity not for hire, an offense which came to the attention of the juvenile courts especially in centers of war industry and military establishments.

The changing definition of the situation with respect to the conduct of girls merits added consideration in itself. Among the effects of the war was an augmented interest in the activities of young girls, particularly those whose activities took the form of increased sexual behavior. The juvenile court statistics are a reflection of that heightened interest. As the Children's Bureau points out, "The increasing proportion of referrals by the police, especially noticeable for girls' cases, suggests that part of the increase in juvenile delinquency as measured by court cases may be due to increased attention of the police to behavior which they have previously ignored."[45] Whether or not there was a direct relationship between the rise in the number of girls' cases disposed of by the courts and a rise in the number and severity of departures from the social norm cannot be directly ascertained. Statistics of juvenile court disposals are not only a measure of the incidence of a particular type of behavior but also a reflection of the changing community conception thereof.

An increased freedom of sex behavior was evident in the decades between the wars. Much of this behavior existed in the years immediately prior to Pearl Harbor but was partially ignored by the police. The social changes of World War II increased the opportunities for such behavior and in addition invested extramarital relationships with an aura of patriotism. At the same time, the interest of the military was aroused by danger to health and efficiency from such promiscuous activities. This interest was communicated to the local authorities who were galvanized into action on the level of law enforcement. In the desire to eradicate prostitution and limit promiscuity not for hire, the police probably arrested and brought into court many young girls who were formerly immune from interrogation concerning their sexual activities. Furthermore, many of the young girls caught in police roundups may have been innocent of any antisocial behavior and may merely have been present in a tavern, café, or roadhouse when the police descended upon the establishment and hailed all of its clients into court. Such cases may or may not have been dismissed upon submission of evidence. The point is that the case was entered upon the records of a reporting court and the number of alleged female delinquents was increased thereby.[46]

This consideration of the sex of juvenile delinquents shows that we are here measuring not only trends in adolescent behavior but also trends in social definition of that behavior. The genesis and relative importance of these social attitudes are impossible to estimate accurately. We can only indicate their existence and suggest their vital role in bringing about the statistics we are attempting to analyze. In this instance, it is probably fair to state that both the behavior itself (i.e., female delinquency) and its social definition (ultimately expressed in the number of cases disposed of by the juvenile courts) increased in number and intensity. But we cannot assign an accurate evaluation to each.

2. *Age of child.* No substantial change was evident in the age of the wartime delinquents, as compared with those of a peacetime decade. In 1943, 4 per cent of the children were under ten when referred to the court, 8 per cent between ten and 12, 17 per cent between 12 and 14, 37 per cent between 14 and 16, and 34 per cent over 16.[47] The 34 per cent were mostly more than 16 and less than 18, since comparatively few juvenile courts have jurisdiction over adolescents who have reached their 18th birthday. The youth of these delinquents is striking, when we consider the behavior to which many of them have become habituated by the time they are brought before the court.

3. *Race of child.* The number of cases of Negro children in 1943 was considerably lower than that of white children (74,439 white boys and 17,400 white girls, as compared to 16,667 Negro boys and 4,443 Negro girls).[48] In relation to the number of both races in the population, however, the Negro commitments were disproportionately high. Such a relationship between the racial rates of reference does not indicate any "inherent" propensity on the part of Negro children to delinquent conduct. It rather reflects the lower economic and social status of the Negro group as a whole. Furthermore, the police tend to arrest Negro children with less solicitude for their civil rights than they display toward the average white child of the same age and degree of suspicion. Underprivileged economically and socially, the Negro race contributes more than its share to the group charged with delinquent behavior.

Negro children, particularly girls, are often referred to the courts on comparatively minor charges and for vague and arbitrary reasons. A considerably larger proportion of Negro girls than white girls have their cases dismissed, adjusted, or held open without further action, especially for such offenses as ungovernable behavior or running away. In many communities, the facilities for housing, detaining, or rehabilitating Negro girls are not as well organized as those for white girls and the court has no recourse but to dismiss the less serious charges among the Negro girls. The high percentage of dismissals for Negro girls would also indicate, in the words of the Children's Bureau, that "Negro girls are referred to court far more frequently than white girls in cases for which there is less evidence of serious misbehavior."[49] The Bureau concludes by suggesting that "The high proportion of cases so disposed of, among both girls and boys whose cases were referred for acts of carelessness or mischief, suggests that in many of these cases there may have been no need in the first place for reference to court."[50]

4. *Reasons for reference.* The largest group of boys referred to the 399 courts in 1943 allegedly committed acts of *stealing*. Forty-two per cent were so charged, a proportion approximating that of the prewar years. This offense was of comparatively minor importance among girls, with 11 per cent so charged in 1943. Acts of *carelessness or mischief* were next in importance among boys' cases in 1943, with 20 per cent in that group. Such charges accounted for only 6 per cent of the girls' cases. *Ungovernable behavior* and *running away*, both closely related to sex offenses in causation as well as official definition, were the chief reasons for reference of girls in 1943. These two reasons, plus the more specifically stated *sex offenses*, comprised 61 per cent of the girls' cases; for the boys, only 11 per cent were referred for ungovernable behavior and running away. Most boys commit acts against property and in related fields; most girls commit acts against the sex mores which are defined as detrimental to social welfare. This centralization of delinquent behavior about property and sex obtained in peace as well as war.[51]

The character of the adolescent population in the juvenile courts during World War II was in general similar to that during peacetime. The striking exception was the increased proportion of girls' cases during the war. The over-all figures for boys and girls increased considerably in the years from 1938-1945, with an increase of 65 per cent in the former and 79 per cent in the latter cases disposed of by 56 courts serving areas with populations of 100,000 or more. The compilations from all groups of courts showed marked increases during the war. The interpretation of these increases is more complicated. The courts were busier during the war, but it is not clear to what extent this activity reflected actual changes in adolescent behavior and to what extent changes in the definition of this behavior. Social problems rest upon social values. When the values change, the problems follow suit. Such changes were clearly evident in World War II.

CHAPTER EIGHT

WAR AND CRIME

The Nature of Crime

A criminal is one who is guilty of a criminal offense. This somewhat tautological definition is the only one that can be strictly applied to criminal behavior. "In modern civilized society," in other words, "a crime is an act forbidden by law which may be punished by death or by fine or by imprisonment in jail, workhouse, reformatory, or prison."[1] The action construed as a crime must generally be accompanied by a culpable intent to commit it, although in certain instances the mere commission of the act is sufficient. Crime thus involves a social relationship within which a particular act takes place, plus a social definition of that act. The social definition gives meaning to the activity, rather than implying any intrinsic significance in the activity itself. Although such offenses as murder, rape, robbery, and treason are ordinarily defined as crimes no matter what the social context, many other offenses are dependent for definition upon the society in which they occur. Furthermore, social definitions change and an action considered criminal at one time, such as profaning the Sabbath, is not so defined by a later generation. In certain countries, criticism of the government is considered an admirable indication of freedom of speech, while in others it is looked upon as detrimental to the general welfare and punished accordingly.[2]

Crime is a clear example of a social problem, since it involves both overt behavior and a value judgment. In addition, society has evolved certain reprisals directed at the criminal, both for the sake of punishing him and of protecting itself against further transgressions. The fundamental values upon which our society is based—respect for life, property, and individual freedom in approximately that order—are endangered by criminal behavior, although the danger may range in severity from minor theft to murder. Steps are taken to keep the individual from endangering these social values and to punish him if he persists in doing so. An understanding of the nature of these values and the appropriate social action to safeguard them is relatively clearer in the case of crime than in certain other forms of activity considered as social problems.

Many problems involving family change and disorganization, adolescent storm and stress, unconventional sex behavior, and even juvenile delinquency are not fully crystallized as social problems. Some persons, for example, consider a high divorce rate to be a social problem, while others consider it a refreshing indication of increasing individual freedom. Premarital sex behavior is condemned by persons who adhere to the conventional moral judgments, while others at least condone such behavior if not actively encourage it. In the matter of crime, however, at least for the more conventional varieties, no such disparity of definition exists. The majority of citizens are sure of what constitutes criminal behavior and are united in its punishment.

Crime is therefore easier to define than family tensions, sexual irregularity, or even juvenile delinquency. Police, judges, probation officers, statisticians, and members of the general public are reasonably certain what they are talking about when they speak of crime. For this reason, the available information on criminal behavior during World War II is considerably more detailed and accurate than is the case with many other social problems. Much still remains to be done in the matter of criminal statistics, but for all practical purposes it is possible to determine the trends in crime with reasonable accuracy. Compared to the available knowledge on family separations, sexual promiscuity, and juvenile delinquency, the existing information on criminal trends constitutes a model of clarity. Hence it is possible— anticipating our analysis for a moment—to say that in general criminal conduct decreased during World War II, a statement impossible to make with the same certainty concerning many forms of related behavior. The dividing line between crime and not-crime is, with the exception of certain "white-collar" crimes,[3] more clearly drawn than is the case with many other social problems.

Within the general framework of criminal conduct, our society classifies persons as criminals and misdemeanants, based upon the type of offense they have committed. Such a classification is often less revealing than at first appears; a person who habitually commits dangerous felonies may be convicted of a misdemeanor and superficially considered less dangerous than a law-abiding person who commits a single felony and is convicted for it. The distinction between a criminal and a misdemeanant is an arbitrary one in borderline cases. In general, the former is one who is "guilty of the more serious offenses punishable by death or by imprisonment in a state or federal penitentiary," while the latter is "one who has committed a petty offense which is punishable by fine or by imprisonment in a local jail."[4] There is virtual unanimity between the several states on the classification of such serious offenses as murder and robbery with a gun as felonies and the violation of minor traffic ordinances as misdemeanors. A considerable sector of antisocial behavior, on the other hand, is defined as a felony in one state and a misdemeanor in another, a situation which renders certain statistical comparisons somewhat suspect. The states do not make such comparisons any easier by occasionally deciding that an erstwhile misdemeanor is now a felony or that a third or fourth misdemeanor automatically becomes felonious. For purposes of the present discussion, however, the existing definitions and compilations are sufficiently clear to indicate the general wartime trends in criminal behavior.

In accordance with the plan followed with reasonable assiduity throughout this discussion, emphasis will be placed upon civilian, as compared to military, crime. This is done for two reasons: *first,* the nature of civilian crime is generally understood and defined as a social problem, while crimes committed by the military are often of a special category and subject to military exigencies; *second,* data are available on civilian crimes from the conventional sources, whereas information on military crimes, committed both in the continental United States and elsewhere, is not so readily available. This situation has an obvious effect upon the population from which civilian criminals are drawn and hence in the comparative rate of civilian crime. With twelve million men in the armed forces, a considerable minority drawn from the age groups habitually contributing the largest number of peacetime criminals, the remaining population was hardly representative of ordinary times. This change in the composition of the wartime civilian population is an important consideration in determining criminal trends.

War and Crime

In the concluding remarks of his study on *War and Crime,* based largely upon World War I, Dr. Hermann Mannheim suggests that war may be a substitute for crime, particularly those crimes involving physical violence: "War and crime may, in some ways, be subject to the principle of indestructibility of matter: if either evil be discouraged in one form it may show itself in the other."[5] Such manifestations of individual violence as murder, manslaughter, or rape may be largely supplanted in time of war by the infinitely greater murders, manslaughters, and rapes conducted under the comforting cloak of war. If war were ever eliminated as the institutionalized outlet for the sadistic impulses of mankind, he maintains, one of the results might be an increase in the individualized crimes of violence among the civilian population.

This generalization was based on past wars and could not anticipate the trends of World War II. Mannheim confines his hypothesis to serious crimes of violence and indicates that crimes of an economic nature show a tendency to thrive both during and after national struggles. The actual situation in World War II in the United States was, however, too complicated to allow such a facile explanation. The number of cases of criminal homicide (murder and negligent manslaughter) known to the police showed a slight decline in 1944 as compared to the prewar average 1939–1941. Cases of rape showed an appreciable increase as military and industrial mobility stirred the tremendous cauldron of America. Robbery showed a slight decrease through 1944 over the period 1939-41, while burglary showed a considerable decline. Larceny declined considerably during the war years, whereas auto theft (partially reflecting the scarcity of automobiles) increased sharply after the manufacture of automobiles was suspended.[6] These general trends in offenses known to the police will be considered in more detail below; the point here is that criminal behavior is so varied that sweeping generalizations on the criminogenic role of war are difficult to sustain in the face of the facts. Although corresponding in some respects to previous wars in its impact upon civilian society, World War II was also a unique phenomenon, with many unique characteristics.

The effect of World War II upon the criminality of the United States involves a further refinement of our definition of war. In a research memorandum on *War and Crime*, a leading criminologist states that in this connection war "means simply that a social change is suddenly initiated which creates either immediate and great, or small and progressive, changes in the lives of persons living in the nation at war. . . . In other words," he continues, "war should be looked upon merely as the occasion which permits us to observe what happens to the conduct norms of persons subjected to strains and stresses, sudden or protracted, called into being or intensified by a social cataclysm."[7] This viewpoint is in accord with the theoretical framework of the present study, namely, the observation of social problems as intensified or modified by wartime social changes. As a result of this conflict, a large minority of the population found themselves doing entirely different things than they had previously done, while the majority experienced some more or less drastic series of changes in their lives. The central question is whether or not these changes increased the criminality of the American nation.

The problem may be approached in terms of a very simple alternative: either criminal behavior increased or it did not. A third possibility is of course that some criminal behavior increased while other behavior did not. The last hypothesis would indicate that war involves certain elements encouraging criminal behavior and certain elements discouraging it. The two general causal sequences have been summarized as follows:[8]

War increases criminal behavior because:

1. The general pattern of war, with its ruthlessness, violence, and disorderliness, closely resembles certain types of crimes and the individual soldier is thus brought into contact with criminal or quasi-criminal patterns of behavior.
2. The mobility of war brings many persons into contact with the social patterns of crime, with which they might otherwise have remained unfamiliar.
3. The physical removal of members of the family from the home, either into the armed forces or the factory, tends to decrease the frequency and intimacy of their association with anticriminal patterns.
4. The increased concentration of community leaders, welfare officers, school teachers, recreational agents, and similar groups in activities related to the war further decreases the frequency and efficiency of community contacts with anticriminal patterns.
5. The disorganization of social life breaks down the accustomed habits of millions of persons and makes them think and act by trial and error, thus increasing the possibility of criminal behavior.

6. War brings about individual tension, worry, and fear, which may predispose the individual to criminal behavior.
7. The uncertainty of wartime life, ranging in degree from that of the front-line soldier to the civilian with no close relatives in the armed forces, tends to weaken the social control arising from the necessity of planning for the future and adapting to such plans. In time of war, the future becomes highly uncertain and many individuals tend to be controlled by immediate impulses and satisfactions which may dispose them to criminal conduct.

War decreases criminal behavior because:[9]

1. The age groups contributing the greatest number of criminals are withdrawn from the civilian population and incorporated into the military.
2. Military service may change the direction of individual aggression from members of one's own national group to external national groups. This hypothesis is somewhat similar to that of Mannheim, in which he surmises that war is a substitute for crimes of violence.
3. Military service may serve as a reformatory agent for the young men who otherwise might commit crimes following their period of service. The allegedly therapeutic effects of military discipline are examples of this point of view.
4. The agencies of social control in the local community so increase their efforts during wartime that behavior which might otherwise become criminal is directed into noncriminal channels.

Some of these hypotheses were verified by the facts and others were not. Criminal behavior is not an entity in itself, standing in a simple cause-and-effect relationship to a given set of social facts. The distinction between crimes against the person and crimes against property is the most obvious case in point. Combinations of social circumstances "causing" one type of behavior do not necessarily have a similar effect upon another type. Wartime increases in crimes against the person, such as rape, involve an entirely different set of social factors from an offense against property, such as larceny. A considerable proportion of the increase in juvenile delinquency was apparently an outgrowth of industrial activity and general wartime prosperity. On the other hand, larceny (defined as including thefts of bicycles, automobile accessories, shoplifting, pocket-picking, or any stealing of property or article of value which is not taken by force and violence or by fraud) decreased considerably over the war years. The civilian age group habitually engaging in larceny was depleted by Selective Service, whereas the group committing juvenile delinquencies was not yet subject to military service. The behavior roughly defined as criminal is extremely involved, and different series of social facts bring about different types of such behavior. The question whether or not "war causes crime" thus becomes impossible to answer categorically.

Other and more general theories of the relationship between war and crime were evolved after World War I. Our interest is primarily in World War II and furthermore general theories of war and crime seem somewhat inappropriate in the face of the facts.[10] Another theory which accounts for the actual wartime variations in criminal behavior is advanced by Sutherland and called the theory of "differential group organization." He suggests that a conviction rate for any type of crime is a product of two variables—the actual criminal behavior and social reactions to it—and each of these is in turn the expression of changes in group organization. These two aspects of organization are called "differential group organization." "The balance between the opposed organizations," he continues, "determines whether the crimes committed, the reactions against crimes, and the conviction rates increase or decrease."[11] The organization against certain types of behavior (prostitution, for example) increased during World War II, with the result that prostitution underwent a considerable decline. Similarly, the decrease in robbery may have resulted from the increased organization against robbery (in addition to the absence of many potential robbers in the armed forces). Organization against auto theft may have decreased and the number of thefts showed a corresponding increase (in addition to the greater value of automobiles after their manufacture was completely suspended).

This orientation of "differential group organization" is in full accord with the theory of social problems followed throughout this discussion. The rate of criminal convictions, like the incidence of any social problem, is a function of behavior *defined* as criminal and the organizations evolved to meet it. War may bring about changes in either or both of these variables, with the result that "crime" increases or decreases at a differential rate. Evidence appeared during World War II of significant changes in social definitions (toward behavior involving promiscuity for hire) as well as the mechanisms established to meet the threat to social values posed by the new definition (increased police attention given to activities culminating in venereal disease). The social definitions of and organization against sexual promiscuity *not for hire*, on the other hand, were weakened under the combined force of patriotic sentiments and social mobility.

These changing definitions and practices and the "differential group organization" resulting therefrom make the interpretation of even the most prosaic statistics on wartime crime a difficult task. Sutherland has posed the general problem as follows: "First, do convictions for crimes in general, for the several types of crimes and for the several classes of the population, increase or decrease in wartime? Second, what do the statistics of conviction mean in terms of the behavior of people? Third, what specific or abstract elements in wars produce the changes in criminal behavior and in convictions?"[12] The first question can be answered with reasonable certainty, allowing for the admitted inadequacy of criminal statistics. The second can be answered only approximately by segregating the complex group of factors operative in wartime criminal behavior. The third has already been answered in that no satisfactory hypothesis has been evolved to explain over-all changes in all of the various forms of criminal behavior.

Social Factors in Wartime Crime

World War II accelerated certain aspects of social disorganization already present in a dynamic peacetime society. Many of these social factors have been considered above and it is not necessary to repeat the analysis here. Peacetime personal disorganization was intensified by the tensions of war to such a degree that, with other things equal, a considerable increase in wartime crime might presumably have been expected. Other things were not, however, equal in a conflict which saw more than twelve million young men and women in the armed forces. If, by some monstrous sleight-of-hand, wartime conditions had been accompanied by the presence of these millions of young men in the civilian population, crime convictions might have equaled or surpassed juvenile delinquency in their upward spiral. The summary removal of these young men from the jurisdiction of the criminal courts so altered the situation that an accurate comparison between war and non-war is out of the question. A per capita analysis of the crime rate based upon the number and age groupings of the civilian population before and during the war would be most revealing. Such data, unfortunately, are not available.

In addition to the general elements of social disorganization, whether in the war or peace, there are certain more specific factors which may affect the amount of crime in a community or a nation. These social factors are offered by the Federal Bureau of Investigation in substantiation of the statement that crime is more than a matter of criminals and police officers. Crime is rather a "charge against the entire community,"—or an entire nation. The suggested factors are as follows:

1. "Population of the city and metropolitan area adjacent thereto.
2. "The composition of the population with reference particularly to age, sex, and race.
3. "The economic status and activities of the population.
4. "Climate.
5. "Educational, recreational, and religious facilities.
6. "The number of police employees per unit of population.
7. "The standards governing appointments to the police force.
8. "The policies of the prosecuting officials and the courts.
9. "The attitude of the public toward law-enforcement problems.
10. "The degree of efficiency of the local law-enforcement agency."[13]

The war brought about significant changes in many of these criteria, from population to police, from economic status to attitudes toward law enforcement. Each of these changes presumably had some bearing upon the degree, severity, and apprehension of criminal behavior both within a particular community and on a nationwide scale. The complexity of these factors indicates the impossibility of a unitary explanation of crime or of a simple explanation of the changes in criminal behavior during World War II. The crime rate of a given country in peacetime is a reflection of its entire culture; in wartime the same is true, with the added complication that the culture is undergoing a rapid change as a result of the war. Change must therefore be explained in terms of itself, a difficult problem under laboratory conditions and an impossible one under social conditions. The explanations of this behavior and such fragmentary data as are available are thus offered with reservations.

A further proviso on the relationship between war and crime is suggested by Walter C. Reckless. He calls this the theory of intervening agencies and holds that "we should look for the effects of war . . . to be strained through intervening changes in conditions, regulations, and policies, and we should not expect war to have a predetermined or a direct effect on criminal and delinquent behavior."[14] Although the influence of these intervening changes is not always readily apparent during a war, he concludes that "it is reasonably safe to assume that they are operating and to withhold contentions that war bears a direct causative relationship to criminal behavior."[15] This is tantamount to saying that war sets in motion changes in a wide variety of institutional relationships and patterns of behavior, which may or may not find ultimate reflection in criminal behavior.

Additional light is thrown upon the wartime problem of crime by the experience of World War I. The best available figures come from England, Germany, and Austria, although some evidence is available from other countries, including the United States. The general situation during the period 1914—1918 may be summarized as follows, with the proviso that certain nations exhibited wide variation from the general pattern:[16]

1. With but one exception, all the countries showed a decline in the absolute number of convictions.
2. All countries showed a decline in the number of convictions of men.
3. Convictions of women and juveniles increased.
4. Convictions for sex offenses and other offenses against the person declined.
5. Convictions for theft and other offenses against property increased.
6. Convictions for "minor crimes" varied more than crimes defined as more serious.
7. The postwar period was almost universally characterized by an increase in crime, with particular emphasis upon crimes against property.
8. Recidivism decreased in Germany and Austria, with a steady decline of persons previously convicted evident during the war.
9. Violations of special war laws (e.g., black market operations) increased considerably, but were handled by special administrative boards rather than by the criminal courts.
10. The special form of white-collar crime known as profiteering increased tremendously, particularly in the United States.

This general experience is revealing as an index to the social conditions pertaining during the first World War, which approached but did not reach the totalitarian character of the second. Much of the summarized behavior applied to the two defeated members of the Central Powers—Germany and Austria. Hence it was not fully typical of victorious France and England and certainly not of the United

States. The impact of war upon the civilian population was greater in Europe than America during World War I and infinitely greater during World War II. The effect of war upon the "intervening agencies" in the two hemispheres was widely different and hence the changes in the lives of the civilian population were neither so drastic nor so devastating in the United States. However interesting such excursions may be into other wars and other countries, however, the central task before us here is to cultivate our own garden.

Indices of Crime

The best indices to crime in the United States are the crimes known to the police and the reports on prisoners in state and federal prisons and reformatories.[17] Crimes known to the police are assembled and published by the Federal Bureau of Investigation in their *Uniform Crime Reports*.[18] The Bureau of the Census publishes an annual analysis of *Prisoners in State and Federal Prisons and Reformatories* showing the movement of population in and out of these institutions.[19] For our purposes, trends in crimes known to the police offer the best available index to wartime criminal conditions. Data on these trends are maintained more currently than the other indices, since this information is easier to report than the institutional population. At the time of writing, information on crimes known to the police was available through the first half of 1945, while information on prisoners was available (in preliminary form) through 1944.

Offenses known to the police include several of the principal crimes within the jurisdiction of the local force, concerning which information is available from reports of police officers, citizens, prosecuting or court officials, or any other official or unofficial source. These offenses include the following classes of crimes generally found to be most completely reported to the police: "Criminal homicide, including (a) murder, nonnegligent manslaughter, and (b) manslaughter by negligence; rape; robbery, aggravated assault; burglary—breaking or entering; larceny—theft; and auto theft."[20] In addition to the crimes actually carried out, the figures include attempted crimes. This total is thus a more complete indication of the amount of criminal behavior within a particular community or throughout the country than any enumeration of cleared cases or even arrests. Complaints which upon investigation by the police proved to be without foundation are not included in the tabulations.

During the calendar year 1944 (the last full year of American participation in World War II), information was available for some 1,078 towns and cities of 10,000 population or over, with a total population of 62,726,936, plus 2,085 cities, villages, and rural townships with a total aggregate population of 10,385,121. The most complete data were available for a group of 318 cities of 25,000 population or over with a total population of 45,062,198; the bulk of the generalizations on wartime criminal trends will be based upon this sizeable sample of the American population. The size and completeness of the sample means that the *Uniform Crime Reports* offer perhaps the most complete index available of any of the major social problems considered in this study.[21]

Certain serious offenses are not included in the "offenses known to the police" and hence are not known with the same finality. Among the crimes not uniformly known to the police are "embezzlement, fraud, forgery, counterfeiting, arson, receiving stolen property, drug violations, and carrying concealed weapons."[22] Other offenses not in the official statistics are desertion and nonsupport, vagrancy and disorderly conduct, public drunkenness, gambling, and driving while intoxicated. Some information does exist on many of these offenses, however, in the form of figures for arrests compiled by the Federal Bureau of Investigation from fingerprint cards submitted by local police departments. We shall consider first the more authoritative trends in crimes known to the police and then some of the less serious crimes on which information exists in the form of arrests.

The *Uniform Crime Reports* throw some definite light upon the criminal character of the American people. During the calendar year 1944, the total number of major crimes committed in the United States was estimated at 1,393,655. This figure breaks down as follows: murder and nonnegligent manslaughter, 6,552; manslaughter by negligence, 3,783; rape, 10,915; robbery, 43,804; aggravated assault, 54,841; burglary, 274,134; larceny, 796,590; and auto theft, 203,036. These estimates were derived from monthly reports from 2,100 cities representing an aggregate population of more than 65,000,000 persons. "With the passing of each hour during 1944," says the Federal Bureau of Investigation, "more than 158 serious crimes were reported to local police authorities in the United States. Each day on the average brought 28 felonious killings, 30 rapes, 150 aggravated assaults, and left 120 persons robbed, 555 with their automobiles stolen, and the homes or business places of 749 others burglarized. In addition, 2,176 larcenies occurred during the average day. . . ."[23] These totals represented a selective change from an average prewar day, with increases in some categories and decreases in others.

A further proviso on using the data from the *Uniform Crime Reports* as an index to wartime criminal behavior lies in the modifications in definition of behavior that accompany a war. The theft of a tire, for example, in the lush days of peacetime might be a simple misdemeanor but in the midst of wartime rationing might become a felony. Other offenses might be overlooked in peacetime and stressed in wartime or vice versa, and the statistical total would be increased or decreased without any corresponding change in behavior. The enumerations of the *Uniform Crime Reports* thus reflect changes in social attitudes, since certain forms of behavior may be reported in one period and not in another. The law-enforcement process, ranging from the initial report of the alleged offense to the final sentence or liberation, reflects the changes in social attitude.[24]

Finally, the *Uniform Crime Reports* make no attempt to measure special wartime crimes—acts specifically defined as crimes by wartime legislation which would not normally be so considered. Violations of the Selective Service Act, the Alien Registration Act, the Foreign Agents Registration Act; acts of espionage, sabotage, and sedition; and denaturalization proceedings against naturalized citizens for membership in un-American organizations are examples of such behavior. These threats to internal security were met with all the legal resources of the Department of Justice, which is the agency specifically concerned with such problems.[25] Prosecutions for these offenses were relatively few in number and do not come within the strict purview of the present discussion. Certain wartime crimes, particularly those involving black market operations, may have been carried on by the criminal or quasi-criminal groups who normally would be engaged in more conventional criminal activities. Such behavior may merely represent the transfer of activity away from the traditional offenses, particularly those against property, toward activities which offer immediate return in wartime.[26]

Wartime Trends in Crime

We are now ready to consider the wartime trends in offenses known to the police. The following data are taken from the *Uniform Crime*

Reports and cover the offenses reported in 318 cities over 25,000 population, with a total population of 45,062,198 people. In each case, the average figures for the prewar years 1939-41 are compared with those for the wartime years 1942-44. These figures are supplemented in a footnote by percentage changes for the first six months of 1945, which for all practical purposes marked the end of our participation in World War II. The six month percentage changes for 1945 represent a different sample of the population than the totals for the years 1942-44, but the general trend is indicated by the percentage increases in most crimes during the six months immediately preceding the surrender of Japan.

1. *Criminal homicide (murder and nonnegligent manslaughter).* —This crime is defined[27] as including "all wilful felonious homicides as distinguished from deaths caused by negligence."[28] Trends for this offense were as follows:

Table XV

Trends in Criminal Homicide (1) 1939–1944*
(Murder and Nonnegligent Manslaughter)

Year	Number of Offenses
Average 1939–41	2,632
1942	2,673
1943	2,345
1944	2,434

* Reports from 392 cities for the first six months of 1945 indicated an increase of 4.3 per cent in murder and nonnegligent manslaughter over the first six months of 1944. *Uniform Crime Reports,* Volume 16, *loc. cit.,* p. 7.

The 1944 figures for murder and nonnegligent manslaughter were 7.5 per cent below the average for the immediate prewar years, although 1944 showed a slight increase of 3.8 per cent over 1943. Part of this over-all decrease may be attributed to the direction of murderous impulses into the socially approved channels of war. This is in accord with the hypotheses which consider war in terms of the redirection of impulses of aggression from members of the internal group to rival groups. The negligible change in the number of such offenses suggests, however, that any such transfer of aggression on a massive scale did not take place. The actual decline may be attributed to the decrease in the age groups in the civilian male population that tend to commit crimes of such a nature.

2. *Criminal homicide* (*manslaughter by negligence*). This crime "includes any death which the police investigation establishes was primarily attributable to gross negligence on the part of some individual other than the victim." Trends in criminal homicide took the following pattern:

Table XVI

Trends in Criminal Homicide (2) 1939-1944*
(Manslaughter by Negligence)

Year	Number of Offenses
Average 1939–41	1,978
1942	2,003
1943	1,796
1944	1,981

* Reports from 392 cities for the first six months of 1945 showed a decrease of 1.6 per cent in manslaughter by negligence over the first six months of 1944. *Uniform Crime Reports, loc. cit.*

Figures for 1944 were almost exactly the same as those for the prewar years, with 1944 showing a 10.3 per cent increase over 1943. Most of these homicides arise from the careless use of automobiles. The use of this lethal weapon was severely curtailed during the war, both by the cessation of its manufacture and the strict gasoline and tire rationing obtaining until the end of the Japanese War. Even with this curtailment, no significant wartime change in behavior was apparent in manslaughter by negligence.

3. *Rape.* This offense "includes forcible rape, statutory rape, (no force used—victim under age of consent), assault to rape, and attempted rape." Annual trends in this form of criminal behavior were as follows:

Table XVII

Trends in Rape 1939-1944*

Year	Number of Offenses
Average 1939–41	4,286
1942	4,764
1943	5,224
1944	5,443

* Reports from 392 cities for the first six months of 1945 showed an increase of 9.0 per cent in rape over the first six months of 1944. *Ibid.*

A considerable increase in cases of rape was evident during the war years, with a slight but consistent increase in each of the years under consideration. The figure for 1944 was 27.0 per cent greater than the average for 1939-41. Part of this rise may be explained by the wartime increase in civilian mobility, whereby large numbers of persons left their former communities and migrated to those in which they were unknown.

Generally speaking, rape declined in areas of the country (like the New England and Middle Atlantic States) which showed a decrease in population and increased in the West and Southwest where the population increased. Part of the wartime increase in rape may have resulted from the changed definition of the offense, as sex behavior came to be considered a source of venereal infection and hence a danger to the war effort. In order to discourage such behavior, the local police may have changed the definition from undesirable behavior to rape, particularly in statutory cases. The number of offenses defined as statutory rape is particularly susceptible to changes of definition. A great deal of sex behavior involving girls under the age of consent takes place at all times, but is normally ignored by the police. In wartime, some of this behavior may have come more formally to their attention and thus swelled the total for such offenses.

4. *Robbery.* Robbery is a crime which includes "stealing or taking anything of value from the person by force or violence or by putting in fear, such as strong-arm robbery, stick-ups, robbery armed. Includes assault to rob and attempt to rob." World War II saw the following trends in this form of criminal behavior:

Table XVIII
Trends in Robbery 1939-1944*

Year	Number of Offenses
Average 1939-41	26,965
1942	24,370
1943	23,894
1944	23,393

* Reports from 392 cities for the first six months of 1945 showed an increase of 10.0 per cent in robbery over the first six months of 1944. *Uniform Crime Reports,* Volume 16, *loc. cit.,* p. 7.

Robbery showed a net decline of 13.2 per cent in 1944 over the prewar average of 1939-41. This is in contrast to the trend evident during World War I in the European countries, where crimes against property increased substantially, while crimes against the person de-creased.[29] The generally high level of employment, industrial activity, and personal income during World War II in the United States, as contrasted to the depressed European economic conditions during World War I, contributed to this change in criminal behavior. Food, clothing, and shelter were all relatively plentiful in America, in con-trast to the situation among the Central Powers during World War I, when these commodities were in extremely short supply. Many of the robberies in Germany and Austria were directed at commodities rather than money, since the value of money was negligible when there were no goods and services to buy.

5. *Burglary (breaking or entering)*. This offense includes "bur-glary, housebreaking, safecracking, or any unlawful entry to commit a felony or a theft, even though no force was used to gain entrance. Includes attempts. Burglary followed by larency is included in this classification and not counted again as larceny." This behavior showed the following wartime trends:

Table XIX

Trends in Burglary 1939–1944*
(Breaking or Entering)

Year	Number of Offenses
Average 1939–41	143,313
1942	124,428
1943	128,656
1944	130,563

* Reports from 392 cities for the first six months of 1945 showed an increase of 12.1 per cent for burglary over the first six months of 1944. *Uniform Crime Reports,* Volume 16, *loc. cit.,* p. 7.

Cases of burglary known to the police showed an over-all percentage decrease of 8.9 in 1944 over the prewar average, despite a slight in-crease in the last two years. The first full year of American participa-tion showed a sharp drop in the number of offenses, from a prewar average of 143,313 in 1939–41 to 124,428 in 1942. The general wartime decrease in this offense was presumably also attributable in large part to the absorption into the armed forces of millions of young men and their removal from possible criminal activity.[30]

6. *Larceny (theft)*. The Federal Bureau of Investigation categorizes larceny as "(a) Fifty dollars and over in value; (b) under $50 in value—includes in one of the above subclassifications, depending upon

the value of the property stolen, thefts of bicycles, automobile acces-sories, shoplifting, pocket-picking, or any stealing of property or article of value which is not taken by force and violence or by fraud." Trends in larceny during World War II were as follows:

Table XX
Trends in Larceny (Theft) 1939–1944*

Year	Number of Offenses
Average 1939–41	388,309
1942	377,105
1943	337,208
1944	336,530

* Reports from 392 cities for the first six months of 1945 indicated an increase of 7.9 per cent in larceny over the first six months of 1944. *Uniform Crime Reports,* Volume 16, *loc. cit.,* p. 7.

The number of cases of larceny known to the police underwent a 13.3 per cent decrease in 1944, compared to the period 1939–41. Taken with the 13.2 per cent decline in robbery and the 8.9 per cent decline in burglary, this reflects a considerable wartime decrease in criminal behavior directed against property. This decline was probably a reflec-tion of the intervening changes of World War II in manpower rather than the economic betterment of increased employment at wartime wages. This hypothesis is suggested by the fact that juvenile delin-quency, contrary to adult crime, tends to increase during times of economic prosperity, a tendency particularly apparent in certain indus-trial centers during World War II.[31]

7. *Auto theft.* This type of larceny "includes all cases where a motor vehicle is stolen or driven away and abandoned, including the so-called joy-riding thefts." World War II saw the following trends in this form of behavior:

Table XXI
Trends in Auto Theft 1939–1944*

Year	Number of Offenses
Average, 1939–41	84,293
1942	79,713
1943	88,897
1944	97,081

* Reports from 392 cities for the first six months of 1945 showed an increase of 4.6 per cent in auto theft over the first six months of 1944. *Uniform Crime Reports,* Volume 16, *loc. cit.,* p. 7.

The first full year after Pearl Harbor saw a considerable decrease in the number of auto thefts known to the police, but in 1943 and 1944 there was a steady increase therein. The figure for 1944 was 15.2 per cent higher than the prewar average for 1939-41. This wartime increase is significant in view of the steady decrease in the total number of automobiles in operation. No new automobiles were manufactured after the first few months of 1942; a large number of usable automobiles were put up for the duration because of the shortage of tires and gasoline; and hundreds of thousands of automobiles annually reached the junk yards after breaking down completely.

In the face of these factors decreasing the available supply of automobiles, the number of thefts nevertheless continued to increase. The shortage was presumably also the most important intervening cause for the increased number of thefts. Automobiles became increasingly valuable commodities which, despite the shortages of tires and gasoline, could be profitably disposed of to eager buyers. Many stolen cars may have been sold to persons engaged in war industry and hence eligible for priorities in the necessaries for their continued operation. The highest rate of increase in auto theft took place in the areas where war industry and military installations were located. The increase was particularly apparent in the Pacific States, where 27 cities with a population of 4,430,816 showed an increase in thefts from 17,531 in 1939-41 to 23,027 in 1944. These areas also underwent considerable increases in population during the war years, which should be considered in any regional study of the trends.

8. *Aggravated assault.* This form of crime against the person includes "assault with intent to kill; assault by shooting, cutting, stabbing, maiming, poisoning, scalding or by the use of acids. Does not include simple assault, assault and battery, fighting, etc." Trends in these assorted forms of violence were as follows:

Table XXII

Trends in Aggravated Assault 1939-1944*

Year	Number of Offenses
Average, 1939-41	21,864
1942	23,533
1943	23,421
1944	26,221

* Reports from 392 cities for the first six months of 1945 indicated an increase of 11.3 per cent in aggravated assault over the first six months of 1944. *Ibid.*

Trends in aggravated assault followed somewhat the same wartime pattern as that other form of physical violence—namely, rape. The 1944 figure for aggravated assault was 19.9 per cent higher than the prewar average for the years 1939-41. This offense was also especially apparent in the sections where war industry and military establishments had encouraged widespread mobility, with consequent increase in population. The cumulative effect of wartime frustrations, inadequate housing conditions, overcrowded transportation facilities, and the mixture of various racial and cultural groups may have increased these varied forms of sadistic behavior. It would be significant to compare the reactions of the British people—who underwent far greater hardships, deprivations, and physical dangers—with those of the American people. The homogeneity of the British people, plus the companionship of shared danger, probably kept down the rate of aggravated assault in that island fortress. The increase of nearly 20 per cent in this country was one of the most significant developments of the war years.

Summary of Wartime Trends

The changes in criminal behavior during World War II in the eight categories of major crimes known to the police were as follows:
1. Murder and nonnegligent manslaughter decreased by 7.5 per cent.
2. Manslaughter by negligence showed practically no change.
3. Rape increased by 27.0 per cent.
4. Robbery showed a net decline of 13.2 per cent.
5. Burglary decreased by 8.9 per cent.
6. Larceny decreased by 13.3 per cent.
7. Auto theft increased by 15.2 per cent.
8. Aggravated assault increased by 19.9 per cent.

These percentage changes represent figures for 1944 compared with the average for the prewar years 1939-41. In general, the number of crimes known to the police during the last full year of American participation represented the culmination of trends evident during the three full war years 1942-43-44, with a fairly consistent tendency in one direction or the other in each case. With the exception of manslaughter by negligence (which showed a decline of 1.6 per cent) all of the above categories showed an increase during the first six months of 1945 over the corresponding period in 1944. The over-all increase for the first six months of 1945 was 8.4 per cent.[32]

There are exceptions to any generalizations concerning either crimes against the person or crimes against property in World War II. *In general,* however, there was an increase in crimes against the person, particularly rape and aggravated assault, although murder and non-negligent manslaughter decreased slightly and negligent manslaughter remained virtually stationary. Crimes against property tended to decrease, with robbery, burglary, and larceny showing varied declines during the war years. The exception lies in the sharp increase in auto thefts, even with the decrease in the available supply of automobiles. Total war involves so many intervening changes in personal, social, and institutional relationships that the changes in criminal behavior do not fall into a simple pattern. Some behavior defined as criminal increased while other behavior decreased. Whether these modifications took place on a per capita basis which allowed for the declining number in the civilian male population is not known. Were the young men left in the civilian population more or less criminal than before the war? Were the crimes known to the police during the war greater or less in proportion to the civilian population of criminal age? These refinements are unknown on a national scale. We can only approximate the per capita rate of criminal behavior during wartime from the above figures.

The decline in crimes against property may be partly explained by the decrease in the civilian population in the younger age groups. Figures for 1944 indicated that youths under 21 committed a disproportionate share of the crimes against property. In that year, males (and a few females) under 21 committed 34.5 per cent of the robberies, 51.8 per cent of the burglaries, 35.4 per cent of the larcenies, and 63.1 per cent of the auto thefts. Extending the list of crimes against property, some 40.1 per cent of the 110,346 persons arrested in 1944 for robbery, burglary, larceny, auto theft, embezzlement, fraud, forgery, counterfeiting, receiving stolen property, and arson were under 21 years of age. Between 1941 and 1944, the number of males from 18–21 arrested and charged with all crimes decreased from 66,689 to 44,234, or 33.7 per cent.[33] The high percentage of crimes against property committed by young men and the sharp decrease in arrests of young men suggest the principal reasons for the decline in crimes against property (with the exception of auto theft) during World War II. Many of the young men who served in the armed forces would have engaged in criminal conduct had they remained in the civilian population. Military service thus served as an unpremeditated agency whereby many young men were restrained (temporarily at least) from criminal careers.

A final comment concerns the relative increase in crimes against the person. In 1944, the violent crimes of criminal homicide, rape, and aggravated assault represented 5.2 per cent of the total offenses reported by 2,161 cities with a total population of 66,776,823. This was an increase from the 4.1 to 4.3 per cent of the total represented by such crimes in the prewar years 1939–40–41. This percentage increase represents the actual increase in such crimes against the person during three years of war, as well as the lower number of crimes of robbery, burglary, and larceny known to the police during the war years.

Although the percentage increase of crimes of violence was slight, the change in behavior of which this figure was an index is significant. Many crimes against property are relatively insignificant and indicate no more drastic offenses than the alleged theft of a bicycle or a small sum of money. Offenses against the person, however, are generally of a more serious nature and (with the exception of some cases of statutory rape) constitute a violent attack upon human life and physical security. "The safety of the person," comments one observer, "is one of the cardinal principles of communal living. In war as in peace, this safety must be assured. The increase (in crimes of violence) . . . suggests that the stay-at-home population is transferring to civilian life procedures and methods which are valuable in meeting and punishing a massed enemy who is not amenable to the more orderly processes which permit people to live in safety."[34] Hence the increase in these crimes from 4.1 per cent to 5.2 per cent of the national total may indicate a significant wartime modification in human relationships.[35]

The decrease in crimes known to the police during the war was reflected in the decline in the prison population. With fewer crimes known to the police, fewer persons were convicted and committed to the state and federal prisons and reformatories. At the end of 1940, the prison population totaled 180,002 persons. At the end of 1941, the number had declined to 171,201 and by the end of 1942 to 154,959 persons. Only 131,289 prisoners were incarcerated at the end of 1943 and by the end of 1944 the number had decreased still further to 127,076.[36]

The reporting institutions comprised all the state and federal institutions for adult civilian offenders. Military prisoners were not included, nor were those in institutions for the training or correction of juvenile offenders. The number of prisoners admitted each year also showed a steady decline during the years of the war, reflecting the same trends evidenced in offenses known to the police. The number of admissions decreased from 84,300 in 1940 to 80,840 in 1941; from 72,381 in 1942 to 63,249 in 1943 and 62,765 in 1944. This is another indication of the decrease in the over-all number of civilian offenders during World War II.

Wartime Trends in "Minor" Crimes

Wartime trends in the eight major offenses known to the police constitute the best available index of criminal behavior during World War II. Other indices are available which give additional insight into other forms of antisocial behavior. These are the trends in *arrests* for a variety of offenses which, although serious in their implications, are not considered as important as those in the first category in *Uniform Crime Reports*. This information is obtained from fingerprint cards submitted by local police departments to the Federal Bureau of Investigation of persons arrested for violations of state laws and municipal ordinances. The figures do not include arrests for violations of federal laws, nor even for all those arrested for state and municipal violations, since an indeterminate number of the latter are not fingerprinted. Furthermore, since two or more persons may be arrested for a single offense or one person arrested and charged with a number of offenses, the figures are not as exact as offenses known to the police. In spite of these limitations, trends in arrests constitute a significant index to wartime criminal conditions. With the number of annual arrests approaching half a million (488,979 in 1944 and 576,920 in 1939), this is a sizeable sample of the criminal population.

The following figures are taken from a list of some 20 offenses against property or the person plus miscellaneous offenses involving violations of the mores incorporated into law. These figures suggest a variety of hypotheses about wartime behavior, which cannot be definitely substantiated in the state of present knowledge. Certain offenses against property, for example, such as embezzlement and fraud, buying or receiving stolen goods, and forging and counterfeiting, appear to have undergone a drastic decline during the war. These offenses involve a lower percentage of young men of military age than some of the more strenuous crimes. Only 27.7 per cent of those arrested for embezzlement and fraud during 1944 were in the age group under 25, while 57.1 per cent of arrests for robbery involved persons under 25. Buying and receiving stolen property likewise showed but 33.1 per cent of arrests among persons under 25, while forgery and counterfeiting had 43.9 per cent.[37]

The sharp decline in these offenses against property thus only partially resulted from the decreased number of young men among the civilian population, since young men do not commit these latter offenses to the same extent as they commit certain of the major offenses. The high rate of employment and national income undoubtedly had something to do with the decrease in these more genteel crimes against property. We may also speculate whether, in the midst of a war in which human life was placed in such large-scale jeopardy, certain changes in other values were not undergone by the civilian population. Money might not have seemed so important and a corresponding decline in illegal methods of attaining it might have evidenced this temporary change in social attitudes.

1. *Embezzlement and fraud.* This offense is defined by the Federal Bureau of Investigation as including "all offenses of fraudulent conversion, embezzlement, and obtaining money or property under false pretenses.[38] Trends in arrests for this form of behavior over the six years from 1939 through 1944 were as follows:[39]

Table XXIII

Trends in Embezzlement and Fraud, 1939-1944*

Year	Number of Arrests
1939	17,586
1940	19,132
1941	14,845
1942	11,018
1943	7,674
1944	8,131

* For the first six months of 1945, arrests for embezzlement and fraud totaled 4,609.

Trends in this offense against property were consistently downward during the war. The rise in arrests in 1940 over 1939 might have been a partial reflection of the material prosperity beginning with the defense program. The year of Pearl Harbor showed a considerable drop from 1940 and the three years of full participation evidenced further declines in this form of illegal enterprise. The attention of many persons was presumably directed during the war from the illegal pursuit of money to other and more patriotic goals. Embezzlement and fraud are twin activities of an age group who were not in the armed forces to the same extent as younger men. These older men either exerted their energies elsewhere or the police were not as zealous in arresting persons for such alleged behavior. In any event, the decline in arrests for embezzlement and fraud constituted one of the most spectacular wartime changes in criminal behavior.

2. *Forgery and counterfeiting.* This includes "offenses dealing with the making, altering, uttering, or possessing, with intent to defraud, anything false which is made to appear true." Arrests for this offense took the following pattern:

Table XXIV

Trends in Forgery and Counterfeiting 1939–1944*

Year	Number of Arrests
1939	7,513
1940	7,105
1941	6,810
1942	5,157
1943	3,880
1944	3,958

* For the first six months of 1945, arrests for forgery and counterfeiting equalled 2,052.

While the decline in forgery and counterfeiting was not as pronounced as that for embezzlement and fraud, it was nevertheless considerable. A larger proportion of the arrests for this offense come from persons under 25 (43.9 per cent in 1944) than is the case with embezzlement and fraud. This factor might have decreased the number of arrests for forgery and counterfeiting, although it does not explain the decline in embezzlement and fraud. The rise in the national income may have contributed to the decline in arrests for forgery and counterfeiting, even as it may have done so for embezzlement and fraud. Definitions of this behavior by the police may also have changed and with them the number of arrests. There is no convincing single explanation for this decline.

3. *Buying or receiving stolen property.* This offense "includes buying, receiving, and possessing stolen property as well as attempts to

commit any of these offenses." The number of arrests for this offense is not large in any one year, but the general wartime trend is significant, since it follows the same pattern as the preceding two general offenses.

Table XXV

Trends in Buying or Receiving Stolen Property 1939–1944*

Year	Number of Arrests
1939	3,786
1940	3,577
1941	2,978
1942	3,104
1943	2,417
1944	2,526

* For the first six months of 1945, arrests for buying or receiving stolen property totaled 1,587.

Explanations for this decline are probably similar to those for embezzlement and fraud and forgery and counterfeiting, reflecting both changes in behavior and changes in its definition. The changes in behavior cannot be completely explained on the basis of available information. All we can do here is to note the changes, with the suggestion that in wartime considerable activity appeared to have been diverted from illegal economic activities into legal ones.

We turn now from some of the less violent crimes against property to a group of offenses against the public morality. These offenses include drunkenness, driving while intoxicated, prostitution and commercialized vice, disorderly conduct, and gambling. An investigation into their incidence—at least insofar as may be estimated by the number of arrests—suggests certain changes in the public morality during World War II. With the exception of driving while intoxicated, which was necessarily curtailed by the rationing of gasoline and tires plus the decreasing number of automobiles on the road, offenses against the mores increased. These wartime increases reflected the rise in the national income, the decline of unemployment, and the material prosperity brought about by the vast federal expenditures. When the citizens are in funds, many of them indulge themselves by getting drunk, engaging in disorderly conduct, consorting with persons other than their wives, and gambling.

4. *Drunkenness.* Drunkenness is one offense for which there is no

need of esoteric definition. The number of arrests for this offense increased rapidly from 1939 through the first full year of our participation in the war and then receded slightly. The figure for 1944 remained, however, considerably higher than that for 1939.

Table XXVI
Trends in Drunkenness 1939–1944*

Year	Number of Arrests
1939	90,989
1940	115,848
1941	142,748
1942	145,946
1943	111,031
1944	104,487

* For the first six months of 1945, arrests for drunkenness totaled 63,182.

The number of persons arrested for drunkenness during the year 1942 was the highest in the six-year cycle which began in 1939 and ended with the climacteric year of 1944. In the year of the surrender of Bataan, the fall of Singapore, and the worldwide series of Axis successes, some 145,946 persons (134,418 males and 11,528 females) stimulated themselves sufficiently to become legally involved on charges of drunkenness. These bibulous characters may have been drowning their sorrows at the reverses of American arms and the then parlous state of the world in general. On the other hand, they may merely have been enjoying the full employment and prevailing high wages in this uninhibited fashion. Much of the increase in drunkenness during 1940 and 1941 may be attributed to the increased spending money in the pockets of the American people accompanying the rearmament program. Wartime tensions presumably relaxed somewhat after the peak year of 1942; the increased rate of induction into the armed forces may have so decreased the male civilian population of a drinking age to account for the decline in 1943 and 1944. At the same time, the police may have become more lenient in their arrests for drunkenness during the later war years. The pattern of wartime arrests for this offense is probably explained by a combination of these and more subtle psychological factors.

5. *Driving while intoxicated.* The behavior subsumed under this heading is also clear without further definition. Arrests for this offense

increased from 1939 through 1941 and then began a steady and precipitous decline which continued through 1944.

Table XXVII

Trends in Driving While Intoxicated 1939–1944*

Year	Number of Arrests
1939	24,309
1940	28,803
1941	34,007
1942	29,197
1943	18,392
1944	17,790

* During the first six months of 1945, arrests for driving while intoxicated were 9,958.

Fortunately only a relatively small proportion of the persons who indulge excessively in alcoholic beverages also endanger themselves and the general public by driving automobiles while in that condition. Otherwise the number of arrests for driving while intoxicated and for negligent manslaughter would be considerably higher. Arrests for driving while intoxicated followed very much the same pattern as those for drunkenness, except that the high point for the former came in 1941 and for the latter in 1942. Increases in driving while intoxicated during the years 1940 and 1941 undoubtedly reflected the increasing affluence of the people, as they amused themselves in public places and then attempted to drive home. The decreases in arrests subsequent to 1941 probably reflected the stringent rationing of tires and gasoline, as well as the complete cessation of automobile manufacture after the first quarter of 1942. The automobile plays such an important role in American culture that its sudden curtailment brings about unexpected social changes.

6. *Disorderly conduct.* Closely allied to the overindulgence in alcohol is the perpetration of other excesses known as disorderly conduct. The two forms of behavior often go hand in hand. A person arrested for disorderly conduct is one accused of "all charges of committing a breach of the peace"—from making a disturbance in a public place to insulting an officer of the law. All persons charged with disorderly conduct are by no means drunk, but the relationship is nevertheless a close one. Trends in arrests for this offense during World War II were as follows:

Table XXVIII

Trends in Disorderly Conduct 1939-1944*

Year	Number of Arrests
1939	27,996
1940	29,403
1941	34,948
1942	38,103
1943	35,319
1944	36,399

* Total arrests for disorderly conduct during the first six months of 1945 were 19,517.

By the second full year of American participation (1943), the early tendencies causing an increasing number of persons to become disorderly had apparently begun to decrease. The years 1943 and 1944 saw a slight decline from the high point of 1942 with, however, an increase in 1944 over 1943. The number of arrests for this offense depends upon police definition to an extent perhaps greater than for any other. Men and women engaging in the same "disorderly" conduct may or may not be arrested by different officers of the law or even by the same officer on different occasions. The changes in the number of arrests over the war years were not sufficient to warrant any strong conclusions about changes in conduct. These changes may rather be explained by the vagaries of social definition of a variety of situations.

7. *Gambling.* This includes gambling as well as the related offenses of "promoting, permitting, or engaging in gambling." World War II saw the following changes in arrests:

Table XXIX

Trends in Gambling 1939-1944*

Year	Number of Arrests
1939	11,214
1940	13,283
1941	13,510
1942	13,398
1943	13,930
1944	14,387

* Arrests for gambling during the first six months of 1945 were 6,363.

The last full year of the war saw a somewhat larger number of arrests for gambling than the year of its outbreak in Europe. The sharp increase in 1940 over 1939 may have reflected the increased national income attending the defense program. From 1940 through 1944, considerable consistency was maintained in arrests, which implies either a similar consistency in the behavior itself or in its definition by the police. A small but devoted minority of the population apparently engage in the fortuitous pursuit of gain, either as participants or promoters, year in and year out. Their involvement with the law is a function of the strictness with which state and municipal statutes are enforced. A series of large raids in one or more metropolitan areas may thus increase the national total to a disproportionate degree. Under these arbitrary conditions, the wonder is not that the total number of arrests in the years under consideration showed some variation but rather that they did not show more.

8. *Prostitution and commercialized vice.* The impact of World War II upon this form of behavior has been considered above. Suffice it to point out here the relationship between arrests for prostitution and commercialized vice and those for other offenses against property and public morality. Prostitution and commercialized vice are defined as including "sex offenses of a commercialized nature, or attempts to commit the same, such as prostitution, keeping bawdy houses, procuring, transporting, or detaining women for immoral purposes." Arrests showed the following variations:

Table XXX

Trends in Prostitution and Commercialized Vice 1939–1944*

Year	Number of Arrests
1939	6,928
1940	8,987
1941	9,273
1942	9,031
1943	9,263
1944	10,787

* Arrests for prostitution and commercialized vice during the first six months of 1945 were 5,495.

Arrests for prostitution and commercialized vice were considerably higher in 1944 than in 1939, with 10,787 arrested in 1944 and only 6,928 in 1939. These figures represent alleged violations of state and municipal statutes only and do not include violations of federal statutes,

LIBRARY OF
Westmar College
199
LE MARS, IOWA

Vol. No.

such as the Mann Act and the May Act. The total figure of 10,787 comprised some 3,155 males and 7,632 females, with a considerable proportion involving the persons who profited from this traffic as well as those physically engaging therein. The 3,155 men arrested represented several times that number of women engaged in the traffic, some of whom were arrested and others not.

This increase in arrests for prostitution and commercialized vice superficially appears as indisputable evidence that such behavior underwent a substantial increase during the defense program and the war. On the contrary, however, other evidence suggests that the practice of prostitution actually decreased during World War II. The police were thoroughly alerted to the danger to the armed forces and the civilian population through the unrestricted practice of prostitution. The officers of the law were more zealous in apprehending persons charged with prostitution during the war than either before or after. The individual decision to arrest a young woman suspected of prostitution rests with the local police, with the final responsibility in most cases upon the individual patrolman. The increase in arrests for this offense reflected the wartime definition of commercialized sex behavior. As that definition changes, the statistics change with it. Crime, like all other social problems, involves both a situation and its definition.[40]

The majority of the crimes known to the police decreased during World War II. The composition of the civilian population also underwent a correspondingly drastic change, with the temporary withdrawal of a large number of young men in the age groups from which the bulk of certain types of criminals are ordinarily drawn. This qualification does not negate the basic fact, however, of the statistical decrease in most forms of crime during the peak years of the conflict. In view of this fact, therefore, we must again qualify our hypothesis by suggesting that, whereas World War II increased the incidence and severity of many social problems, it also modified or curtailed other problems. This change constitutes additional data for our final consideration, when we decide whether the original hypothesis should be retained, amended, or rejected.

CHAPTER NINE

WAR AND PERSONAL DIS-
ORGANIZATION

The Nature of Personal Disorganization

Personality is a social product. The individual comes into the world with various hereditary potentialities and the form they take is ultimately determined by the social situation. The social environment is the final determinant of personality as we know it and the individual reflects the patterns of his society. When the society is stable and serene, the individual will presumably reflect this stability and serenity in his own personality. When the society is confused and disorganized, certain reflections thereof are often apparent in the lives of its members. In practice, the relationship between personal and social disorganization is more complicated, with many persons becoming disorganized for reasons largely or wholly remote from the confusion of the society. Nevertheless, there is a sufficiently close reciprocity between the individual and his world to look for disorganization in the one if there is disorganization in the other. The nature of this personal-social relationship is so complex that only the roughest comparisons are possible in the present state of knowledge. But we do know the relationship is there.

The disorganization of the individual may take three general forms. These forms are not strictly comparable either in causation or severity, but they do represent different ways in which the distracted individual may turn, whether consciously or unconsciously. The individual may become neurotic, he may develop a psychosis, or he may commit suicide. From many points of view—the casual sequence, degree of disorganization, the completeness of the break with "normal" society, and the finality of the transition—the three aspects of personal disorganization are not conterminous. They all represent in a rough way, however, the breakdown of the personality and the resultant inability to live under conditions of normal social intercourse. This chapter attempts to summarize the general trends in such personal failures and semifailures which took place within the civilian population of the United States during World War II. Neither the treatment nor the analysis pretends to be exhaustive.

Personal disorganization has always been defined as a social problem, particularly that involving psychotic behavior. Neuroses have traditionally been accepted as a more common aspect of the stresses and strains of a world admittedly not the best of all possible worlds. Suicide as a final denouement of individual life has been variously defined in different cultures, sometimes as a social problem and sometimes as an honorable, if regrettable, way out of a deplorable situation. But the individual afflicted with a psychosis—commonly called insane—has, with negligible cultural exceptions, always been viewed as a difficult social problem. Whether the mental derangement were considered as emanating from an evil spirit which had mysteriously possessed the body and soul of the afflicted one, or whatever the explanation for the bizarre and frightening conduct, it was defined as a threat to social stability. The insane person was ordinarily treated with extreme harshness because the vicious spirit lurking within him justified no other treatment. In recent years, the science of medicine has combined with the growing spirit of humanitarianism to improve the lot of the "madman" and undertake some systematic efforts toward the cure or alleviation of his discomfort. But whether possessed by the devil or afflicted with an illness considered no more reprehensible than pneumonia, the psychotic person remains a serious social problem.

Central to our conception of a social problem is the process of social definition. A given situation or form of behavior comes to the attention of a large number of people, who consider it a threat to social values. The definition constitutes the deciding factor in whether the situation is or is not a social problem. The initial decision that something is wrong and the subsequent decision to do something about it can come only from society. In this sense, there is nothing either good or bad (or a social problem) unless thinking makes it so. The judgment of the group is the deciding factor.

There is no rigidly fixed definition of human behavior or of the social problems which arise therefrom. This flexibility is especially apparent in the field of mental maladjustment. The norm of human behavior on this level is both arbitrary and flexible—arbitrary in that there is no exact measure of mental normality and flexible in that the norms differ within the same society at different times and from one society to another at the same time. The insane person is one whose behavior is sufficiently divergent from the norm to be adjudged incapable of satisfactory adjustment. The neurotic is one whose aberrations from the norm are not ordinarily considered sufficiently dangerous to necessitate his physical separation from the normal world. There is no wish at this point to explore the thorny intricacies of abnormal psychology, but merely to indicate that mental difficulties present peculiar claims to consideration as social problems from the point of view of genesis and diagnosis alike.

War and Personal Disorganization

The close relationship between personality and society suggests that the greatest crisis in history would produce a corresponding harvest of disorganized persons. Among the civilian population of the United States, however, World War II apparently levied no such toll, at least as indicated by the conventional indices of such behavior. The mental havoc wrought upon the civilian population of Europe, with its heritage of horror, is another matter altogether, whose extent and severity will never be fully known. The civilian population of this country was spared the personal crises of millions of Europeans, with the exception of the anxiety and interruption of emotional relationships caused by service in the armed forces. Civilians moreover were stimulated by the fervor of a great national crusade. Many of their petty annoyances appeared insignificant in the gravity of the national peril. The resulting spirit of co-operation in a joint effort of unprecedented scope apparently was a therapeutic influence for numbers of persons who might otherwise have succumbed to an outrageous fortune on a more personal level.

"Group morale," it will be remembered, "exists as a disposition to act together toward a goal."[1] Such a disposition is absent in peacetime, when a variety of pressure groups and individual self-interests make national consensus difficult to attain. In wartime, however, many group interests are temporarily subordinated to the great task of winning the war. On this level, the citizens find it comparatively easy "to act together toward a goal" and thus purge the attitudes which cause men to work at cross purposes. Under these conditions, the individual tends to be diverted from his own problems, whose unsuccessful solution in peacetime may disorganize him. The neophyte neurotic, the potential psychotic, and the would-be suicide become so enveloped in the national euphoria that they thereby solve their own personal problems. The length of this solution is problematical and the difficulty of personal adjustment may reappear after the crisis is over. World War II appeared to act as a great but probably temporary catharsis for the civilian population by diverting their physical and psychic energies toward a common goal.

In a preliminary study undertaken while American participation was still in its early stages, Professor H. Warren Dunham suggested a possible relationship between national morale and mental disease. "As the morale of a nation at war," he suggests, "develops to the extent that all persons within the population become aware of the major aims of the war and have a role to play in carrying it out, the personality breakdowns of individual members of the population will diminish in frequency."[2] This hypothesis was difficult to verify, since the rise in morale after Pearl Harbor was complicated by the industrial activity and high level of employment. The prolonged unemployment and economic insecurity of the depression years apparently had an adverse effect upon mental health, particularly in the functional psychoses. These forms of mental disease are closely related to social and environmental factors and there appears to be a direct relationship between economic conditions and the principal functional psychoses. In a study of first admissions to the New York Civil State Hospitals undertaken during the depression, Dr. Benjamin Malzberg concluded that ". . . the economic factors, whether primary or not, do act as inciting and precipitating influences in functional mental disorders."[3]

The adverse effect of the depression upon mental health was partially counterbalanced by the economic security of the defense and war periods. The first five years of the 1940's were years of economic expansion and general prosperity; for the first and perhaps the only time in modern history, employment reached an absolute maximum. Although complete information is not available, it is believed that mental disease is relatively higher in the lower economic groups than in the higher.[4] With the fear of unemployment and loss of security temporarily removed, a lowering of the rate of functional mental disorders in the marginal economic groups might be expected.

The second wartime hypothesis offered by Professor Dunham is that "The development of a national morale high in quality and sound in purpose would be the means of including those persons who in a peace situation would suffer a mental breakdown. Thus a high national morale serves as a preventive device for the development of certain types of functional mental afflictions."[5] The personal problems of many young men who might have become criminals in civil life were apparently solved temporarily by service in the armed forces. The marital problems of thousands of dissatisfied husbands and wives may likewise have been solved for the time being by military service. The high emotionalism of World War II may similarly have saved many persons from the morbid self-absorption which leads to mental disease.

In the individualistic society of the United States, a heavy premium is placed upon personal success, whether in love, marriage, economic accumulation, or professional attainment. World War II was marked by new opportunities for civilians to fall in love, marry, achieve temporary economic success, and rise to the top in professions whose best men were often engulfed in the vast anonymity of the armed forces. Especially important were the high rate of employment, the rise in wages, and the opportunities for businessmen to make money on government contracts or find congenial employment in war work. These possibilities for individual success, even in the midst of a great national crisis, were apparently so outstanding that they counterbalanced the interruption of personal lives, the anxieties of family separation, and the fear for the national safety. In partial explanation, an eminent psychiatrist suggests that "A cynic might well say that men and women fear individual financial disaster and social disaster more than they do the communal injury inflicted by war, if at the same time there is employment. It is probable that employment is a more important factor in the maintenance of mental and physical health than any one single social circumstance."[6]

Many of the individuals who suffer maladjustment or complete breakdown in personality may be influenced by the economic contradictions of a pecuniary society. The resultant frustrations are greater in time of acute economic depression, with unemployment either an actuality or a threat to tens of millions of individuals and their families.[7] Many of these frustrations were removed, temporarily at least, by the billions of dollars poured into the economic system by the Federal Government during the years of World War II. Both the etiology and the measurement of personal disorganization are so complex that no direct correlation between mental disease and employment is necessarily suggested. The two phenomena cannot, however, be entirely unconnected.

The total number of first admissions to hospitals for the permanent care of psychiatric patients increased from 93,357 in 1939 to 111,325 in 1944.[8] These figures alone suggest a substantial increase in mental disease during the defense period and the first three years of the war. These trends will be considered in more detail below; at this point, our interest is only in the broad outlines. It is difficult to attribute these increases to the personal crises induced by World War II, however, for at least two reasons: (a) The figures may reflect an increase in hospitalization facilities for mental disease rather than the incidence of such disease; (b) the figures may also reflect the increased hospitalization of persons with symptoms predisposing them to mental disease who were brought to light in the general social insecurity. It is difficult to say that the war "caused" these personal breakdowns or whether they would have occurred without any national crisis at all.[9] The number of first admissions increased by almost 20 per cent between 1939 and 1944. That is all we can say with certainty.

The discussion has been largely confined to the social problems arising among the civilian population during World War II. This approach will be continued here as far as possible, although the military and civilian groups cannot be rigidly separated. The principal source of information on trends in mental disease is the number of persons on the books of and admitted to mental hospitals, not including those operated directly by the armed forces. However, the enumerations do include the veterans' hospitals, which ultimately receive most of the mental patients from the military hospitals. The number of mental patients on the books of the veterans' hospitals increased from 32,871 in 1942 to 34,976 in 1943 and 38,872 in 1944. These figures may be compared with the totals on the books of all mental hospitals (including veterans' hospitals) of 556,476 in 1942, 567,423 in 1943, and 572,251 in 1944.[10] The statistics hereinafter cited are thus largely, although not wholly, descriptive of the civilian rather than the military population during World War II. Trends in the various psychoses will be considered below. We are concerned here only with the broad outlines of the mental health of the nation.

War and Neurotic Behavior

The neurotic is a person who is not well-adjusted to his environment. The maladjustment may arise from certain drives or wishes which cannot be reconciled with social controls or from the demands of a complex modern society. The maladjustment may also arise from a combination of social and constitutional factors, the exact nature of which is not clearly understood. Whatever the explanation, the neurotic has desires and interests which are not adjusted to his social group. The resulting maladjustment produces mental conflicts which take the form of chronic worry, unusual fatigue, ungrounded fears, irrational compulsions and aversions, and various other peculiarities of behavior. The neurotic is ordinarily able to conform with the rudimentary demands of society. His behavior is often bizarre and curious but usually is not sufficiently abnormal to warrant his incarceration in a mental hospital. The symptoms of neurotic behavior further number "chronic fatigue, inability to concentrate, phobias, obsessions and gross emotional instability . . . complaints of physical ailment for which no organic basis can be found."[11] In short, the neurotic is one whose inner life is far from "normal," but who can nevertheless adjust sufficiently well to insure his continuance as a functioning member of the group.

This is precisely the sort of behavior which might logically increase because of the fears, frustrations, anxieties, and hallucinations of total war. The lives of millions of persons were seriously interrupted, their loved ones were called into service, and many found themselves in a new community or a bomber factory. The visions of destruction conjured up in the minds of sensitive persons about concentration camps, rocket missiles, and atom bombs, not to mention the conventional horrors of warfare, must have accentuated the personal instability already present or initiated new instability in many otherwise normal persons. Even for the civilian population of the United States, with only a vicarious experience of the physical horrors of total war, the mental images stimulated by the radio, news reels, war correspondents, and reports of returning soldiers should have intensified the mental instability of thousands of sensitive stay-at-homes. For persons with vivid imaginations, horrors experienced thus vicariously may have more emotional reality than the actual experience had for men of more stolid stuff.

The principal difficulty with this seductive hypothesis is that we have no way of proving it. The nature of his behavior precludes the average neurotic from coming in contact with any agency which would enumerate, much less treat, his mental difficulty. The majority of such persons do not vary sufficiently from the norm to make their hospitalization either necessary or desirable, even if they could be initially detected. Society recognizes the absolute need for hospitalizing the psychotic or insane person for the physical protection of the group, if for no other reason. Attempts are also made to improve the mental health of the hospitalized psychotic, but the fundamental reason for his segregation is social protection. The neurotic presents no such clear and present danger and is not officially singled out from the mass of the population.[12] There were, to be sure, approximately 5,000 cases of psychoneurosis annually admitted to mental hospitals during the first three years of the war. But these represented only a small fraction of the total number so afflicted. Any attempt to estimate this total is met first with the difficulty of defining neurotic behavior and then with the absence of any nationwide enumeration of persons suffering therefrom.

Trends in first admissions for pychoneuroses from 1940-1944 showed little variation, except for a substantial increase in 1944 over 1943.

Table XXXI

First Admissions to Hospitals for Mental Disease for Psychoneuroses 1940–1944*

Year	Number of First Admissions
1940	4,423
1941	4,606
1942	4,470
1943	4,767
1944	5,809

* Taken from Bureau of the Census, *Patients in Mental Institutions; 1940*, Washington, 1943; *Patients in Mental Institutions; 1941*, Washington, 1944; *Characteristics of Patients Admitted to Mental Hospitals; 1943 and 1942, loc. cit.*; and *Characteristics of Admissions and Separations: Mental Hospitals, 1944, loc. cit.*

Some of these slight yearly variations resulted from changes in the numbers of hospitals reporting. For whatever they may be worth, these figures do not indicate a widespread increase in neurotic behavior during World War II.

This apparent maintenance of mental health may be partly explained by the spirit of participation in a great joint undertaking. The importance of participation was demonstrated repeatedly throughout the conflict, with boys and girls, adult men and women, and old people all participating to the extent of their abilities. Boys and girls took the places of soldiers and warworkers in the service activities; women left home to work in factories or engage in volunteer activities related to the war; and older men came out of retirement to lend their skills to the national effort. "For one individual whom the war depresses into withdrawal," suggests Dr. Abraham Myerson, "there are several, I think, who come back to community participation through the feeling of emergence and need. . . . Again, we come to the factor of communal participation as it lessens the individual struggle and even paralyzes the effort for individuality and thus acts as a factor for mental health in the face of other circumstances which would seem to operate against sanity and stability."[13]

In peacetime, the sentiments of nationalism are comparatively quiescent and play a relatively unimportant role in the mental processes of the individual. The person is motivated by individual sentiments and emotions, whose ultimate solution may be difficult in the face of social convention. The peacetime contradictions between individual and social welfare may be so great as to cause the maladjustment of many individuals, who ultimately may swell the unrecorded total of neurotics and the recorded admissions to mental hospitals.[14] In wartime, individual sentiments are temporarily superseded by nationalistic emotions, mobilized and dramatized by the manipulation of powerful symbols. In this way, the potential neurotic may merge his individuality into the national consensus and by so doing save himself.

World War II was by no means a universal therapeutic agent for neurotic behavior among the civilian population. Many of the wartime changes in social situation and role undoubtedly had unfortunate results upon the organization of the personality. Such fragmentary information on civilian war neuroses as we have suggests that change of equilibrium may cause the individual to become mentally ill if he cannot measure up to the expectations of other persons. The war situation called for an intensification of aggressive behavior on the part of society. Certain persons seemed unable to overcome their inertia or their fear of aggression sufficiently to adjust to the new situation. Attempting to compensate for their failure to measure up, they developed a "civilian war neurosis."[15]

The other general factor in civilian neuroses appears to be the danger to a member of the family and the corresponding loss of family equilibrium. "The foremost impression derived from our observations," remarks a member of the Psychiatry Clinic of the Boston Psychoanalytic Institute, "is that 'civilian war neurosis' is a family neurosis, par excellence, centered around the individual directly involved in the military matter, who is then either the contagious member, or becomes the target and victim of the neurotic action of the environment . . . the treatment . . . reaches out to a group of people whose shaken equilibrium must . . . be reëstablished."[16] Most of the twelve million men and women in the armed forces were members of at least one family group, with central roles of son, daughter, brother, sister, husband, father, wife, or mother. With the millions of individual family situations disorganized by the separation of the war years, the wonder is that more stay-at-home members did not develop neurotic symptoms. The general failure to do so is a striking indication of the power of participation, consensus, and morale in a modern nation at war.

War and Psychotic Behavior

While the neurotic may find difficulty in adjusting himself to the demands of normal society, the psychotic finds it almost impossible to do so. His behavior is not adjusted to the expectations of other people, who consider him irrational and incomprehensible because they cannot understand his motives. His mental world is to a large extent his own, cut off from that of normal men by strange interpretations, emotions, and desires. The psychotic does not react "normally" to social stimuli; a hand extended in friendship may be interpreted as an attempt at bodily injury; an invitation to dinner as a wish to poison. The logic of the normal world often makes no impression upon the psychotic, or at least not a "normal" impression. Other methods of control such as persuasion, suggestion, or force are interpreted in a fashion strange to the normal person. The psychotic is thus one whose behavior is so far removed from ordinary standards and whose reactions are so unpredictable that he must be segregated from the rest of society. He is the one who has suffered a virtually complete personal disorganization.[17]

The psychoses are divided into two general categories, the organic and the functional. The *organic psychoses* are those forms of mental derangement with a demonstrable physical or organic foundation, such as physical deterioration from old age or the destruction of brain tissues by disease. The most important organic psychoses are senile dementia, cerebral arteriosclerosis, general paresis, and alcoholic psychosis. In each of these diseases, a specific organic factor or combination of factors is present to impair the functioning of the mental processes. The majority of these afflictions are the end result of a long process of disease or deterioration. The effect of the war upon this general type of psychosis would presumably be comparatively negligible, at least in terms of immediate changes in first admissions to mental hospitals. If World War II had any immediate and cataclysmic impact upon the mental health of the civilian population, it must be sought elsewhere.

The second general category comprises the so-called *functional psychoses*, in which there is no demonstrable organic pathological condition and the difficulty presumably arises from a combination of mental conflict and possible hereditary predisposition. The functional psychoses are probably precipitated by failure to make a satisfactory social adjustment and involve a consequent flight from normal reality into a reality which exists only for the harassed individual. The circumstances under which these flights take place are not completely understood, but it is reasonable to assume that the more frustrating the world the more difficult is the adjustment. The period of World War II, when the world was undergoing such a massive series of changes, presumably registered its shocks on large numbers of persons who otherwise would have lived their lives in normal adjustment. The number of first admissions to mental hospitals for the functional psychoses should thus logically have increased during the war, as men and women were unable to adjust to a world in which they were strangers and afraid.

It is not altogether clear whether or not this hypothesis was justified by the facts. The principal functional psychoses are dementia praecox, manic-depressive psychosis, involutional melancholia, and paranoia. The situation on first admissions for these psychoses was extremely mixed, with a marked increase in dementia praecox and inconclusive changes in some of the others. In 1939, there were 20,876 first admissions of patients with dementia praecox, representing 22.4 per cent of the total admissions for all psychoses. By 1944, this number had increased to 29,010 cases and 26.1 per cent of the total, which would suggest some relationship between war and functional maladjustment. The trend for manic-depressive psychosis, however, showed a slight decline during the period 1939–44, at least in percentage terms. First admissions were 11,132 in 1939 and 11,811 in 1944, representing a decline from 11.9 to 10.6 per cent of the total admissions.[18] The relationship, if any, between World War II and the functional psychoses is thus a devious one.

The functional psychoses ordinarily have a long history of development which, although not involving any apparent organic deterioration, nevertheless does not occur in a completely unpredictable fashion. The individual who develops unmistakable symptoms of dementia praecox in his early twenties, for example, usually has a history of personal maladjustment behind him. Difficulties within the family group, rejection by one or both of the parents, or excessive affection in the home may be a part of his personal history. The adolescent may feel himself rejected by his playmates and retire into a world of his own, increasingly remote from other people. The young person may be unable, for a variety of reasons, to emancipate himself from his infantile dependence upon the emotional security of the family. While he may make the physical plunge into adulthood, he may be unable to make the mental adjustment and remain forever in the limbo of emotional immaturity.

Thousands of men and women at any time are on the ragged edge of personal disorganization. Some of them may eventually work out an adequate adjustment or at least an armed truce with the forces within and without which may destroy them. Others may break down and unconsciously seek the security found only in a world of their own fashioning. Still others may find themselves unable to adjust to a new and accelerated way of life, such as that of a nation at war. In this sense, the war may precipitate the personal disorganization, but it does not initiate it. The individual who breaks down in the midst of war can never know for certain whether he would have mentally survived in a world at peace. In this sense, war may possibly aggravate the conditions in a dynamic society which predispose some people to mental derangement.[19]

As noted above, war and depression represent changes in social organization affecting many members of an interdependent society. The shock of the depression, bringing loss of employment and security, apparently had an adverse effect upon mental health.[20] The shock of war, with its frustrations, separations, and anxieties, apparently did *not* have a similar effect upon the mental health of the nation as a whole. The individual crisis of the depression was not counterbalanced by any such increase in national morale as characterized the channeled aggression of war. The emotional influence of the New Deal may have stimulated certain segments of the population during the depression, but for the most part the struggle for security was individual in character. In World War II, the individual was taken out of himself by his participation in a common cause, which had the high emotional sanctions of a world of competing nationalisms.

The therapeutic effect of the war upon the mental health of the individual took a different tone in the United States from the other countries of the great coalition. The emphasis in this country was directed largely toward the preservation of national safety and the perpetuation of national ideals. The threat of the Axis powers was defined largely in terms of their physical challenge to the independent existence of the United States. The war was thus a gigantic social problem to the American people, representing a menace to the social values embodied in the national existence. All the symbols of nationalism were employed, consciously and unconsciously, to direct the national effort toward maximum efficiency in the prosecution of the war. The success of this effort was measured in a number of ways—in the acceptance of conscription, the tremendous war production, the individual sacrifices of millions of working men and women, and apparently by the betterment of the aggregate mental health of the nation.

While the national morale was stimulated in the United States by the symbols of nationalism, in other countries it was stimulated by anti-Fascism, economic democracy, and freedom from prejudice. Apropos of morale in this country during the war, Blumer remarked that "the American people do not harken to the urgings that the war should be won to establish a new order of life or to extend and materialize an ideal philosophy. They are not animated by the sense of a cause, of engaging in a crusade, of carrying out a sacred mission. . . ."[21] For the average American, in or out of uniform, the war was not so much *against* Fascism as it was *for* the physical safety of the United States. Many of the issues were so confused that millions of Americans were wholly or partially unsympathetic to certain of the implications of a complete democracy. In the present context, this ideological confusion was apparently not so important as the positive rallying powers of a nation in danger of aggression. At this level, the sacred values of *la patrie* (American style) were sufficiently powerful to mobilize the nation for victory and apparently did much to stabilize its mental health.

The comparatively small increase in the number of admissions for mental disease among the civilian population may further indicate that the "reality" of World War II was not such as to cause a serious mental breakdown among many potential candidates. The "reality" of war to the people of Britain was incomparably greater, but even here the number of mental breakdowns, at least during the early days of the Blitz, did not materially increase. Dr. R. D. Gillespie, who served in the dual capacity of physician for psychological medicine in one of the large London hospitals and Wing Commander in the Royal Air Force Volunteer Reserve, commented on this situation as follows: "It can be said at once that one of the most striking things about the effects of the war on the civilian population has been the relative rarity of pathological mental disturbances among the civilians exposed to air raids."[22] Working in a large hospital in the district which underwent some of the heaviest bombing in 1940 and 1941, Dr. Gillespie nevertheless could state that "the psychiatric out-patient department which still functions there records very few cases of neuroses attributable to war conditions. The patients who do come, with few exceptions, present mainly the same problems as in peacetime."[23]

The testimony of British experience, which can doubtless be duplicated by other nations when the reports become available, demonstrates the tenacity of the individual in the face of harrowing personal experiences—provided he is sustained by co-operative activities and similarity of values. The American people might similarly have undergone greater hardships and personal dangers and still have come out with flying colors. Comparisons between the homogeneous British and the heterogeneous Americans are difficult, but in spite of racial and ethnic differences the average person in America apparently participated in the national effort and received corresponding mental reinforcement. At some stage in the vicissitudes of modern war, the point is presumably reached when mental breakdowns begin to appear, first among those whose mental adjustment is marginal and then among those whose adjustment is increasingly normal. In the United States, this danger point was not approached.

In the countries which suffered the humiliation of military defeat, occupation by the Axis powers, and the tortures and inhumanities which accompanied this enforced servitude, the situation was undoubtedly different. The degree of such personal breakdown will never be completely known, however, in the confusion and social disorganization following the liberation. Records were destroyed, hundreds of thousands of men, women, and children were lost without a trace, and the normal life of the occupied countries was interrupted for a generation. The personal disorganization which accompanied this unprecedented debacle was infinitely greater than that undergone by the United States, or even Great Britain. Its exact extent will never be known.

The Measurement of Psychotic Behavior

There are two principal methods of measuring the incidence of mental disease: the number of first admissions to mental hospitals and the resident population therein at the beginning of the calendar year. The number of *first admissions* is the criterion usually used to enumerate the yearly trends and signifies the number of patients admitted for the first time to mental hospitals. After the patient has been discharged or paroled, he may be readmitted and numbered among the "total admissions," which include both first and subsequent admissions. The *resident-population* (more properly, the number of patients "on the books" of mental hospitals at the beginning of each year) includes those actually in hospitals as well as those in family and other forms of extramural care. The resident population represents the residue after the dead, discharged, and paroled have been subtracted.[24] There were 576,448 patients on the books of the hospitals for the permanent care of the mentally deranged at the end of 1944. Of this total, 506,346 were actually in the hospitals, 2,164 in family care, and 67,938 in some other form of extramural care. This total figure represented a slight net increase of 4,595 patients (about 1 per cent) over the first of the year 1944.[25]

The statistics include all hospitals offering mental care for chronic patients over an unlimited period and thus include state, veterans', county and city, and private hospitals. In addition to the hospitals operated by the Veterans' Administration, the compilations also include statistics for two hospitals operated by the United States Public Health Service, opened during the war to care for psychiatric casualties from the armed forces. The statistics do *not* include the psychiatric facilities of general hospitals, or the station and general hospitals operated by the armed services. The patients admitted to these civilian and military hospitals and requiring permanent mental care eventually appear on the books of the hospitals offering permanent care and are enumerated in the Census Bureau data. Some time may elapse between initial treatment in a military hospital and eventual appearance in a civilian hospital. The figures thus represent primarily the civilian trends, since mental cases in the armed forces did not appear in large numbers until toward the end of the war.[26]

The majority of the mental patients are in hospitals operated by the several states. Of the 506,346 resident patients at the end of 1944, 434,209 were in state hospitals. Veterans' hospitals numbered only 38,623 at that time, although this figure will presumably increase rapidly in the early postwar years. City and county hospitals housed 21,259 mental patients, while private hospitals sheltered 12,255. The problem is thus primarily in the hands of the states, whose standards and practices vary widely. The resident psychiatric population in the veterans' hospitals increased from 28,653 in 1939 to 38,623 in 1944. Nevertheless, the problem of caring for the mentally deranged still rests largely with the states.[27]

Trends in hospitalization for mental disease have long been on the increase and will in all probability continue so for some time. In 1923 there were 267,617 patients in the various state, veterans', county and city, and private hospitals for the mentally ill. By 1941, this number had increased to 480,741 and at the end of 1944 the resident population had reached 506,346.[28] This apparently represents a pronounced secular trend toward an absolute increase in mental disease. Such a conclusion, however, is not so certain. The only thing the statistics actually represent is the trend in *hospitalization* for mental disease. The incidence in the population as a whole can only be inferred from the trends in hospitalization. The Bureau of the Census points out that these figures "reflect only in part the true extent and incidence of mental disease in the general population. Usually hospitalization rates are higher when facilities are available in greater abundance, when they are readily accessible, and when the type of treatment that a hospital provides is well thought of in the community."[29]

Other factors were present in this increase in hospitalizations over the two decades prior to World War II. Beds for mental patients were provided in increasing numbers and in every case were promptly filled. The period was also characterized by the movement from the open country and the small town to the metropolitan area. This migration was accompanied by a change in housing facilities from large rural homes to crowded urban apartments. Facilities for caring for the mentally disabled in the home rapidly declined and many persons were institutionalized because there was no other place to put them. This was particularly true of the aged and infirm, who formed the large group suffering from the various senile psychoses. The rise in the average age of the population further contributed to the increased hospitalization for mental disorders, with their greater prevalence among the aged.[30]

Another index to secular trends in mental disease is the rate of hospitalization per 100,000 of the population. In 1923, the rate per 100,000 of the population stood at 241.7; in 1932 it had increased to 300.9; in 1936 to 337.5; by 1939 it had grown to 360.9; and on July 1, 1941 it was 368.2. Comparable figures for the war years showed slight and inconclusive fluctuations, with an increase in resident patients per 100,000 of the population to 369.8 in 1942, followed by a decrease to 366.7 in 1943 and 366.7 in 1944.[31] The secular trend has pointed to an increase in hospitalization for mental disease, both in absolute and relative terms. This trend was not greatly advanced during World War II.

In considering the rates of hospitalization, it is also important to note that all forms of mental disorder do not lead with the same inevitability to the institution. Certain psychoses—notably general paresis and the other diseases involving organic derangements of the nervous system—require hospitalization sooner or later. Some of the functional disorders—notably certain types of dementia praecox—may never disorganize the personality sufficiently to make hospital treatment mandatory. Hence the rate of first admissions for the various psychoses and the numbers of the resident population suffering therefrom may not be a completely reliable index to their incidence among the general population. The functional psychoses may be more generally prevalent than the figures suggest.[32] The effects of World War II may therefore not appear in their true proportion, since most war-induced or war-precipitated psychoses are presumably functional.

Age differentials offer a further complication to the interpretation of wartime figures. In 1944, 26.1 per cent of all first admissions were diagnosed as dementia praecox, which is by definition a disease of the comparatively young. The median age of first admissions for dementia praecox in 1944 was 30.7 years, as compared to 38.9 for manic-depressive psychosis and 69.9 years for cerebral arteriosclerosis.[33] The changes in the age composition of the civilian population during the war years may thus have had some effect upon the rate of civilian admissions to mental hospitals. Millions of young men were transferred from the civilian to the military population. Many potential neurotics and psychotics were initially rejected for military service, but a considerable number found their way into the armed forces. Some of these young men suffered mental difficulties after military service and were sent first to military hospitals and finally to hospitals for the permanent treatment of mental patients. Only at this last institution were they enumerated by the Bureau of the Census. It is impossible to say how many of these young men would have undergone a mental breakdown in civilian life, either under peacetime conditions or as nonsoldiers in a total war.

These and other statistical vagaries again raise the recurring question of measurement and definition. Are we measuring actual changes in behavior, changes in definition, or both? The answer is both. The nature of social problems, especially mental problems, is such that a process of definition has gone on before the behavior is adjudged a social problem. Only within recent years has mental disease become widely accepted as a social rather than a religious or moral problem. Defining any form of behavior as a social problem means that something can be done about it. Great strides have been made in recent decades in the treatment and cure of mental disease and high claims have been made for the therapy perfected during the war. When we measure the trends in first admissions during World War II, we are measuring behavior widely accepted as a social problem. It is difficult, however, to determine if the figures actually measure the changing incidence of mental disease among the civilian population, since its composition changed tremendously during the war. Hundreds of thousands of young men were considered a bad risk for military service but were still able to make an adequate adjustment to civilian life. These are a few of the imponderables in any tentative excursion into the cloudy mysteries of mental disease.

Wartime Trends in Psychotic Behavior

The following discussion is based upon first admissions for patients with psychosis to hospitals for the permanent care of psychiatric patients for the years 1939 through 1944. The following psychoses will be briefly considered: general paresis, alcoholic psychosis, psychosis with cerebral arteriosclerosis, senile psychosis, manic-depressive psychosis, and dementia praecox (schizophrenia).

The over-all trends should first be considered. Following are the total first admissions with psychosis:

Table XXXII

Total First Admissions With Psychosis*

1939–1944

Year	Total First Admissions
1939	93,357
1940	90,940
1941	97,288
1942	98,424
1943	102,104
1944	111,325

* Bureau of the Census, *Characteristics of Patients Admitted to Mental Hospitals: 1943 and 1942, loc. cit.;* Bureau of the Census, *Characteristics of Admissions and Separations: Mental Hospitals, 1944, loc. cit,* Table 2.

The war years showed a gradual increase in the number of first admissions from 1939 through 1944. The only exception was evident in 1940, when reports were not received for three state hospitals and one veterans' hospital. If these institutions were included, the number of first admissions would have been considerably higher. The growing war clouds in Europe, the actual outbreak of the war, the increasing involvement of the United States, the rapid defense preparations, and finally our total participation apparently did not seriously disrupt the mental health of the nation, as measured by the first admissions to mental hospitals.[34]

1. *General paresis.* We may now consider the trends in wartime first admissions for the various psychoses, starting with the organic. General paresis is perhaps the best-known of the mental difficulties which have a demonstrable organic foundation. Paresis is the progressive deterioration of the central nervous system as a result of syphilitic infection. The mental and emotional life of the individual usually shows a similar deterioration, which grows more devastating as the physical involvement runs its course. The paretic becomes more and more childlike, unco-ordinated, and unable to control his mental as well as his bodily functions. In the final stages of the disease, he loses many of the characteristics of a human being and retrogresses toward the animal level.

As medical treatment for syphilis is perfected and knowledge of the existence of the treatment correspondingly disseminated, presumably the incidence of general paresis will decline. Such changes will take many years, however, before they will substantially affect the first

admissions for this form of psychosis. Wartime trends for paresis were
as follows:

Table XXXIII

First Admissions for General Paresis*

1939–1944

Year	First Admissions
1939	7,998
1940	7,196
1941	7,501
1942	7,281
1943	6,751
1944	6,605

* Unless otherwise noted, the following tables of first admissions are taken from
Bureau of the Census, *Characteristics of Admissions and Separations: Mental Hospitals,
1944, loc. cit.,* Table 1.

World War II saw a considerable decrease in the number of first
admissions diagnosed as general paresis. During the five years prior
to 1939, the number had remained relatively constant, varying from
7,294 in 1934 to 7,827 in 1938. In the war period, the percentage of such
first admissions decreased from 8.6 of the total in 1939 to 5.9 in 1944.
This decline had no demonstrable relationship to the war, since the
seeds for this form of physical and mental deterioration were planted
many years before.

2. *Senile psychosis.* As the name implies, the senile psychoses involve mental diseases accompanying the deterioration of the physical
structure in old age. The difficulty takes various forms, ranging from
simple loss of memory, decline in powers of concentration, and inability to carry an ordinary train of thought to extreme agitation, melancholy, or delusions of persecution and grandeur. The majority of persons suffering from these difficulties are 65 years and over, judging
from the median age of first admissions (70 years) to the mental
hospitals. Some of the forms included in the blanket category of senile
psychoses are apparently induced by organic changes and others are
apparently functional in character. Trends in first admissions for the
senile psychoses during the war years are shown in Table XXXIV.

The number of first admissions suffering from senile psychosis increased steadily during the six years under consideration. This increase
took place at a considerably faster rate than was evident during the

previous five years, when the number increased from 8,120 in 1934 to 8,576 in 1938. Over the war years, these psychoses rose from 9.0 to 11.5 per cent of total first admissions. There seems to be no ready explanation for this wartime change, if indeed any increased incidence of such difficulties actually took place. The change may have been one of definition, whereby an increasing percentage of patients were diagnosed as suffering from senile psychoses rather than from some other psychosis or combination thereof.

Table XXXIV
First Admissions for Senile Psychosis
1939–1944

Year	First Admissions
1939	8,440
1940	8,707
1941	9,781
1942	10,889
1943	11,978
1944	12,771

The disruption of normal housing facilities, brought about by the extreme mobility of the war years, may have been an additional factor in the increased hospitalization of senile psychotics. Many families living in houses in the country or small towns where they could take care of their old people moved to the centers of war production where the housing facilities were more crowded. Some of the grandfathers and grandmothers, in their declining mental and physical health, may have been placed in mental hospitals. The increasing age level of the population also undoubtedly continued its long-range effect upon the number of persons suffering from the mental diseases of old age. This effect was remarked by the Bureau of the Census in its summary of trends in hospitalization through 1941. "As the prevalence of mental disorders is greater among those of more advanced years," suggested the Bureau, "the fact that the median age of the general population is steadily advancing will ultimately be responsible for a tremendous increase in the incidence of mental diseases, that is, unless methods of prevention and treatment of old-age psychoses undergo a revolutionary change."[35]

3. *Psychosis with cerebral arteriosclerosis.* This form of mental impairment results from interference with the passing of the blood to

the brain, brought about by hardening of the cerebral arteries. The speech areas of the brain are often impaired, as are the motor functions. The patient is understandably apprehensive about his physical condition and this apprehension may develop into delusions of various kinds. Many of the symptoms of cerebral arteriosclerosis are similar to those of the senile psychoses, but the causes differ considerably. Senile psychosis ordinarily reflects an intensification of the physiological deterioration of old age, while cerebral arteriosclerosis is brought about by impairment of the cerebral circulation of the blood.[36]

Like the senile psychoses, diagnoses for cerebral arteriosclerosis showed a considerable increase from 1939–1944:

Table XXXV

First Admissions for Psychosis with Cerebral Arteriosclerosis, 1939–1944

Year	First Admissions
1939	12,625
1940	12,319
1941	13,441
1942	13,986
1943	14,308
1944	15,132

This increase was a continuation of the trend evident since the midthirties, with first admissions for cerebral arteriosclerosis showing a steady rise from 9,106 in 1934 to 11,989 in 1938. This diagnosis has also represented an increasing percentage of the total first admissions, although the increase was not so marked during the war years. In 1934, the percentage of the total was 11.0; by 1938 it had grown to 12.8; in 1939 it had risen to 13.5; and in 1944 it was 13.6, after reaching a high point of 14.2 in 1942.

This increase in cerebral arteriosclerosis also reflected the increasing age of the population as a whole. Like the senile psychoses, difficulties of this type appear to be the inevitable accompaniment of an aging population. Unless new therapeutic techniques for the diseases of old age are introduced, the percentage of such hospitalizations will continue to increase. During World War II, the interest of medical science was directed elsewhere. In wartime, the physical and mental welfare of the young is more important than that of the old.

4. *Alcoholic psychosis.* Alcoholics belong among the group suffer-

ing from the toxic psychoses, caused by poisons generated within the body or induced from without. Drug addiction is one form of toxic psychosis induced from without, but that induced by alcohol is more prevalent. Persons who indulge to excess in alcohol do not necessarily become psychotic, and considerable variations exist between individuals in this regard. In a continued attempt to escape from an unpleasant reality, however, the alcoholic may develop such pathological symptoms as "the loss of powers of inhibition, the decline in mental activity and physical strength . . . unusually violent emotional disturbances . . . uncontrollable and hysterical rages . . . ideas of persecution and hallucinations. . . ."[37] When these attacks become increasingly frequent and violent, the individual is usually hospitalized. The majority of alcoholic patients ultimately recover and are discharged from mental hospitals. In 1944, the proportion of patients discharged as recovered was 54.0 per cent for the alcoholic psychoses, as compared to 7.9 per cent for the senile psychoses.[38]

Trends in first admissions for alcoholic psychosis were as follows:

Table XXXVI
First Admissions for Alcoholic Psychosis
1939–1944

Year	First Admissions
1939	4,788
1940	4,845
1941	5,319
1942	5,054
1943	5,036
1944	3,873

The increase in alcoholic psychosis during the troubled early years of World War II was so small as to be negligible, in spite of the fact that millions of persons were receiving higher incomes than ever before. Wartime economic conditions were such as would normally bring about a considerable increase in alcoholism and alcoholic psychosis. These improved conditions were reflected in the increase in police arrests for drunkenness, which rose from 90,989 in 1939 to 124,914 in 1945, after reaching a high point of 145,946 in 1942.[39]

Such behavior was apparently a relatively harmless euphoria, induced by high wages and full employment. The alcoholic indulgence of the war years was sufficiently serious to bring the participants into conflict with the police, but it was apparently not such as to precipitate a large-scale increase in psychotic behavior induced or aggravated by alcohol. The negligible increase in alcoholic psychosis measured in terms of first admissions is remarkable in view of the simultaneous presence of high wages and widespread worry, both factors which presumably stimulate overindulgence in alcohol. The decrease from 5,036 in 1943 to 3,873 in 1944 is difficult to explain on any terms.

5. *Manic-depressive psychosis.* We turn from the organic to the functional psychoses. Manic-depressive psychosis is, as the name suggests, ordinarily characterized by alternating fits of extreme excitement and deep depression. All persons experience some oscillations in their emotional reactions, but these fluctuations in the normal individual have some basis in fact. The normal person is happy if something happens to him which other persons would agree is pleasant; similarly, he is sad when something sad occurs. The manic-depressive, however, often reacts in completely bizarre fashion, appearing highly elated at an event the normal person would consider melancholy, and vice versa.

The psychotic constructs a mental world of his own and reacts to it. While in the manic state, the patient is abnormally excited and indulges in excessive motor activity not warranted by the occasion. In the depressive state, his low spirits are customarily equaled only by his aversion to mental or physical activity, a state which is often accompanied by extreme melancholy. Some patients may become more or less permanent manics or depressives and exhibit the chronic symptoms of each form of behavior. The "classic" manic-depressive, however, is the mixed type, who vacillates between extreme excitement and depression, with intermediate periods of lucidity. During the latter interludes, he may show no evidence of mental disease.[40]

First admissions for manic-depressive psychosis were as follows:

Table XXXVII

First Admissions for Manic-Depressive Psychosis
1939–1944

Year	First Admissions
1939	11,132
1940	10,433
1941	10,551
1942	11,026
1943	10,562
1944	11,811

The trend in manic-depressive psychosis during the war was an approximate extension of the trend before it. In the period from 1934 through 1938, admissions remained fairly stable, ranging about the 12,000 annual level. The percentage of the total represented by manic-depressive psychoses underwent a decline from 14.6 in 1934 to 13.1 in 1938. This decline continued during the war years, until 1944 admissions were only 10.6 per cent of the total. In ten years, the percentage had decreased from more than 14 to slightly more than 10, a considerable decline in such a short period.

In spite of the events of the war, which superficially would be expected to induce mental disease involving depression, no increase took place in such difficulties, at least as measured by first admissions. Manic-depressive psychosis is a functional difficulty and thus is presumably not unrelated to the world in which the individual lives, but apparently the exact relationship is more devious than might be expected. With a world at war and millions of young men exposed to its dangers, worry might be expected to precipitate mental depressions of all kinds. In this instance, such was apparently not the case.

6. *Dementia praecox.* This is both the most prevalent and the most perplexing form of mental disease. In 1944, 26.1 per cent of all first admissions were suffering from dementia praecox, a percentage which had shown a slow but steady increase over the preceding decade. The symptoms of this disease, also known as schizophrenia, are almost as diverse as its suggested causes. The dementia praecox patient is said to be suffering from a "split personality," whereby he lives to a greater or lesser extent in a world of his own. The definitions, reactions, and understandings of the schizophrenic are not those of normal people, from whom he is separated by an invisible but often impenetrable mental barrier. He is not a part of the normal group; its world is not his world, its insights are not his insights, and its symbols are not his symbols. The process by which he becomes cut off from the group is ordinarily a gradual one, first apparent in the relatively early years; the median age for first admissions for dementia praecox in 1944 was 30.7 years. The isolation slowly becomes more complete as the years go on. Among the patients discharged from mental hospitals in 1944, only 18.4 per cent of the dementia praecox patients were listed as "recovered," as compared to the 50.7 per cent of the manic-depressives in this category.[41]

Dementia praecox takes four general forms: (a) *The simple type,* whereby the patient suffers from early mental deterioration which leaves him "apathetic, careless, and untidy." (b) *The hebephrenic type*, wherein the patient exhibits behavior which has no meaning for the normal person, in the sense that it is "bizarre, fantastic, and irrelevant." His responses to social stimuli have little or no basis in fact, and he may laugh or cry for no visible reason. (c) *The catatonic type*, in which the patient is often completely mute and in a stuporous condition, during which he may become physically rigid or abnormally flexible. (d) *The paranoid type*, in which the patient hears voices, entertains delusions of grandeur and persecution, and reacts in a manner completely unreal to the normal person.[42] The latter is the type of dementia praecox most familiar to the layman, in which the patient may engage in his most spectacular flights from reality.

Wartime trends in this form of mental derangement were as follows:

Table XXXVIII

First Admissions for Dementia Praecox
1939–1944

Year	First Admissions
1939	20,896
1940	20,457
1941	22,155
1942	22,643
1943	24,939
1944	29,010

World War II saw a considerable increase in first admissions for dementia praecox, with an especially large increase in 1944 over 1943. This wartime rise continued a trend apparent over the five years immediately preceding the war, when the number rose from 18,397 in 1934 to 21,279 in 1938. The relative proportion of dementia praecox has also shown a slow but steady increase over the period 1934–1944, rising from 22.3 per cent of the total in 1934 to 26.1 in 1944. The civilian increase during the war took place despite the presence in the armed forces of large numbers of young men in the age groups most susceptible to dementia praecox. The veterans' hospitals, which provide institutional care for the majority of mental disease cases discharged from the armed forces, had an abrupt increase in first admissions for dementia praecox in 1943 and again in 1944. In 1942, the number admitted was 1,336; in 1943 it was 4,997; and in 1944 the figure had risen to 8,821. The percentage of first admissions to veterans' hospitals for dementia praecox also increased from 21.3 in 1942 to 42.0 in 1944. These figures will be further increased when results of the final year of the war and the immediate postwar years are added. A considerable number of young men, who might or might not have become psychotic if they had remained permanently in civilian life, suffered a mental breakdown as members of the armed forces.

The causes of dementia praecox are so complex and little known that it is difficult to relate the increase in first admissions to any specific change in the social climate during World War II. The high national morale might have been expected to solidify the close ties between the individual and the larger group and thus minimize the isolation which is such a persistent attribute of this disease. The changes in the way of life of millions of persons, the necessity of adjusting to new situations, the difficulty of making new decisions for which no precedent existed, and the individual worry for close relatives in the service— these and other wartime factors may have increased the number of those who could not make a satisfactory social adjustment. The figures appear to indicate a slow but steady continuation during the war of the prewar trend toward increasing hospitalization for dementia praecox.

Suicide and Personal Disorganization

Suicide is the final and irrevocable step in the process of personal disorganization. The suicide has reached such a pass that he sees no other way out of his personal dilemma than to do away with himself. The factors which cause the individual to take this most drastic of all steps in the chain of personal disorganization are highly involved. Economic reverses, poverty, frustrated romance, blasted marriage, mental disease, and ill health are the principal elements which take their toll and cause the individual to deny the most elemental of all natural forces. Religious training, racial background, ethnic heritage, and sexual differences all play a role in the suicide process, each influencing in its own way the predisposition of the individual to self-destruction or the forces which keep him from it. Properly speaking, however, the ramifications of this complex human problem do not belong in the present context.[43] Our principal concern is with the changes, if any, which took place in this most violent form of personal disorganization during World War II.

Between 15,000 and 20,000 persons annually commit suicide in the United States. Many thousands more make the attempt but, through the conscious or unconscious choice of inefficient methods, do not succeed. During World War II, the number of suicides decreased to the smallest figure on record, with 13,000 recorded cases of self-destruction in a representative war year.[44] Even more revealing than the absolute number of wartime suicides was the trend in the relative proportion of such deaths to the total. The Metropolitan Life Insurance Company gathers such vital statistics from the records of its millions of industrial policy holders; these figures constitute an accurate sample of suicidal trends.

Table XXXIX

Death Rates per 100,000 Industrial Policy Holders,
Metropolitan Life Insurance Company, for Suicide*

Year	Rate Per 100,000
1938	9.4
1939	8.6
1940	8.7
1941	7.6
1942	7.3
1943	6.5
1944	6.3
1945	6.2

* Adapted from *Statistical Bulletins*, Metropolitan Life Insurance Company.

These figures are most revealing. They indicate a steady decline in the suicide rate from 9.4 per 100,000 deaths in 1938 to 6.3 in 1944 and 6.2 in 1945.[45] The war apparently had a marked influence upon the members of the general population who might otherwise have chosen suicide as a solution of their personal difficulties. The factors combining to exert this influence upon the mental health of the population have been considered above. We need only enumerate them as follows:

1. *Economic factors.* Economic difficulties are a frequent cause of suicide. These difficulties may involve the loss of wealth and social status or threaten minimum economic security. The suicide rate tends to vary inversely with the business cycle, an increase in suicide accompanying a decline in the general price level and vice versa. The war years were marked by full employment, high wages, and ample rates of profit. The number of suicides showed a corresponding decrease.

2. *Psychological factors.* Psychological factors also play their part in the suicide rate. Many suicides grow out of isolation from the larger group, as men and women feel themselves deprived of the warming social contacts which make life worth living. In wartime, the intense spirit of national solidarity brings many people back into the emotional orbit of the group and thereby strengthens their will to live. In the face of the national danger, personal difficulties become less significant and the individual is not so prone to take the suicidal way out.[46]

This decline in the suicide rate is the final example in this study of a drastic, although temporary, modification of a social problem during World War II. Starting with the initial hypothesis that war merely accelerates the rate of change and does not substantially modify the nature of social problems, we have perforce modified our position before the facts of wartime behavior. The morale engendered by the national crisis introduced new psychological elements into the situation, with the result that the national rate of self-destruction underwent a substantial decline in the years 1940–1045. The evidence points to the transitory character of this subtle but unmistakable change in the national ethos; a sharp increase in the suicide rate was apparent after the end of hostilities in Europe.[47] For the duration, however, the national crisis acted upon the civilian population by strengthening the will to live.

CHAPTER TEN

SUMMARY AND CONCLUSIONS

War and Social Problems

We come now to a summary of the role of World War II in initiating, intensifying, or modifying certain social problems in the United States. Total war brought about at least a minimum of change in the behavior of every man, woman, or child in the country; it remains to recapitulate the principal forms of the changes insofar as they relate to social problems. By modifying all social behavior to some extent, the war set in motion changes in the collective actions of large numbers of people. The rapidity with which they modified their peacetime activities during the war represents the rate of social change. This rate was greater than was evident in peacetime. Social change was thus accelerated by World War II.

This acceleration did not take place uniformly in all segments of society. Cultural lag was intensified by the war. Technological change in certain fields took place at the most rapid rate in history, climaxed by the advancements in atomic energy. Changes in social institutions, attitudes, values, and ideologies did not take place at a similar rate. This disparity produced a widening gap between technological possibilities and their social implications, and constituted perhaps the most significant cultural lag that has yet existed. The maladjustment between different aspects of society was never so apparent as it was in the days when the smoke was still settling over Hiroshima and Nagasaki.

Social problems result from a situation and its definition. The differential rate of wartime change between the different parts of our society was not universally recognized as a social problem, particularly when these changes did not palpably encroach upon cherished social values. If everybody had the same set of values, many social problems would obviously disappear altogether, since there would then be complete unanimity about their solution. If war were viewed as the most devastating of all social problems, especially in the atomic age, such

229

values as national sovereignty would be so curtailed that war would be impossible. In many fields, however, there was unusual unanimity during World War II concerning the extent to which the war aggravated other social problems.

In the introductory chapter we suggested that the normal processes of social change are merely intensified, rather than materially changed, by total war. As a result of this acceleration, it was further suggested that the principal difficulties of social adjustment are basically similar under conditions of peace and war, with the difficulties considerably enhanced by accelerated wartime change. Our initial hypothesis was that war produced essentially the same social problems as peace, only in an accelerated and therefore presumably more serious form. Conditions adjudged detrimental to social values would therefore be exaggerated in number and degree but not materially changed. From time to time throughout the discussion, this hypothesis has been questioned. Let us look at the record more thoroughly.

War and the Acceleration of Social Problems

Considerable evidence was found to justify this hypothesis. We shall merely list the evidence here, since we have already considered it in some detail. World War II intensified certain social problems which were already present before the war. These problems may be summarized as follows:

1. The rate of social change was increased.
2. Certain technological changes were accelerated.
3. Corresponding changes in the adaptive culture lagged farther behind than ever before.
4. The rate of social mobility was intensified, with 15 million civilians and 12 million soldiers and sailors on the move.
5. Social congestion was intensified in certain industrial and military centers.
6. The gradual decline in the traditional functions of the family was accelerated.
7. The trend toward the employment of women was intensified by the wartime shortage of labor.
8. Many of the tensions which lead to the peacetime disorganization of the family were increased.
9. Desertion probably increased.

10. The long-term trend toward a higher divorce rate and a greater yearly number of divorces was accelerated.
11. The emotional deprivation of children caused by the employment of mothers was increased.
12. Adolescence adjustment was complicated by the accelerated differences between the generations.
13. The trend toward increased sexual freedom was intensified by the wartime decline in the mores.
14. The number of illegitimate births increased, but not as fast as legitimate births.
15. Juvenile delinquency increased sharply, especially among girls.
16. Certain crimes against the person showed a considerable increase.
17. Various minor crimes and offenses against the public morality increased.
18. First admissions to mental hospitals for all psychoses increased.
19. First admissions to mental hospitals for certain organic psychoses of old age increased.
20. First admissions to mental hospitals for the functional psychoses showed a mixed trend, with manic-depressive psychosis decreasing slightly and dementia praecox increasing substantially.

Some of these changed social conditions were general, while others were more specific. Each condition, however, represents a situation or combination thereof considered a threat to social values. Each of these problems represents a familiar situation in the dynamic society of peacetime; the war intensified these problems without materially changing them.

War and the Modification of Social Problems

These were not the only problems arising from the war. Many problems arose which were either substantially new or represented considerable modifications of old ones. Our initial hypothesis was thus gradually questioned by many situations not found in prewar society or else reversing completely (if only temporarily) the peacetime trends. The new or drastically modified situations included:

1. The increased national consensus on the necessity of winning the war.
2. The high morale resulting from the clear and present danger to national symbols.

3. The increase in prejudice, despite the fact that the war was presumably fought for its abolition.

4. The high level of employment, made possible by the demands for manpower and war production.

5. The high income level, particularly in the manufacturing industries, but partially shared by other employed persons.

6. The large-scale and prolonged separation of millions of families, which was unique both in extent and duration and which brought about significant changes in family roles.

7. The sense of participation in the adolescent generation, whose older brothers had but little possibility for participation during the depression.

8. The increased employment of children and adolescents, which reversed a secular trend toward the progressive abolition of child labor.

9. The decrease in promiscuity for hire (prostitution) because of the more efficient social control thereof.

10. The conflicting trends in venereal disease, with syphilis decreasing and gonorrhea increasing among the civilian population.

11. The decrease in total crimes known to the police, particularly offenses against property.

12. The decline in the suicide rate to its lowest figure in recent years, as many persons merged their personal troubles into the national effort.

The Nature of Wartime Change

We must therefore modify our original hypothesis that war merely intensifies the social maladjustments of peacetime society and hence has no fundamental effect upon social problems. World War II instead exerted a differential effect upon the social structure of the United States, intensifying some problems and temporarily reversing others. Certain trends long evident in peacetime were modified by introducing variables which changed the situation in wartime. Even these variables, however, were not something new under the sun, but evolved out of the general cultural and social situation. These wartime variables assumed three general forms, each with its effect upon social problems.

1. *Economic.* In the period from July 1, 1940, to July 1, 1945, the Federal Government spent 323 billions of dollars, largely upon the war and related activities.[1] These expenditures produced virtually full

employment, with a minimum low of 630,000 estimated unemployed in October, 1944.[2] These expenditures influenced, directly or indirectly, the following social conditions: individual and national morale; the level of employment and income; the gainful employment of women, children, and adolescents; the rise in the marriage rate; the rise in the birth rate; the decrease in crimes against property; the increase in juvenile delinquency; the increase in offenses against the public morality; and the decline in the number of suicides.

These Federal expenditures and the accompanying boom of the national economy seemingly represented a new situation resulting from World War II. On closer analysis, however, the source of the expenditures emerges as part of a previously established pattern, even if the extent of the expenditures was unprecedented. The spending undertaken by the Federal Government during the depression stimulated business activity by placing a floor under which consumer purchasing power theoretically could not go. These expenditures did not approach in size those made for the prosecution of the war, although many persons expressed alarm lest the national debt become unmanageable when it was less than one-tenth the size of the wartime figure. The purpose of the wartime expenditures was the winning of the war and not the maintenance of employment or increased purchasing power. Some of the effects of this wartime program, however, were similar to those of the depression program. Only in wartime, however, is full employment at high wages considered sufficiently important to warrant adequate Federal expenditures to bring it about.

2. *Psychological.* Co-operative activity toward a common goal is the distinctive feature of high morale.[3] World War II engendered sufficient national sentiment to win the war expeditiously. The principal social groups co-operated in this effort, whether on the battlefield, in the factory, or in the home. The differential effects of wartime consensus were apparent upon such social situations as the widespread participation in the labor force, the adolescent euphoria toward the war, the decrease in prostitution, the decline in certain crimes against property, the merely nominal increase in neurotic behavior, the comparative stability in the rate of certain functional psychoses, and above all in the decreased number of suicides. Many of these problems were also influenced by economic factors, a situation not inconsistent with the multiple causes of social problems.

In a society which places such a premium upon individualism, the high collective morale of World War II at first seemed something new. Not since World War I had the nation been mobilized both physically and psychologically in such a supreme effort. The symbols of nationalism have more emotional content during wars than between them. Nevertheless, the psychological mobilization of World War II did not arise full-blown from the great crusade against Fascism. The efforts of the Federal Government during the depression aroused the spirit of national co-operation and individual responsibility. This feeling of participation had a considerable effect upon many social problems through the growing realization that the bell tolled for everyone. National co-operation was not an entirely new phenomenon when the nation entered the perilous decade of the 1940's.

3. *Familial.* The most exceptional effect of World War II upon social problems was the prolonged and extensive separation of families. The total number of broken families during these years is not known exactly, but by April, 1944, the Bureau of Labor Statistics estimated more than 3 million.[4] This figure was later augmented by the induction of married men following the invasion of Europe and the heavy fighting on the continent. Whatever the final figure—whether three and one-half or four million—this situation was unique. Never before were so many American families broken for so long. Many families had been broken during World War I, but for shorter periods and in smaller numbers. Others had been temporarily broken during the depression, as fathers sought work in distant centers. In scope and intensity, however, World War II was the most serious situation the American family ever faced.

The effects of this massive separation were difficult to measure, since they took the form of modifications in family roles. Many effects will not be apparent until the children and adolescents who underwent several years of paternal deprivation have become adults. Many families had developed patterns of reciprocal roles before the war, wherein the relationships between husband and wife and father and children were clearly established. Other families were so recently founded that no such pattern was possible prior to the departure of the husband. Adjustments were necessary, both for the childless wives and those with small children. A considerable segment of the new generation grew up with little initial contact with their fathers.

We have examined our original hypothesis that World War II merely intensified and did not substantially modify certain representative social problems. The industrial activity of wartime solved (if only temporarily) many problems related to income and employment, while adding other problems growing out of the composition of the newly employed groups. The high national morale mitigated many existing barriers to co-operation, if only for the duration. The family underwent the most drastic, widespread, and novel changes of any institution we have examined. A revised hypothesis must be offered to explain these and many other new facts. World War II had a differential effect upon social problems, intensifying some, alleviating others, and creating still others in a society made more dynamic by the pressures of total war.

FOOTNOTES

Chapter One

[1] This volume is one of a number of studies sponsored by the Committee on War Studies of the Social Science Research Council, depicting various phases of the impact of World War II upon American society.

[2] Quincy Wright, *A Study of War*, The University of Chicago Press, Chicago, 1942, vol. I, p. 8 (Italics those of Wright).

[3] *Ibid.*, vol. II, p. 698.

[4] *Ibid.*, vol. I, p. 311.

[5] Richard C. Fuller and Richard R. Myers, "Some Aspects of a Theory of Social Problems," *American Sociological Review*, 6:24-32 (February, 1941).

[6] *Ibid.*

[7] Louis Wirth, (Editor), *Contemporary Social Problems*, University of Chicago Press, Chicago, 1939, p. 5.

[8] The ramifications of housing as a social problem are explored by Louis Wirth, *op. cit.*, chap. III.

[9] Richard C. Fuller and Richard R. Myers, "The Natural History of a Social Problem," *American Sociological Review*, 6:320-329 (June, 1941).

[10] *Ibid.*

[11] *Ibid.*

[12] Report of the Subcommittee on Technology, National Resources Committee, *Technological Trends and National Policy*, United States Government Printing Office, Washington, 1937.

[13] Cf. Mabel A. Elliott and Francis E. Merrill, *Social Disorganization*, Harper & Brothers, New York, 1941, (Revised Edition).

[14] Cf. Agnes E. Meyer, *Journey Through Chaos*, Harcourt, Brace and Company, New York, 1944.

[15] "Increasing Productivity and Technological Improvements in Defense Industries," *Monthly Labor Review*, 54:34-48 (January, 1942).

[16] Shelby C. Davis, "Coordinating Production for War," *Journal of the American Statistical Association*, 38:417-424 (December, 1943).

[17] William F. Ogburn, *Social Change*, B. W. Huebsch, New York, 1922.

[18] W. Edgar Gregory, "The Idealization of the Absent," *American Journal of Sociology*, 50:53-54 (July, 1944).

[19] Dixon Wecter, *When Johnny Comes Marching Home*, Houghton Mifflin Company, Boston, 1944.

[20] Walter Lippmann, *Public Opinion*, The Macmillan Company, New York, 1922.

[21] Cf. Bernhard J. Stern, "Resistances to the Adoption of Technological Innovations," *Technological Trends and National Policy, loc. cit.*, pp. 39-66.

[22] Walter Lippmann, *op. cit.*, p. 15.

[23] For a study of the housing situation in a representative defense area, cf. Alexander

C. Findlay, "Occupancy of Privately Financed Houses in Bridgeport," *Monthly Labor Review*, 54:1073-1083 (May, 1942).

[24] For statements of the wartime housing situation, cf. Kathryn R. Murphy, "Housing for War Workers," *Monthly Labor Review*, 54:1257-1277 (June, 1942); "Housing Provided in 138 Defense Areas," *Monthly Labor Review*, 55:1203-1212 (December, 1942).

[25] For a concise and authoritative analysis of certain of these changes, cf. William F. Ogburn (Editor), *American Society in Wartime*, The University of Chicago Press, Chicago, 1943.

[26] William I. Thomas, *The Unadjusted Girl*, Little, Brown & Company, Boston, 1923, pp. 42-43.

[27] "Sources of Wartime Labor Supply in the United States," *Monthly Labor Review*, 59:264-278 (August, 1944).

[28] Data taken from "Sources of Wartime Labor Supply in the United States," *loc. cit.*, pp. 272, 273, 278.

[29] Bureau of the Census, Sixteenth Census of the United States: 1940, *Population: Internal Migration 1935 to 1940, Color and Sex of Migrants*, Government Printing Office, Washington, 1943, p. 2.

[30] Bureau of the Census, Population—Special Reports, *Civilian Migration in the United States: December, 1941 to March, 1945*, Series P-S, No. 5, September 2, 1945. An interim report on migration from 1940 to 1943 was brought out by the Bureau of the Census, with estimates for November 1, 1943 based upon registrations for *War Ration Book Four*. Bureau of the Census, Population—Special Reports, *Interstate Migration and Other Population Changes: 1940 to 1943*, Series P-44, No. 17, August 28, 1944.

[31] Bureau of the Census, *Civilian Migration in the United States: December, 1941 to March, 1945, loc. cit.*

[32] Bureau of the Census, *Number of Marriages, by States: 1937 to 1943*, Series PM-1, No. 2, October 6, 1944.

[33] Bureau of the Census, *Civilian Migration in the United States: December, 1941 to March, 1945, loc. cit.*

[34] *Ibid.*

[35] *Ibid.*

[36] *Ibid.*

[37] For a description of the impact of migration upon a small California city, cf. Z. Parker, "Strangers in Town," *Survey*, 79:170-171 (June, 1943).

[38] Robert E. Park and Ernest W. Burgess, *Introduction to the Science of Sociology*, The University of Chicago Press, Chicago, 1924, chap. X, "Accommodation."

[39] Alfred M. Lee and Norman D. Humphrey, *Race Riot*, The Dryden Press, Inc., New York, 1943.

[40] Jane M. Hoey, "The Conservation of Family Values in Wartime," *The Family*, 24:43-49 (April, 1943).

[41] Cf. William F. Ogburn, "Marital Separations," *American Journal of Sociology*, 49:316-323 (January, 1944).

[42] Cf. Jeanette Hanford, "Some Case-Work Notes on the Impact of the War on Family Relationships," *Social Service Review*, 17:354-361 (September, 1943).

[43] J. H. S. Bossard, "Family Backgrounds of Wartime Adolescents," *Annals of the American Academy of Political and Social Science*, 236:33-42 (November, 1944).

44 Edmund N. Bacon, "Wartime Housing," *Annals of the American Academy of Political and Social Science,* 229:128-137 (September, 1943).

45 Cf. Thomas Minehan, *Boy and Girl Tramps of America,* Rinehart and Company, Inc., New York, 1934.

46 Mary Skinner and Alice Scott Nutt, "Adolescents Away from Home," *Annals of the American Academy of Political and Social Science,* 236:51-59 (November, 1944).

47 Jerome S. Bruner, "How Much Post-War Migration?", *American Journal of Sociology,* 49:39-45 (July, 1943), p. 45.

48 Edwin M. Lemert, "Social Participation and Totalitarian War," *American Sociological Review,* 8:531-536 (October, 1943).

49 Alexis de Tocqueville, *Democracy in America,* New York, 1899, vol. I, p. 398.

50 Herbert Blumer, "Morale," in William F. Ogburn (Editor), *American Society in Wartime, loc. cit.,* p. 211.

51 *Ibid.,* p. 228.

Chapter Two

1 Bureau of the Census, *Marriage and Divorce Statistics,* Release March 11, 1939.

2 Mabel A. Elliott and Francis E. Merrill, *Social Disorganization,* Harper & Brothers, New York, 1941 (Revised Edition), chap. 23, "The Romantic Fallacy."

3 William F. Ogburn, *Social Change,* B. W. Huebsch, New York, 1922.

4 Bureau of the Census, Joint Report of Population Division and Special Surveys Division, *Marital Status of the Civilian Population: February, 1944,* Series P-S, No. 1, June 20, 1944.

5 Ernest R. Mowrer, "War and Family Solidarity and Stability," in *The American Family in World War II, Annals of the American Academy of Political and Social Science,* 229:100-106 (September, 1943), p. 104.

6 Harriet R. Mowrer, *Personality Adjustment and Domestic Discord,* American Book Company, New York, 1935, chaps. IX-X.

7 Lewis M. Terman, *Psychological Factors in Marital Happiness,* McGraw-Hill Book Company, New York, 1938.

8 Ernest W. Burgess, "The Family," in William F. Ogburn (Editor) *American Society in Wartime,* University of Chicago Press, Chicago, 1943, p. 35.

9 Bureau of the Census, Population, *Wartime Changes in Population and Family Characteristics, Detroit-Willow Run Congested Production Area: June, 1944,* Series CA-2, No. 9, September 17, 1944.

10 Florence Hollis, "The Impact of the War on Marriage Relationships," *Proceedings of the National Conference of Social Work, 1943,* Columbia University Press, New York, 1943, pp. 108-109.

11 *Ibid.*

12 Bureau of the Census, *Monthly Report on the Labor Force,* Special Surveys: MRLF No. 33, March 9, 1945.

13 Bureau of the Census, *Detroit-Willow Run Congested Production Area, loc. cit.*

14 Bureau of the Census, *San Francisco Bay Congested Production Area: April, 1944,* Series CA-2, No. 3, July 15, 1944.

15 In the Detroit-Willow Run Area, for example, the number of families in Detroit City increased during the war by 9.4 per cent, while the population as a whole increased only 1.9 per cent. Drastic modifications in housing demands would result from

this change in the marital status of the population, even if uncomplicated by other factors. Bureau of the Census, *Detroit-Willow Run Congested Production Area, loc. cit.* p. 7.

[16] Hope Tisdale Eldridge, "Migrants in Congested Production Areas," *Paper read at meeting of Population Association of America,* November 11, 1944, Washington, D.C., p. 6.

[17] For a more inclusive statement of the nature and causes of desertion, cf. Mabel A. Elliott and Francis E. Merrill, *op. cit.* pp. 703-713.

[18] Bureau of the Census, Joint Report of Population Division and Special Surveys Division, *Marital Status of the Civilian Population: February, 1944, loc. cit.;* Also Bureau of the Census, *Marital Status of the Civilian Population: February, 1946,* Population, Series P-S, No. 10, October 14, 1946.

[19] Bureau of the Census, Population, *Total Population of Ten Congested Production Areas: 1944,* Series CA-1, No. 11, September 20, 1944.

[20] Bureau of the Census, *Wartime Changes in Population and Family Characteristics: San Francisco Bay Congested Production Area:* April, 1944, Series CA-2, No. 3, July 15, 1944, p. 8.

[21] Bureau of the Census, *Wartime Changes in Population and Family Characteristics: Detroit-Willow Run Congested Production Area:* April, 1944, Series CA-2, No. 9, September 17, 1944, p. 7.

[22] Bureau of the Census, *Wartime Changes in Population and Family Characteristics: Los Angeles Congested Production Area:* April, 1944, Series CA-2, No. 5, August 4, 1944, p. 8.

[23] Bureau of the Census, *Marriage and Divorce Statistics, loc. cit.*

[24] Kingsley Davis, "Social and Statistical Analysis," in *Children of Divorced Parents,* Special Issue of *Law and Contemporary Problems,* School of Law, Duke University, 10:700-720 (Summer, 1944).

[25] *Ibid.,* p. 718.

[26] Bureau of the Census, *Marriages in the United States: 1914 to 1943,* Series PM-1, No. 1, July 4, 1944.

[27] Kingsley Davis, *op. cit.,* pp. 715-716.

[28] Ernest W. Burgess, *op. cit.,* p. 25.

[29] *Ibid.*

[30] Army Service Forces, *Annual Report of the Office of Dependency Benefits for the Fiscal Year 1944,* Washington, 1945, p. 34.

[31] *Ibid.,* p. 68.

[32] Kingsley Davis, *op. cit.,* p. 716, note 32.

[33] David M. Levy, "The War and Family Life," *American Journal of Orthopsychiatry,* 15:140-152 (January, 1945).

[34] Constantine Panunzio, "War and Divorce," *Sociology and Social Research,* 28:15-19 (September-October, 1943).

[35] David M. Levy, *op. cit.,* p. 141.

[36] Calvin Hall, "The Instability of Post-War Marriages," *Journal of Social Psychology,* 5:523-530 (November, 1934).

[37] Constantine Panunzio, *op. cit.,* p. 17.

[38] Metropolitan Life Insurance Company, "Will Divorce Increase in the Postwar Years?", *Statistical Bulletin* (October, 1943).

[39] Bureau of the Census, *Marital Status of the Civilian Population: February, 1944, loc. cit.*

[40] Mabel A. Elliott and Francis E. Merrill, *op. cit.*, chap. 23, "The Romantic Fallacy."

[41] Kingsley Davis, *op. cit.*, p. 716.

[42] Metropolitan Life Insurance Company, *op. cit.*

[43] Kingsley Davis, *op. cit.*, p. 717.

[44] Hornell Hart and Henrietta Bowne, *op. cit.*

[45] Kingsley Davis, *op. cit.*, p. 718.

[46] Bureau of the Census, *Estimates of Number of Families in the United States: 1940 to 1960*, Population-Special Reports, Series P-46, No. 4, June 1, 1946.

[47] Paul C. Glick, "Future Family Estimates and Some of Their Implications," *Paper read before the Population Association of America*, Princeton, New Jersey (June 1, 1946).

[48] Alfred Cahen, *Statistical Analysis of American Divorce*, Columbia University Press, New York, 1932, p. 113.

[49] Kingsley Davis, *op. cit.*, pp. 712-713.

[50] Metropolitan Life Insurance Company, *op. cit.*

Chapter Three

[1] *Children in a Democracy—General Report Adopted by the White House Conference on Children in a Democracy, January 19, 1940*, Children's Bureau, Washington, 1941, pp. 5-6.

[2] Emma O. Lundberg, *Our Concern—Every Child*, Children's Bureau Publication 303, Washington, 1944, p. 6.

[3] *The Child*, 8:149-151 (April, 1944).

[4] "State Committees on Children in Wartime," *The Child, loc. cit.*, pp. 152-156.

[5] Among these publications were *To Parents in Wartime*, Children's Bureau Publication 282, Washington, 1942; *Protecting the Health of Young Workers in Wartime*, Children's Bureau Publication 291, Washington, 1943; *Community Action for Children in Wartime*, Children's Bureau Publication 295, Washington, 1943; *Controlling Juvenile Delinquency: A Community Program*, Children's Bureau Publication 301, Washington, 1943; *Goals for Children and Youth in the Transition from War to Peace*, Children's Bureau Publication 306, Washington, 1944.

[6] *Children in a Democracy loc. cit.*, p. 12.

[7] Metropolitan Life Insurance Company, "War and the Birth Rate," *Statistical Bulletin* (October, 1944).

[8] For an authoritative summary of these problems and efforts made to ameliorate them, cf. Katharine F. Lenroot, "Current National Developments and Problems in Public-Welfare Services for Children," *The Child*, 9:103-106 (January, 1945).

[9] *To Parents in Wartime, loc. cit.*, pp. 2-4.

[10] *Ibid.*, p. 8.

[11] Charlotte Towle, "The Effect of the War Upon Children," *Social Service Review*, 17:144-158 (June, 1943).

[12] Quoted from Dr. Robert D. Gillespie, Salmon Memorial Lectures delivered before the New York Academy of Medicine, November 18–19, 1941 by E. C. Ciccarelli, "Measures for the Prevention of Emotional Disorders," *Mental Hygiene*, 26:383-393 (July, 1942), pp. 384-385.

242 *Footnotes*

¹³ Quoted from Dr. Anna Freud by E. C. Ciccarelli, *op. cit.*, p. 387.

¹⁴ Emma O. Lundberg, *op. cit.*, p. 20.

¹⁵ *Ibid.*

¹⁶ Charlotte Towle, *op. cit.*, p. 153.

¹⁷ Cf. Martha W. MacDonald, "Security for Children in the World Today," *American Journal of Orthopsychiatry*, 13: 514-516 (July, 1943).

¹⁸ *Ibid.*, p. 146.

¹⁹ "Care of Infants Whose Mothers Are Employed," *The Child*, 9:131-132 (February, 1945), p. 131.

²⁰ *Ibid.*

²¹ Eleanor S. Boll, "The Child," *Annals of the American Academy of Political and Social Science*, 229:69-78 (September, 1943).

²² Unpublished report on war-conditioned delinquency prepared for the North Central Regional Conference, American Orthopsychiatric Association, Chicago, December 12, 1942, quoted by Charlotte Towle, *op. cit.*, p. 149.

²³ Dr. Karl A. Menninger, *Bulletin of the Menninger Clinic*, 5:188-194 (September, 1941), quoted by Eugene C. Ciccarelli, "Measures for the Prevention of Emotional Disorders," *Mental Hygiene*, 26:383-393 (July, 1942).

²⁴ Charlotte Towle, *op. cit.* Cf. also Lois B. Murphy, "The Young Child's Experience in Wartime," *American Journal of Orthopsychiatry*, 13:497-501 (July, 1943).

²⁵ Margaret W. Gerard, "Problems of a Wartime Society: The Clinical Picture," *American Journal of Orthopsychiatry*, 13:600-604 (October, 1943).

²⁶ V. W. Bernard, "Detection and Management of Emotional Disorders in Children," *Mental Hygiene*, 26:368-382 (July, 1942), p. 372.

²⁷ Cf. Dr. Jean A. Thompson, "Pre-School and Kindergarten Children in War Time," *Mental Hygiene*, 26:409-417 (July, 1942).

²⁸ Dr. Emanuel Kline, "The Influence of Teachers' and Parents' Attitudes and Behavior Upon Children in War Time," *loc. cit.*, pp. 434-445.

²⁹ Dr. George E. Gardner, Director, Judge Baker Guidance Center in Boston, tends to minimize the role of World War II in the emotional life of the child. "No children," he states, "have been treated at our clinic because of imaginary fears of injury to themselves or to their families." George E. Gardner, "Child Behavior in a Nation at War," *Mental Hygiene* 27:353-369 (July, 1943).

³⁰ Lauretta Bender and John Frosch, "Children's Reactions to the War," *American Journal of Orthopsychiatry*, 12:571-586 (October, 1942), p. 585.

³¹ *Ibid.*

³² Bureau of the Census, *Civilian Migration in the United States: December, 1941 to March, 1945*, Population-Special Reports, Series P-S, No. 5 (September 2, 1945).

³³ John N. Webb and Malcolm Brown, *Migrant Families*, Works Progress Administration, Division of Social Research, Research Monograph XVIII, Washington, 1938.

³⁴ Bureau of the Census, *Characteristics of the Population, Labor Force, Families, and Housing*, Series CA-3, Washington, 1944.

³⁵ Ione L. Clinton and Ella A. Merritt, "Young Agricultural Workers in 1944," *The Child*, 9:119-125 (February, 1945).

³⁶ Walter H. Gaumnitz, "Ways of Extending Educational Opportunities to Migrant Children," *The Child*, 9:141-142 (March, 1945).

[37] Dr. Hope Tisdale Eldridge, "Migrants in Congested Production Areas," *Paper read at meeting of Population Association of America,* November 11, 1944, Washington, D.C.

[38] Katharine F. Lenroot, *op. cit.,* p. 104.

[39] Hazel A. Fredericksen, "The Program for Day Care of Children of Employed Mothers," *Social Service Review,* 17:159-169 (June, 1943).

[40] Leonard W. Mayo, "What We Can Learn from National Experience in Day Care," *Proceedings of the National Conference of Social Work 1943,* Columbia University Press, New York, 1943, pp. 126-132.

[41] Hazel A. Fredericksen, *op. cit.,* p. 161.

[42] David M. Levy, "The War and Family Life," *American Journal of Orthopsychiatry,* 15:140-153 (January, 1945), pp. 147-148.

[43] *Ibid.*

[44] *Ibid.*

[45] Margaret W. Gerard, "Psychological Effects of War on the Small Child and Mother," *American Journal of Orthopsychiatry,* 13:493-496 (July, 1943).

[46] Kingsley Davis, "Social and Statistical Analysis," in *Children of Divorced Parents,* Special Issue of *Law and Contemporary Problems,* Duke University, 10:700-720 (Summer, 1944).

[47] Special estimate by the Bureau of the Census contained in a letter by J. C. Capt, Director, and dated March 28, 1945.

[48] Army Service Forces, *Annual Report of the Office of Dependency Benefits for the Fiscal Year 1944,* Washington, 1945, p. 34.

[49] George E. Gardner, *op. cit.,* p. 359.

[50] Amelia Igel, "The Effect of War Separation on Father-Child Relations," *The Family,* 26:3-9 (March, 1945).

[51] *Ibid.*

[52] Margaret W. Gerard, "Psychological Effects of War on the Small Child and Mother," *loc. cit.,* p. 495.

[53] Elisabeth R. Geleerd, "Psychiatric Care of Children in Wartime," *American Journal of Orthopsychiatry,* 12:587-593 (October, 1942).

[54] Margaret W. Gerard, "Psychological Effects of War on the Small Child and Mother," *loc. cit.,* p. 495.

[55] Ralph Linton *The Study of Man,* D. Appleton-Century Company, New York, 1936, Chapter X, "The Family."

Chapter Four

[1] Caroline B. Zachry, "Customary Stresses and Strains of Adolescence," *Annals of the American Academy of Political and Social Science,* 236:136-144 (November, 1944).

[2] Cf. William I. Thomas, *Primitive Behavior,* McGraw-Hill Book Company, Inc., New York, 1937, chap. 12.

[3] Margaret Mead, *Coming of Age in Samoa,* William Morrow & Company, New York, 1928, chaps. 13 and 14.

[4] Kingsley Davis, "Adolescence and the Social Structure," *Annals of the American Academy of Political and Social Science,* 236:8-16 (November, 1944) p. 9.

[5] Warren S. Thompson, "Adolescents According to the Census," *Annals of the American Academy of Political and Social Science,* 236:17-25 (November, 1944).

[6] Charlotte Towle, "Some Notes on the War and Adolescent Delinquency," *Social Service Review*, 17:67-73 (March, 1943).

[7] Marion Cowin and Alma Paulsen, "Adolescents in War Time," *Mental Hygiene*, 26:418-424 (July, 1942).

[8] Caroline B. Zachry, *op. cit.*, p. 141.

[9] Ella A. Merritt and Floy Hendricks, "Trend of Child Labor, 1940-44," *Monthly Labor Review*, 60:756-775 (April, 1945). Figures for April, 1945, indicate that approximately the same number (three million) boys and girls 14 through 17 were employed on the eve of V-E Day. Cf. "Youth Employment on the Eve of V-E Day," *The Child*, 10:93 (December 1945).

[10] "Teen-Age Youth in the Wartime Labor Force," *Monthly Labor Review*, 60:6-17 (January, 1945).

[11] John Slawson, "The Adolescent in a World at War," *Mental Hygiene*, 27:531-548 (October, 1943), pp. 544-545.

[12] Ernest R. Groves and Gladys H. Groves, "The Social Background of Wartime Adolescents," *Annals of the American Academy of Political and Social Science*, 236:26-32 (November 1944).

[13] Dorothy Ellsworth, "Precocious Adolescence in Wartime," *The Family*, 25:3-13 (March, 1944), p. 4.

[14] *Ibid.*, p. 13.

[15] *Ibid.*

[16] Ernest R. Groves and Gladys H. Groves, *op. cit.*, p. 27.

[17] "Teen-Age Youth in the Wartime Labor Force," *loc. cit.*, Table 2.

[18] *Ibid.*, Table 6.

[19] *Protecting the Health of Young Workers in Wartime*, Children's Bureau Publication 291, Washington, 1943.

[20] "Teen-Age Youth in the Wartime Labor Force," *loc. cit.*, pp. 6-7.

[21] Ernest R. Groves and Gladys H. Groves, *op. cit.*, pp. 28-29.

[22] "Sources of Wartime Labor Supply in the United States," *Monthly Labor Review*, 59:264-278 (August, 1944), Table 4.

[23] Henry L. Zucker, "Working Parents and Latchkey Children," *Annals of the American Academy of Political and Social Science*, 236:43-50 (November, 1944).

[24] Hope Tisdale Eldridge, "Migrants in Congested Production Areas," *Paper read at the Meeting of the Population Association of America*, November 11, 1944, Washington, D.C.

[25] James H. S. Bossard, "Family Backgrounds of Wartime Adolescents," *Annals of the American Academy of Political and Social Science*, 236:33-42 (November, 1944).

[26] Mary Skinner and Alice Scott Nutt, "Adolescents Away from Home," *Annals of the American Academy of Political and Social Science*, 236:51-59 (November, 1944).

[27] "Teen-Age Youth in the Wartime Labor Force," *loc. cit.*, p. 7.

[28] Dorothy Hankins, "Mental Hygiene Problems of the Adolescent Period," *Annals of the American Academy of Political and Social Science*, 236:128-135 (November 1944).

[29] *Ibid.*, pp. 134-135.

[30] James H. S. Bossard, *op. cit.*, p. 39.

[31] *Ibid.*, pp. 38-39.

[32] Dorothy Hankins, *op. cit.*, pp. 128-135.

[33] Margaret Mead, "The Cultural Picture," *American Journal of Orthopsychiatry,* 13:596-599 (October, 1943).

[34] Dorothy Hankins, *op. cit.*

[35] John Slawson, *op. cit.*, p. 532.

[36] *Ibid.*

[37] Ella A. Merritt and Floy Hendricks, *op. cit.*, p. 756.

[38] *Ibid.* Employment figures for April, 1944, were obtained by the Bureau of the Census which, at the request of various interested Federal agencies, included the pertinent questions in its monthly sample survey of labor supply and employment. Cf. also "Youth Employment on the Eve of V-E Day," *loc cit.*

[39] Golda G. Stander and Edith S. Gray, "Young Workers in the Wartime Labor Market," *The Child,* 9:72-76 (November, 1944), Table 4.

[40] Ella A. Merritt and Floy Hendricks, *op. cit.,* Table 2.

[41] "Sources of Wartime Labor Supply in the United States," *loc. cit.*

[42] "Teen-Age Youth in the Wartime Labor Force," *loc. cit.,* Table 1.

[43] Gertrude F. Zimand, "The Changing Picture of Child Labor," *Annals of the American Academy of Political and Social Science,* 236:83-91 (November, 1944).

[44] *Goals for Children and Youth in the Transition from War to Peace,* Children's Bureau Publication 306, Washington, 1944, p. 5.

[45] "The Effect of the War on Child-Labor Legislation During 1943," *The Child,* 8:69-73 (November, 1943) p. 73.

[46] *Ibid.*

Chapter Five

[1] Richard C. Fuller, *Social Problems,* in Robert E. Park (Editor), *An Outline of the Principles of Sociology,* Barnes & Noble, Inc., New York, 1939, p. 7. (Italics those of Fuller.)

[2] Walter Clarke, "A Year of Great Progress: Report on the Work of the American Social Hygiene Association: 1944," *Journal of Social Hygiene,* 31:164-183 (March, 1945), p. 173.

[3] "Sex Delinquency Among Girls," *Journal of Social Hygiene,* 29:492-501 (November, 1943), p. 493.

[4] Richard A. Koch and Ray Lyman Wilbur, "Promiscuity as a Factor in the Spread of Venereal Disease," *Journal of Social Hygiene,* 30:517-529 (December, 1944).

[5] Eliot Ness, "Sex Delinquency as a Social Hazard," *Proceedings of the National Conference of Social Work, 1944,* Columbia University Press, New York, 1944, p. 280.

[6] Robert D. Weitz and H. L. Rachlin, "The Mental Ability and Educational Attainment of Five Hundred Venereally Infected Females," *Journal of Social Hygiene,* 31:300-302 (May, 1945).

[7] Mary Edna McChristie, "Girls Are Different," *Cooperation in Crime Control, 1944 Yearbook National Probation Association,* New York, 1945, pp. 74-83.

[8] Lewis M. Terman, *Psychological Factors in Marital Happiness,* McGraw-Hill Book Company, New York, 1938; Dorothy Dunbar Bromley and Florence Haxton Britten, *Youth and Sex,* Harper & Brothers, New York, 1938.

[9] Bureau of the Census, Sixteenth Census of the United States: 1940, *Population: Internal Migration 1935 to 1940, Color and Sex of Migrants.* Washington, 1943.

246 *Footnotes*

[10] Bureau of the Census, Population-Special Reports, *Civilian Migration in the United States: December, 1941 to March, 1945,* Series P-S, No. 5, September 2, 1945.

[11] Willard Waller, "War and Social Institutions," in *War in the Twentieth Century,* edited by Willard Waller, The Dryden Press, New York, 1940, p. 486.

[12] *Ibid.,* p. 492.

[13] Ernest R. Groves and Gladys H. Groves, "The Social Background of Wartime Adolescents," *Annals of the American Academy of Political and Social Science,* 236:26-32 (November, 1944), p. 30.

[14] George E. Gardner, "Sex Behavior of Adolescents in Wartime," *Annals of the American Academy of Political and Social Science,* 236:60-66 (November, 1944).

[15] Ernest R. Groves and Gladys H. Groves, *op. cit.,* p. 30.

[16] Elsa Castendyck, "Helping to Prevent Sex Delinquency," *Proceedings of the National Conference of Social Work,* Columbia University Press, New York, 1943, p. 141.

[17] *Ibid.*

[18] *Ibid.,* p. 142.

[19] Eliot Ness, *op. cit.,* p. 280.

[20] Cf. Josephine D. Abbott, "The Community and its Youth in Wartime," *Journal of Social Hygiene,* 29:511-518 (November, 1943).

[21] "Juvenile-Court Statistics, 1943," *Social Statistics,* Supplement to vol. 9, no. 12 (June, 1945) of *The Child,* Washington, 1945, p. 12.

[22] *Ibid.*

[23] *Ibid.*

[24] Federal Bureau of Investigation, *Uniform Crime Reports,* vol. 15, no. 2, Washington, 1945, p. 101.

[25] *Ibid.,* Table 26, pp. 63-64.

[26] *Ibid.,* "Monthly Variations Offenses Known to the Police," Figure 10, p. 65.

[27] *Ibid.,* p. 94.

[28] Elsa Castendyck, *op. cit.,* p. 142.

[29] "Juvenile-Court Statistics, 1940-42," *Social Statistics,* Supplement to vol. 8, no. 6 (December, 1943) of *The Child.*

[30] *Ibid.*

[31] Mabel A. Elliott and Francis E. Merrill, *Social Disorganization,* Harper & Brothers, New York, 1941 (Revised Edition), p. 214.

[32] *Ibid.,* pp. 214-215.

[33] Bureau of the Census, *Vital Statistics, Special Report, 1937,* Released March 24, 1939.

[34] Cf. Norman E. Himes, "Birth Control and Social Work," *The Survey,* 75:74-75 (March 15, 1939) for estimate of the yearly number of abortions in the United States.

[35] Florence Clothier, "Psychological Implications of Unmarried Parenthood," *American Journal of Orthopsychiatry,* 13:531-549 (July, 1943), p. 548.

[36] Bureau of the Census, Vital Statistics-Special Reports, *Illegitimate Live Births By Race: United States, 1942,* vol. 19, no. 12 (April 27, 1944), p. 141. The majority of the births in 1942 represented conceptions during the prewar year of 1941.

[37] Federal Security Agency, National Office of Vital Statistics, Vital Statistics-Special Reports, *Illegitimate Births By Race: United States and Each State, 1944,* vol. 25, no. 14 (October 31, 1946).

[38] Federal Security Agency, National Office of Vital Statistics, Vital Statistics-Special

Reports, *Illegitimate Births By Race: United States and Each State, loc. cit.* Table 2, p. 255.

[39] Federal Security Agency, *op. cit.*

[40] *Ibid.*

[41] Richard A. Koch and Ray Lyman Wilbur, *op. cit.,* Table III.

[42] Mary Louise Webb, "Delinquency in the Making," *Journal of Social Hygiene,* 29:502-510 (November, 1943).

[43] *Ibid.,* pp. 506-507.

[44] Elsa Castendyck, *op. cit.,* pp. 146-147.

[45] Mary Louise Webb, *op. cit.,* pp. 507-508.

[46] "Teen-Age Youth in the Wartime Labor Force," *Monthly Labor Review,* 60:6-17 (January, 1945), Table 2.

[47] "Sex Delinquency Among Girls," *loc. cit.,* p. 498.

[48] *Ibid.*

Chapter Six

[1] Mabel A. Elliott and Francis E. Merrill, *Social Disorganization,* Harper & Brothers, New York, 1941 (Revised Edition), p. 242.

[2] Wilbur C. Curtis, "The Prostitute Before the Court," *Federal Probation,* 7:34-37 (April–June, 1943).

[3] Walter C. Reckless, "A Sociologist Looks at Prostitution," *Federal Probation,* 7:12-16 (April–June, 1943), p. 13.

[4] *Ibid.*

[5] Helen Hironimus, "Survey of 100 May Act Violators Committed to the Federal Reformatory for Women," *Federal Probation,* 7:31-34 (April–June, 1943), p. 31.

[6] Adapted from Helen Hironimus, *op. cit.*

[7] Laura Waggoner, "Girls and Women Apprehended by Police in San Antonio, Texas, for Prostitution and Allied Offenses," *Journal of Social Hygiene,* 28:390-396 (October, 1942).

[8] Marjorie F. Kennedy, "An Individual Study of Women Held in the Tacoma City Jail and Pierce County Detention Home," *Journal of Social Hygiene,* 28:398-402 (October, 1942).

[9] Richard A. Koch and Ray Lyman Wilbur, "Promiscuity as a Factor in the Spread of Venereal Disease," *Journal of Social Hygiene,* 30:517-529 (December, 1944).

[10] Cf. Joel T. Boone, "The Sexual Aspects of Military Personnel," *Journal of Social Hygiene,* 27:113-124 (March, 1941).

[11] Paul M. Kinsie, "The Prostitution Racket Today," *Journal of Social Hygiene,* 27:327-334 (October, 1941).

[12] G. F. McGinnis and Henry Packer, "Prostitution Abatement in a Venereal Disease Control Program," *Journal of Social Hygiene,* 27:355-363, (October, 1941), p. 356.

[13] Bascom Johnson, "When Brothels Close, V.D. Rates Go Down," *Journal of Social Hygiene,* 28:525-535 (December, 1942).

[14] Taken from "Teamwork in Venereal Disease Prevention: A Report of 1943 Activities to the Friends of the American Social Hygiene Association," *Journal of Social Hygiene,* 30:107-127 (March, 1944), p. 116.

[15] *Ibid.*

248   *Footnotes*

[16] Walter Clarke, "A Year of Great Progress: Report on the Work of the American Social Hygiene Association: 1944," *Journal of Social Hygiene,* 31:164-183 (March, 1945), p. 172.

[17] L. R. Pennington, "The Challenge to Law Enforcement," *Journal of Social Hygiene,* 30:530-537 (December, 1944), p. 532.

[18] "Social Protection—A Summing Up," *Journal of Social Hygiene,* 31:303-307 (May, 1945).

[19] Federal Bureau of Investigation, *Uniform Crime Reports,* Annual Bulletin 1944, Washington, 1945, p. 102.

[20] *Ibid.,* Table 38, p. 91.

[21] Adapted from Gaylord W. Anderson, "Venereal Disease Education in the Army," *Journal of Social Hygiene,* 30:20-28 (January, 1944).

[22] C. S. Stephenson and George W. Mast, "Venereal Disease Education in the U. S. Navy," *Journal of Social Hygiene,* 30:29-39 (January, 1944).

[23] Jean B. Pinney, "How Fares the Battle Against Prostitution?" *Social Service Review,* 16:224-246 (June, 1942). An Act of Congress, signed by President Roosevelt in September, 1944, abolished all punishment of members of the armed forces for venereal infection, *provided* that they complied with regulations concerning reporting and treatment. *Journal of Social Hygiene,* 31:65 (January, 1945).

[24] Lt. Colonel Thomas H. Sternberg and Captain Granville W. Larimore, "Army Contribution to Postwar Venereal Disease Control Planning," *Journal of Social Hygiene,* 31:26-33 (January, 1945); Commander Walter H. Schwartz, "Venereal Disease Control in the U. S. Navy," *ibid.,* pp. 34-43 (January, 1945).

[25] Lt. Colonel Thomas H. Sternberg and Captain Granville W. Larimore, *op. cit.,* p. 26.

[26] *Ibid.*

[27] Commander Walter H. Schwartz, *op. cit.,* p. 38.

[28] Thomas Parran, "The Role of the United States Public Health Service in Venereal Disease Control," *Federal Probation,* 7:3-7 (April–June, 1943), p. 3.

[29] *Ibid.*

[30] "Teamwork in Venereal Disease Prevention," *Journal of Social Hygiene,* 30:107-127 (March, 1944), p. 110.

[31] Thomas Parran, "Promised Victory: A Progress Report on Venereal Disease Control," *Journal of Social Hygiene,* 31:133-137 (March, 1945).

[32] Walter Clarke, "Postwar Social Hygiene Problems and Strategy," *loc. cit.*

[33] Cf. Jean B. Pinney, *op. cit.*

[34] Gaylord W. Anderson, "Venereal Disease Education in the Army," *Journal of Social Hygiene,* 30:20-28 (January, 1944).

[35] C. S. Stephenson and George W. Mast, "Veneral Disease Education in the U.S. Navy," *Journal of Social Hygiene,* 30:29-39 (January, 1944).

[36] Thomas Parran, "Promised Victory: A Progress Report on Venereal Disease Control," *loc. cit.*

[37] Raymond F. Clapp, "Social Treatment of Prostitutes and Promiscuous Women," *Federal Probation,* 7:23-27 (April–June, 1943).

[38] Mark A. McCloskey, "V. D. Control—A War on Many Fronts," *Journal of Social Hygiene,* 31:44-51 (January, 1945).

[39] These statutes are the Mann Act, enacted in 1910 and the May Act, enacted in 1941 (Public Law 163—77th Congress, H. R. 2475).

[40] L. R. Pennington, "The Challenge to Law Enforcement," *Journal of Social Hygiene*, 30:530-537 (December, 1944).

[41] Cf. Walter Clarke, "A Year of Great Progress: Report on the Work of the American Social Hygiene Association: 1944," *loc. cit.*

Chapter Seven

[1] Cf. Richard C. Fuller, "The Nature and Study of Social Problems," chap. I in Robert E. Park (Editor), *An Outline of the Principles of Sociology*, Barnes & Noble, Inc., New York, 1939.

[2] William I. Thomas, *The Unadjusted Girl*, Little, Brown & Company, Boston, 1923, pp. 42-43.

[3] Children's Bureau, *Social Statistics: Juvenile-Court Statistics, 1940-42*, Supplement to vol. 8, no. 6 (December, 1943) of *The Child*.

[4] Mabel A. Elliott and Francis E. Merrill, *Social Disorganization*, Harper & Brothers, New York, 1941 (Revised Edition), p. 103.

[5] Children's Bureau, *op. cit.*, p. 5.

[6] Lowell J. Carr, *Delinquency Control*, Harper & Brothers, New York, 1941, pp. 57-61.

[7] Victor H. Evjen, "Delinquency and Crime in Wartime," *Journal of Criminal Law and Criminology*, 33:136-146 (July–August, 1942), p. 137.

[8] *Ibid.*

[9] *Understanding Juvenile Delinquency*, Children's Bureau Publication 300, 1943, pp. 17-18.

[10] Martin H. Neumeyer, "Delinquency Trends in Wartime," *Sociology and Social Research*, 29:262-275 (March–April, 1945).

[11] *Social Statistics* (Supplement no. 4 to *The Child*), United States Children's Bureau, Washington, June, 1939, vol. 3, p. 3.

[12] Cf. Mabel A. Elliott and Francis E. Merrill, *op. cit.*, chaps. 5 and 6 for a discussion of the principal factors bringing about juvenile delinquency.

[13] Bureau of the Census, Sixteenth Census of the United States: 1940, *Population: Internal Migration 1935 to 1940, Color and Sex of Migrants*, Washington, 1943.

[14] Bureau of the Census, Population-Special Reports, *Interstate Migration and Other Population Changes: 1940 to 1943*, Series P-44, No. 17 (August 28, 1944).

[15] Bureau of the Census, Population-Special Reports, *Civilian Migration in the United States: December, 1941 to March, 1945*, Series P-S, No. 5 (September 2, 1945).

[16] *Understanding Juvenile Delinquency, loc. cit.*, p. 19.

[17] Maurice A. Bigelow, "Social Hygiene and Youth in Defense Communities," *Journal of Social Hygiene*, 28:437-447 (November, 1942).

[18] *Ibid.*, p. 439.

[19] David Bogen, "Juvenile Delinquency and Economic Trend," *American Sociological Review*, 9:178-184 (April, 1944).

[20] David Bogen, "Trends in Juvenile Delinquency," *Federal Probation*, 9:25-28 (January–March, 1945), p. 27.

[21] *Ibid.*

[22] Paul Wiers, "Wartime Increases in Michigan Delinquency," *American Sociological Review*, 10:515-523 (August, 1945), p. 515.

[23] "Sources of Wartime Labor Supply in the United States," *Monthly Labor Review*, 59:264-278 (August, 1944), p. 270.

[24] *Understanding Juvenile Delinquency, loc. cit.,* p. 20.

[25] Ella A. Merritt and Floy Hendricks, "Trend of Child Labor, 1940–44," *Monthly Labor Review,* 60:756-775 (April, 1945), pp. 756-757.

[26] *Understanding Juvenile Delinquency, loc. cit.,* p. 19.

[27] *Ibid.,* pp. 12-14.

[28] Richard L. Jenkins, "Factors Influencing Wartime Increase in Juvenile Delinquency," *1944 Yearbook National Probation Association,* New York, 1945, p. 166.

[29] Henry L. Zucker, "Working Parents and Latchkey Children," *Annals of the American Academy of Political and Social Science,* 236:43-50 (November, 1944).

[30] "Sources of Wartime Labor Supply in the United States," *loc. cit.,* Table 4.

[31] *Ibid.*

[32] *Ibid.*

[33] *Ibid.,* p. 270.

[34] *Controlling Juvenile Delinquency,* Children's Bureau Publication 301, Washington, 1943, p. 10.

[35] Lowell J. Carr, *op. cit.,* p. 37.

[36] David Bogen, "Trends in Juvenile Delinquency," *loc. cit.,* p. 25.

[37] Lowell J. Carr, *op. cit.,* p. 63.

[38] U. S. Department of Labor, Children's Bureau, *Juvenile-Court Statistics, 1944* (Preliminary Statement), February 24, 1945.

[39] Children's Bureau, *Social Statistics: Juvenile-Court Statistics, 1940–42, loc. cit.*

[40] U. S. Department of Labor, Children's Bureau, *Juvenile-Court Statistics, 1944, loc. cit.*

[41] *Ibid.*

[42] Bureau of the Census, *Population: Estimates of the Civilian Population by Counties, May 1, 1942,* Series P-3, No. 33, Washington, February 25, 1943, p. 1.

[43] U. S. Department of Labor, Children's Bureau, *Juvenile-Court Statistics, 1943,* Supplement to vol. 9, no. 12 of *The Child* (June, 1945), pp. 19-21.

[44] Cf. also Elsa Castendyck and Sophia Robison, "Juvenile Delinquency Among Girls," *Social Service Review,* 17:253-264 (September, 1943), p. 254.

[45] Children's Bureau, *Social Statistics: Juvenile Court Statistics, 1940–42, loc. cit.,* p. 5.

[46] *Ibid.*

[47] U. S. Department of Labor, Children's Bureau, *Juvenile-Court Statistics, 1943, loc. cit.,* Table 2.

[48] *Ibid.,* Table 1.

[49] Children's Bureau, *Social Statistics: Juvenile-Court Statistics, 1940–42, loc. cit.,* pp. 3-4.

[50] *Ibid.*

[51] U. S. Department of Labor, Children's Bureau, *Juvenile-Court Statistics, 1943, loc. cit.,* Table 3.

Chapter Eight

[1] Mabel A. Elliott and Francis E. Merrill, *Social Disorganization,* Harper & Brothers, New York, 1941 (Revised Edition), p. 152.

[2] *Ibid.,* pp. 152-154.

[3] Edwin H. Sutherland, "White-Collar Criminality," *American Sociological Review*, 5:1-12 (February, 1940).

[4] Mabel A. Elliott and Francis E. Merrill, *op. cit.*, p. 159.

[5] Hermann Mannheim, *War and Crime*, Watts & Co., London, 1941, pp. 204-205.

[6] Federal Bureau of Investigation, *Uniform Crime Reports*, vol. 15, no. 2, Washington, 1945, pp. 63-64.

[7] Thorsten Sellin, *War and Crime: A Research Memorandum*, Prepared for the Committee on Reasearch on Social Aspects of the War, Social Science Research Council, New York, 1942.

[8] Adapted from Edwin H. Sutherland, "Some Hypotheses Regarding War and Crime," in Thorsten Sellin, *ibid.* pp. 13-15.

[9] *Ibid.*

[10] The two principal theories were those of Franz Exner, *Krieg und Kriminalität in Oesterreich*, New Haven, 1927; and Mortiz Liepmann, *Krieg und Kriminalität in Deutschland*, Stuttgart, 1930.

[11] Edwin H. Sutherland, "Crime," in William F. Ogburn (Editor), *American Society in Wartime*, University of Chicago Press, Chicago, 1943, p. 203.

[12] *Ibid.*, p. 185.

[13] Federal Bureau of Investigation, *Uniform Crime Reports*, *loc. cit.*, p. 72.

[14] Walter C. Reckless, "The Impact of War Upon Crime, Delinquency, and Prostitution," *American Journal of Sociology*, 48:378-386 (November, 1942).

[15] *Ibid.*

[16] Adapted from Edwin H. Sutherland, "Crime," *loc. cit.*, pp. 185-193.

[17] The field of criminal statistics is a complex and controversial one, in which the nontechnical reader need not become involved. Cf. Walter A. Lunden, *Statistics on Crime and Criminals*, Stevenson and Foster Company, Pittsburgh, Pa., 1942.

[18] Cf. Federal Bureau of Investigation, *Uniform Crime Reports*, vol. 16, no. 2, Washington, 1946.

[19] Cf. Bureau of the Census, *Prisoners in State and Federal Prisons and Reformatories; 1944*, Series PN, No. 4 (December 31, 1945).

[20] Federal Bureau of Investigation, *Uniform Crime Reports*, vol. 15, Washington, 1945, p. 57.

[21] *Ibid.*, p. 58.

[22] *Ibid.*, p. 88.

[23] *Ibid.*, p. 56.

[24] Thorsten Sellin, *op. cit.*, p. 5.

[25] Wendell Berge, "The Enforcement of the Criminal Laws of the United States in Time of War," *Journal of Criminal Law and Criminology*, 33:297-305 (November–December, 1942).

[26] Lowell S. Selling, "Specific War Crimes," *Journal of Criminal Law and Criminology*, 34:303-310 (January–February, 1944).

[27] The following definitions and classifications of offenses are taken from *Uniform Crime Reports* vol. 15, *op. cit.*, pp. 101-102, unless otherwise noted.

[28] This crime does not include "attempts to kill, assaults to kill, suicides, accidental deaths, or justifiable homicides." *Ibid*.

[29] Edwin H. Sutherland, "Crime," *loc. cit.*, pp. 189ff.

[30] Walter Bromberg, "The Effects of the War on Crime," *American Sociological Review*, 8:685-691 (December, 1943).

[31] Paul Wiers, "Wartime Increases in Michigan Delinquency," *American Sociological Review*, 10:515-523 (August, 1945).

[32] *Uniform Crime Reports*, vol. 16, Washington, 1945.

[33] *Uniform Crime Reports, loc. cit.*, pp. 93-94.

[34] Harry Willbach, "Crime in New York as Affected by the War," *Journal of Criminal Law and Criminology*, 34:371-376 (March–April, 1944), p. 376.

[35] *Uniform Crime Reports, loc. cit.*, p. 60.

[36] Bureau of the Census, Population, *Prisoners in State and Federal Prisons and Reformatories; 1942* (Preliminary Statistics), Series PN, No. 1 (April 12, 1944); Bureau of the Census, Population, *Prisoners in State and Federal Prisons and Reformatories: 1944, loc. cit.*

[37] *Uniform Crime Reports, loc. cit.*, p. 98.

[38] Unless otherwise noted, the following definitions are taken from *Uniform Crime Reports, loc. cit.*, pp. 101-102.

[39] These and subsequent figures are compiled from *Uniform Crime Reports* for the years under consideration.

[40] During the first six months of 1945, arrests for all the above offenses against property and public morality occurred at a higher rate than that manifested for the full year 1944—with the single exception of gambling. The last six months of our participation in the war thus saw a considerable increase all along the line in offenses of this character. *Uniform Crime Reports*, vol. 16, *loc. cit.*, p. 65.

Chapter Nine

[1] Herbert Blumer, "Morale," in William F. Ogburn (Editor), *American Society in Wartime*, University of Chicago Press, Chicago, 1943, p. 211.

[2] H. Warren Dunham, "War and Personality Disorganization," *American Journal of Sociology*, 48:387-397 (November, 1942).

[3] Dr. Benjamin Malzberg, *Social and Biological Aspects of Mental Disease*, State Hospitals Press, Utica, New York, 1940, p. 281.

[4] *Ibid.*, pp. 281ff.

[5] H. Warren Dunham, *op. cit.*, p. 397.

[6] Dr. Abraham Myerson, in a personal communication, quoted by H. Warren Dunham, *op. cit.*, pp. 390-391.

[7] Karen Horney, *The Neurotic Personality of Our Time*, W. W. Norton & Company, Inc., New York, 1937.

[8] Bureau of the Census, *Characteristics of Admissions and Separations: Mental Hospitals, 1944*, Series MP, No. 9 (August 7, 1946).

[9] H. Warren Dunham, *op. cit.*, p. 391.

[10] Bureau of the Census, *Characteristics of Patients Admitted to Mental Hospitals: 1943 and 1942*, (Preliminary Data), Series MP, No. 4 (April 30, 1945); Bureau of the Census, *Movement of Patients in Mental Hospitals: 1944*, (Preliminary Data), Series MP, No. 7 (May 29, 1946).

[11] Carney Landis and James D. Page, *Modern Society and Mental Disease*, Rinehart and Company, Inc., New York, 1938, pp. 9-10 and 14.

[12] *Ibid.*, p. 10.

[13] Dr. Abraham Myerson, quoted by H. Warren Dunham, *op. cit.*, p. 396.

[14] Karen Horney, *op. cit.*, chaps. I and XV.

[15] Dr. Felix Deutsch, "Civilian War Neuroses and Their Treatment," *The Psychoanalytic Quarterly*, 13:300-312 (July, 1944).

[16] *Ibid.*, p. 301.

[17] Carney Landis and James D. Page, *op. cit.*, p. 10.

[18] Bureau of the Census, *Characteristics of Admissions and Separations: Mental Hospitals, 1944, loc. cit.*

[19] H. Warren Dunham, "War and Mental Disorder: Some Sociological Considerations," *Social Forces*, 22:137-142 (December, 1943).

[20] Dr. Benjamin Malzberg, *op. cit.*, chap. XI.

[21] Herbert Blumer, *op. cit.*, p. 223.

[22] Dr. R. D. Gillespie, *Psychological Effects of War on Citizen and Soldier*, W. W. Norton & Company, New York, 1942, p. 106.

[23] *Ibid.*, pp. 106-107.

[24] Carney Landis and James D. Page, *op. cit.*, pp. 14-15.

[25] Bureau of the Census, *Movement of Patients in Mental Hospitals: 1944, loc. cit.*

[26] *Ibid.*

[27] *Ibid.*

[28] Bureau of the Census, *Movement of Patients in Mental Hospitals: 1944, loc. cit.*

[29] Bureau of the Census, *Patients in Mental Institutions: 1941*, Washington, 1944, p. 2.

[30] *Ibid.*, p. 9; Cf. also Carney Landis and James D. Page, *op. cit.*, chap. XII, "Are Mental Diseases Increasing?"

[31] Bureau of the Census, *Movement of Patients in Mental Hospitals: 1944, loc. cit.* All measurements from 1935 on were based upon the number of resident patients as of July 1 of the specified year.

[32] Bureau of the Census, *Patients in Mental Institutions, 1941, loc. cit.* p. 2.

[33] Bureau of the Census, *Movement of Patients in Mental Hospitals: 1944, loc. cit.*, Table 4.

[34] Bureau of the Census, *Characteristics of Admissions and Separations: Mental Hospitals: 1944, loc. cit.*

[35] Bureau of the Census, *Patients in Mental Institutions: 1941, loc. cit.*, p. 9.

[36] Carney Landis and James D. Page, *op. cit.*, p. 12.

[37] Mabel A. Elliott and Francis E. Merrill, *Social Disorganization*, Harper & Brothers, New York, 1941 (Revised Edition), pp. 522-523.

[38] Bureau of the Census, *Characteristics of Admissions and Separations: Mental Hospitals, 1944, loc. cit.*, Table 6.

[39] Federal Bureau of Investigation, *Uniform Crime Reports: 1939-1945*. The figures are for the number of fingerprint cards submitted to the Federal Bureau of Investigation by the police departments for persons arrested for violations of state laws and municipal ordinances.

[40] Mabel A. Elliott and Francis E. Merrill, *op. cit.*, pp. 525-526.

[41] Bureau of the Census, *Characteristics of Admissions and Separations: Mental Hospitals, 1944, loc. cit.*, Table 6.

[42] Carney Landis and James D. Page, *op. cit.*, p. 13.

[43] For a detailed discussion of the many phases of suicide, see Mabel A. Elliott and Francis E. Merrill, *op. cit.,* chap. 20.

[44] Metropolitan Life Insurance Company, "Why Do People Kill Themselves?" *Statistical Bulletin,* (February, 1945).

[45] The suicide rate showed a significant increase following the end of hostilities in Europe in May, 1945. For the first quarter of 1946, the rate among the insured of the Metropolitan Life Insurance Company was 7.8 per 100,000, as compared with 5.7 in the same period of 1945. Metropolitan Life Insurance Company, "Postwar Increase in Suicide," *Statistical Bulletin* (April, 1946).

[46] Metropolitan Life Insurance Company, "Suicides Decline to New Low Level," *Statistical Bulletin,* (July, 1944).

[47] Metropolitan Life Insurance Company, "Postwar Increase in Suicide," *loc. cit.*

Chapter Ten

[1] Statement of Daniel W. Bell, Under Secretary of the Treasury, in an address before the Association of Stock Exchange Firms, quoted in the *New York Times,* November 25, 1945.

[2] Bureau of the Census, *Monthly Report on the Labor Force,* Population: MRLF, No. 38, August 15, 1945.

[3] Herbert Blumer, "Morale," in William F. Ogburn (Editor), *American Society in Wartime,* University of Chicago Press, Chicago, *1943.*

[4] "Sources of Wartime Labor Supply in the United States," *Monthly Labor Review,* 59:264-278 (August, 1944), p. 270.

INDEX

Adolescence, cultural basis of, 74-75; education and, 83-84; nature of, 73-76; war and, 76-82; wartime conflict and, 81-82

Adolescent, adjustment of, 74-76; employment of, 78-80, 84-85; family relations of, 89-92; imminent changes for, 88-89; in armed forces, 79; maturity of, 78-79; mobility and, 86-88; number of, 76; participation of, in World War II, 92-96; school attendance of, 83-84; unsettlement of, 82-83; working mothers of, 86

Child, age levels and, 55-59; neglect of, 66-68; social problems of, 51-55; total war and, 49-51; wartime mobility and, 59-63; working mothers and, 63-68

Children, age groups among, 55-59; homemaker care for, 64-65; in agricultural labor, 61-62; in England, 53, 58; neglect of, 66-68; number of, 50-51; of working mothers, 63-68; physical security of, 52; without fathers, 68-69

Crime, against property, 188-190; against the person, 190; aggravated assault, 187-188; arrests and, 191-199; auto theft, 186-187; burglary, 185; buying or receiving stolen property, 193-194; criminal homicide, 182-183; defined, 169-171; differential group organization and, 175-176; disorderly conduct, 196-197; driving while intoxicated, 195-196; drunkenness, 194-195; during World War I, 178-179; embezzlement and fraud, 192-193; extent of, 180-181; forgery and counterfeiting, 193; gambling, 197-198; indices of, 179-181; larceny,

185-186; local factors in, 176-177; prostitution and commercialized vice, 198-199; rape, 183-184; robbery, 184-185; war and, 171-176; wartime trends in "major," 181-191; wartime trends in "minor," 191-199

Criminal, defined, 170; number of, 180-181; prison population of, 190-191; types of, 170-171; wartime behavior of, 188-191

Desertion, extent of, 34-37; mobility and, 35-38; nature of, 33-34. *See also* Divorce, Family disorganization

Divorce, postwar factors operating against, 47-48; postwar factors operating for, 44-47; secular trend in, 38-40; wartime factors operating against, 41-43; World War II and, 38-43. *See also* Desertion, Family disorganization

Employment, adolescent participation and, 92-96; changing standards of, 94-96; juvenile delinquency and, 154-155; new forms of, 13-14; of adolescents, 79-80, 84-85, 92-96; of married women, 30-31; of mothers, 63-68; of parents, 86; World War II and, 13-14, 93-96

Family, adolescent and, 89-92; bereavement of, 69-72; broken, 68-72; child and, 54-55; cohesive factors in, 41-43; doubling-up of, 32-33; juvenile delinquency and, 156-159; mobility and, 19-20; sex offender and, 116-119; social change and, 234-235; war neurosis and, 208-209; wartime separation of, 35-38; World War II and, 25-27

255

family background of, 125; marital status of, 126; work history of, 126

Prostitution, arrests for, 134-135; as a crime, 198-199; as a social problem, 144, 199; case study of, 130-131; causes of, 123-124; characteristics of girls entering, 124-127; community studies of, 132-134; defined, 122; methods of, 127; military attitude toward, 135-138; military nature of, 128-131; nature of, 122-124; social control of, 142-144; venereal disease and, 130, 138-140; wartime trend of, 132-134

Psychosis, alcoholic psychosis, 221-223; defined, 209; dementia praecox, 224-226; first admissions for, 210, 218; functional, 210-211; general paresis, 218-219; hospitalization for, 215-216; manic-depressive psychosis, 223-224; measurement of, 214-217; organic, 209-210; psychosis with cerebral arteriosclerosis, 220-221; schizophrenia, 224-226; senile psychosis, 219-220; types of, 209-210; war and, 209-214; wartime trends in, 217-226. *See also* Mental disease, Neurosis

Sex behavior, illegitimacy and, 111-116; increased freedom of, 166; juvenile delinquency and, 165-166; of adolescent girls, 80-82, 97-102; prewar changes in, 29-30; war and, 103-104

Sex offender, arrests of, 110; broken home and, 116-117; definition of, 107; family and, 116-119; identification of, 99-100; mental capacity of, 100-101; number of, 107-109; participation and, 104-105; school and, 119-121; truancy and, 119-121; types of, 100

Sex offense, abortion and, 112; adolescent participation and, 104-106; arrests for, 110, 198-199; as a social problem, 97-98; extent of, 107-111; family relations and, 116-119; girls involved in, 100-102; illegitimacy and, 111-116; meas-

urement of, 106-107; nature of, 97-102; promiscuity as, 99-100; rape as, 109-111, 183-184; school and, 119-121; social change and, 105-106; unmarried mother and, 111-113; venereal disease and, 99

Social change, child and, 55-59; cultural lag and, 10-13; defined, 2; economic factors in, 232-233; familial aspects of, 234-235; family disorganization and, 25-27; family ties and, 89-90; nature of, 1-3; process of, 2-3; psychological factors in, 233-234; war and, 8-10, 172-173, 232-235

Social disorganization, crime and, 169-171, 176-179; social change and, 2-3; war and, 1-3

Social mobility, adolescent and, 86-88; agricultural labor and, 61-62; child and, 59-63; delinquency and, 151-152; desertion and, 34-35; extent of, 15-16; family and, 19-20; into congested production areas, 60-63; person and, 20-22; regional differences in, 16-18; sex offenses and, 102-103; society and, 18-19; World War II and, 15-18

Social problem, acceleration of, by World War II, 230-231; child and, 51-55; crime as, 169-171; defined, 3-4; examples of, 5-6; juvenile delinquency as, 145-146; mental disease as, 217; mobility and, 18-22; modification of, by World War II, 231-232; nature of, 3-8; personal disorganization as, 200-202; prostitution as, 144; role of World War II in, 234-235; sex offenses as, 97-98; social values and, 4-7; suicide as, 226-228; war and, 229-235

Social value, conflict and, 7-8; crime and, 169-170; defined, 5; social problems and, 4-7

Suicide, economic factors in, 227; extent of, 227; factors in, 226; psychological factors in, 228; reasons for wartime decline in, 227-228; wartime trends in,

WESTMAR COLLEGE LIBRARY

315/49

FEB 27 50